A Conversation with God for Women

IF YOU COULD ASK GOD ANY QUESTION, WHAT WOULD IT BE?

Marcia Ford

THOMAS NELSON
Since 1798

NASHVILLE   DALLAS   MEXICO CITY   RIO DE JANEIRO

Published in Nashville, Tennessee, by Thomas Nelson. Thomas Nelson is a registered trademark of Thomas Nelson, Inc.

Thomas Nelson, Inc. titles may be purchased in bulk for educational, business, fund-raising, or sales promotional use. For information, please e-mail SpecialMarkets@ ThomasNelson.com.

Scripture quotations marked CEV are from the Contemporary English Version. © 1991, 1992, 1995 by American Bible Society. Used by permission.

Scripture quotations marked ESV are from The Holy Bible, English Standard Version, © 2001 by Crossway Bibles, a division of Good News Publishers. Used by permission. All rights reserved.

Scripture quotations marked MSG are from *The Message: The New Testament in Contemporary English*. Copyright © 1993, 1994, 1995, 1996, 2000, 2001, 2002. Used by permission of NavPress Publishing Group.

Scripture quotations marked NASB are from the NEW AMERICAN STANDARD BIBLE®, © Copyright The Lockman Foundation 1960, 1962, 1963, 1968, 1971, 1972, 1973, 1975, 1977, 1995. Used by permission.

Scripture quotations marked NCV are taken from the New Century Version®. © 2005 by Thomas Nelson, Inc. Used by permission. All rights reserved.

Scripture quotations marked NIV are taken from the HOLY BIBLE, NEW INTERNATIONAL VERSION.® NIV®. © 1973, 1978, 1984 by International Bible Society. Used by permission of Zondervan. All rights reserved.

Scripture quotations noted NKJV are from THE NEW KING JAMES VERSION. © 1979, 1980, 1982, Thomas Nelson, Inc., Publishers.

Scripture quotations marked NLT are taken from the *Holy Bible,* New Living Translation, ©1996, 2004. Used by permission of Tyndale House Publishers, Inc., Wheaton, Illinois 60189. All rights reserved.

Library of Congress Control Number: 2010940135

ISBN: 978-0-7852-3179-0

Editor: Lila Empson Wavering

Associate Editor: Jennifer McNeil

Design: Whisner Design Group

Printed in the United States of America

11 12 13 14 15 QGT 9 8 7 6 5 4 3 2 1

If you don't know what you're doing,

pray to the Father. He loves to help.

You'll get his help, and won't be

condescended to when you ask for it.

Ask boldly, believingly, without

a second thought.

James 1:5–6 MSG

Contents

INTRODUCTION 11

GOD

People are in awe of God. He created the universe out of nothing. But it's hard for some women to understand that God wants to have a relationship with them.

1. God, why don't You just reveal Yourself? 17

2. Why do we have to face temptation? 21

3. Why should we trust You? 25

4. How are we made in Your image? 29

5. How can Your Spirit live in us? 33

6. Who's controlling our lives—You or us? 37

7. Why don't You prevent disasters from happening? 41

JESUS

Though He lived more than two thousand years ago, Jesus is considered the greatest person in history. His followers believed him to be both fully God and fully human while He was on earth.

8. Jesus, are You really God's Son? 49

9. Why did You come to earth anyway? 53

10. Why was a virgin birth necessary? 57

11. Did You physically rise from the dead? 61

12. Did You experience human emotions on earth? 65

13. Is it true that You never sinned? 69

14. Did You really die to save everyone? 73

THE BIBLE

Many women grew up with the Bible but now aren't sure what to think of it. They want to know whether the Bible relates to their lives today—and if so, how.

15. Who actually wrote the Bible? 81

16. Must we obey everything in the Bible? 85

17. Did all those miracles really happen? 89

18. Which biblical promises apply to us today? 93

19. How can the Bible still be relevant? 97

20. What can Bible women teach us? 101

LIFE

God gave the gift of life to the first humans and all who would come after them. Understanding the purpose of life makes all the difference in how people use this gift.

21. Is there a purpose to life? 109

22. How do we know what You want? 113

23. Can we ever be free of guilt? 117

24. Jesus, what does following You involve? 121

25. God, do You really forgive and forget? 125

26. Do we have to go to church? 129

27. What about women in ministry? 133

28. How can we do it all? 137

29. How can we stop worrying so much? 141

30. Is it possible to find genuine peace? 145

31. How can we share our faith inoffensively? 149

PRAYER

Some women have a tough time praying. When things are going okay, there doesn't seem to be much reason to pray. And when things are rough, prayer isn't the first thing on their minds.

32. God, how can we know You're listening? 157

33. Do You hear everybody's prayers? 161

34. Why aren't some prayers answered? 165

35. Can prayer really make a difference? 169

36. Is there one right way to pray? 173

37. Should we pray only about major problems? 177

38. Is it okay to pray repetitious prayers? 181

RELATIONSHIPS

Relationships are often the best part of life, but they can also be the hardest. It isn't always easy to love others, especially when they don't play by the rules or when they treat people badly.

39. How can we love unlovable people? 189

40. How can we trust anyone following betrayal? 192

41. How can You expect us to forgive? 196

42. How can we have deeper friendships? 200

43. What's so bad about gossip? 204

44. Why are there restrictions on sex? 208

45. What's wrong with relationships with unbelieving men? 212

46. God, why did You create families? 216

47. What's up with the teaching on submission? 220

48. How can we respect an ungodly boss? 224

GOOD AND EVIL

Evil abounds in the world, and it sccms to be getting more pervasive. It sometimes seems as if good is being squeezed out. People question whether good is powerful enough to kccp evil at bay.

49. How can evil coexist with Your love? 231

50. Why do Your followers have to suffer? 235

51. Are all sins the same to You? 239

52. How can some unbelievers be so good? 243

53. How can You forgive truly evil criminals? 246

54. What about people who continue to sin? 250

55. How can anybody find good in tragedy? 254

Notes 259

Introduction

In order to reach the deepest levels of relationship to God, one has to put imagination to work and to start upon the daring venture of seeking a God who is loving beyond any experience we have and fulfilling in a way that few of us have ever dreamed of.

Morton T. Kelsey

Wouldn't it be great if you could sit down and have a heart-to-heart conversation with God, confident that He would answer the questions that you've been thinking long and hard about? You know the ones. They're the questions that many women need to have answered so they can better understand the God with whom they long to be intimately connected: questions about life and relationships, prayer and the Bible, good and evil—and questions about God Himself.

In *Conversations with God for Women*, we've taken fifty-five of the most common questions women would like to ask God. We've then used them as springboards to discussions designed to deepen your understanding of God and the way He works in the world and in the lives of His people. Of course, all the answers to those questions are found in the Bible. But instead of simply listing the chapter and verse references, we've created conversations in which God provides answers from His eternal perspective, while Jesus elaborates on those answers using examples from His teachings and experiences during His time on earth.

The conversations weave together insights from the entire Bible, allowing you the opportunity to examine the answer to each question from a more comprehensive angle than a single Bible verse may provide. And that's significant, because the questions we've tackled aren't the kind that can be rushed through with a fill-in-the-blank mentality. These are questions whose answers are likely to make you think deeply about the issues involved, such as why God allows disasters to happen, whether Jesus died for everyone, if the miracles in the Bible really happened, whether women should be allowed to preach, why some prayers aren't answered, why God placed restrictions on sex, and how any good can coexist with all the evil on earth. Each conversation is intended to encourage you to explore for yourself the topic it addresses and perhaps discover even more biblical evidence that answers the specific question related to the topic.

Joining in the conversations are women from the Bible whose names you already know, such as *Eve*; *Mary Magdalene*; and *Mary, the mother of Jesus*; along with lesser-known women like *Hannah*, the mother of the prophet Samuel; and the New Testament prophet *Anna*. Their insights offer a female perspective on the way God interacts with women and the impact He had on the lives of women in the patriarchal societies that existed in Bible times.

For example, as a leader of the church that Paul established in Philippi, a woman named *Lydia* was in a unique position to witness and comment on the positions of responsibility that women held among the followers of Christ. In his account of the work of the apostles after the resurrection of Jesus, Luke described a vision in which Paul saw a man who asked him to travel to Macedonia and help the people there. When they arrived in Macedonia, they sought out those who believed in God—and discovered Lydia and some other women praying outside the city gates. Paul shared the good news about Jesus with them and accepted an invitation to stay with Lydia's household. Later, the believers began meeting in her house, affording Lydia an opportunity to participate fully in the life of the early church.

You'll also hear from *Priscilla*, who along with her husband, Aquila, worked closely with Paul and also held a position of prominence during the formative years of Christianity. Her exposure to the teachings of Paul—in a society that offered few opportunities for women to receive an education—placed her in a position to clarify those teachings when they were misunderstood. Her comments on the transformational nature of a relationship with Christ stem from a direct understanding of what Paul wrote about the possibility that our minds could be renewed.

And then there's *Martha*, a woman from the Bible that many women today can relate to. She was the sister of Mary of Bethany and Lazarus, and she was also the one who had a knack for occasionally blurting out all the wrong things when she spoke to Jesus. Who better to comment on Jesus' kindness and tenderness, even after she scolded Him for not preventing Lazarus's death? Martha's role in *Conversations with God for Women* provides hope for every woman who has wished she could take back the words she just uttered.

The *woman caught in adultery* and *the town harlot*—both are also a part of these conversations. When it comes to a discussion about forgiveness, these are the women you want to hear from, women whose sins were so heinous that the punishment was death by stoning. If you have any doubts about God's willingness and power to forgive *your* sins, just eavesdrop on their conversations and see if you're not convinced that God *wants* to forgive you for very single sin you've ever committed—or will commit.

Sarah, the wife of Abraham, whose late-in-life pregnancy taught her to trust in God; *Naomi*, a widow who learned the meaning of faithfulness and deep friendship from a daughter-in-law; *Deborah*, who taught a nation that God means what He says and will do what He promises—they are some of the other women whose stories appear in answer to the questions that modern-day women would like to ask God. So listen in as God, Jesus, and a number of women from the Bible offer insights into those difficult issues that nag at you, puzzle you, or keep you from fully trusting God. You may want your Bible at your side to do some deeper study, although the scriptural support for each answer may be found in the endnotes that follow the last chapter.

May the LORD show you his favor and give you his peace.

Numbers 6:26 NLT

God is greater than our feelings, and he knows everything. Dear friends, if we feel at ease in the presence of God, we will have the courage to come near him. He will give us whatever we ask, because we obey him and do what pleases him. God wants us to have faith in his Son Jesus Christ and to love each other. This is also what Jesus taught us to do. If we obey God's commandments, we will stay one in our hearts with him, and he will stay one with us. The Spirit that he has given us is proof that we are one with him.

1 John 3:20−24 CEV

GOD

> *People are in awe of God. He created the universe out of nothing. But it's hard for some women to understand that God wants to have a relationship with them.*

1. God, why don't You just reveal Yourself? 17

2. Why do we have to face temptation? 21

3. Why should we trust You? 25

4. How are we made in Your image? 29

5. How can Your Spirit live in us? 33

6. Who's controlling our lives—You or us? 37

7. Why don't You prevent disasters from happening? 41

I
God, why don't You just reveal Yourself?

It's an age-old question and one that challenges the very existence of God: If God actually exists, why doesn't He just come out of hiding and show Himself to the world? It's one thing to believe that God is simply an abstraction like energy or universal consciousness, but skeptics maintain that to expect people to believe in the Judeo-Christian concept of a personal deity requires God to become visible to those He claims to want a relationship with.

Even those women whose hearts seem to be naturally inclined toward God sometimes wish they could have some proof that He is there. Faith would be so much easier if they could see God, or some evidence of His existence, just once.

Q **God, I know You're there. At least, most of the time I know You're there. I'm like that person who once said, "Lord, I believe; help my unbelief!" I want You to come out from the shadows and show who You really are. Why don't You reveal Yourself to us?**

GOD

Believers and skeptics have been asking that question of Me for thousands of years, and those who are certain I don't exist have been asking that question about Me for just as long. Some scientists demand proof of My existence; some theologians manufacture proof to try to convince the scientists. And some philosophers don't want to be convinced; they're much more interested in the ongoing debate.

What most people fail to realize is that I have revealed Myself numerous times and in many different ways, and yet the skepticism persists. Remember, I gave people the freedom of choice, and, more often than not, they choose to turn away from Me, refuse to acknowledge My presence, and deny the proof of My existence that is evident right before their very eyes. Let Me explain the various ways I've revealed Myself.

I've revealed Myself in person. There were those who saw Me and never doubted My existence—those who walked with Me and talked with Me in the perfect world I created for them. But look what happened: They hid from Me! After they disobeyed Me, Adam and Eve were so ashamed to be in My presence that they sought the shelter of the trees when they heard Me approaching them.[1]

Later, I appeared to Abraham[2] and to Jacob,[3] both of whom remained faithful to Me. But then I appeared to Moses. I had a special, one-on-one, face-to-face relationship with him,[4] and I wanted the same kind of relationship with the Israelites. On Mount Sinai as I spoke to them and gave them the Ten Commandments, Moses stood between the Israelites and Me because they were afraid of the fire that encompassed me.[5] They heard My voice; they knew who I was and what I had said to them. But they kept their distance and decided that hearing My voice for themselves was too much for them; they chose to have Moses speak for Me.[6]

In the Bible, you can find other accounts of My appearances to individuals and to the nation of Israel. And although some of My people did turn to Me after I revealed Myself to them, the fact is that never did My obvious presence cause the masses to turn to Me.

I've also revealed Myself through Creation.[7] Look at the sky. Go ahead—right now. What do you see? Do you see a pitch-black void, a swath of midnight blue filled with shimmering stars, streaks of lightning illuminating the darkness? Or do you see an expanse of bright blue broken only by a dazzling sun, distant thunderclouds encroaching on a gray and misty vastness, glittering snow quietly falling from an unknown source? The heavens reveal My glory and My workmanship,[8] as does all Creation, from the smallest atom to the most majestic mountain on earth—and beyond, throughout the entire universe.

For millennia, humanity has tried to make sense of My Creation—or explain away My hand in it—by intense scientific investigation. I welcome their scrutiny and delight in their curiosity, because I know that their search will ultimately lead to Me, whether they recognize Me or not. My Creation is filled with wonder and complexity and much that My people have yet to discover, things that cannot be seen through the lens of the most powerful microscope or telescope, things that can be seen only in the Spirit.

And I've revealed Myself through My people and their moral conscience.

Think about your own human nature. Does forgiveness come naturally to you? What about loving your enemies? Those are not natural inclinations; those are supernatural inclinations that overcome your natural tendencies when you live in full cooperation with My Spirit. Without My Spirit leading, guiding, and empowering My people, the world would be overrun by hatred and every evil thing. The fact that it isn't is evidence of My existence.

Finally, I've revealed Myself in the person of Jesus Christ. People who demand that I reveal Myself forget that I already have. I came to earth in human form, demonstrated My love and compassion to you, showed you how you could live an extraordinary life on earth, and even performed signs and wonders and miracles, and yet many people who knew Me in the form of Jesus still rejected Me.

JESUS

I am the best evidence of the existence of God, and I am also the best evidence that if God were to reveal Himself to your culture today, people would still ask for more evidence. They did that when I was on earth even though I walked among them, healed their sick and raised their dead, and ate and drank with them as a good friend and neighbor. And they've continued to do that ever since.

When I drove out demons, religious leaders called Me the prince of demons.[9] As I began to attract a large group of followers, those same leaders tried to trap Me into proving I was "only human" by asking Me difficult questions.[10] And when the people began to recognize Me for who I am, the religious leaders told Me to rebuke them[11]—I couldn't possibly be who they thought I was! So the very people who knew the Jewish scriptures and were responsible for teaching them to the people refused to see that I was the Son of God, even though the prophecies they knew so well pointed directly to Me.

One of the many stories I told was about a rich man who had died and gone to hell. He pleaded with Abraham to send someone back from the dead to warn his family about the torment they would experience if they ended up in hell with him. Abraham reminded the rich man that they already had the teachings of Moses and the prophets to convince them that God's way is the right way. The rich man said they wouldn't listen to Moses and the prophets but would change their ways if someone rose from the dead and appeared to them. Abraham said that wouldn't make a bit of difference.[12] Not long after, I would rise from the dead—and many of those who refused to listen to Moses and the prophets remained unconvinced despite the evidence of My resurrection.

God

Do you see the pattern here? I revealed Myself in person, and people refused to believe. I revealed Myself in creation, and people refused to believe. I revealed Myself through Moses and the prophets, and people refused to believe.

I revealed Myself through My Son, Jesus Christ, and people refused to believe.

In this day, more than ever before in history, you have a vast amount of technology that can create what previous generations never dreamed would be possible. What do you think would happen if I were to reveal Myself in some miraculous way today? People would claim that My appearance was a trick of technology, and they would marvel at the technology while dismissing the possibility that it was really I who appeared.

The reality is this: People who don't want to believe I exist will not believe in Me no matter how I reveal Myself to them. Those who do believe I exist do so because they have *faith*—the one essential element that the skeptics and unbelievers lack. My people trust Me because I have proven Myself to be trustworthy, and through the eyes of faith, they have seen the abundance of evidence that I exist. They don't need to hear My voice thundering from Mount Sinai. They only need to have faith that I am with them here and now.

2
Why do we have to face temptation?

The temptation to sin can be overwhelming at times, especially when the sin in question is a specific one that a woman has wrestled with all her life. It doesn't matter whether it's a temptation to manipulate other people, shoplift an expensive silk scarf, or return to a promiscuous lifestyle, the desire to give in to that sin can threaten to control a woman's thoughts—or lead her to act on those thoughts.

Some people believe an all-powerful God should eliminate all temptation. After all, not only must people suffer the natural consequences of their sin, like possibly being arrested for shoplifting, they also must face punishment from the God who allowed the temptation in the first place.

Q **God, I cannot control the tempting thoughts that harass me every single day. I haven't given in to the temptation—yet—but sometimes it feels as if dealing with the sin would be easier than dealing with the thoughts. Why do we have to face temptation anyway?**

GOD

My daughter, I know the struggle you are experiencing. You are not alone in that experience; every one of My people struggles with the temptation to sin. Understand that neither sin nor the temptation to sin was part of My original plan, nor am I the one who tempts you to do wrong.[1]

Bear in mind that temptation is not sin—only giving in to the temptation is sinful. And even though you, and other women, struggle with a particular sin that seems to be yours alone, every temptation is universal. There isn't a single temptation out there that is unique to you; others have had to face it as well. But never forget My faithfulness. I will never allow you to be tempted beyond your endurance limit, but instead I will show you the way out of the situation that is tempting you.[2]

21

That way out is, and will always be, through My Spirit. When you live your life controlled by My Spirit, you won't give in to temptation, because My Spirit will not lead you into sin. You'll still feel the conflict within you, but as you yield more and more control to the Spirit, you'll be able to overcome the conflict.[3]

Even though the Spirit offers you a way out, however, don't wait until you face temptation to yield your life to the Spirit. I've seen My people enter into tempting situations completely unprepared for the attack they're about to face. If you live your life in the Spirit all day every day, then finding that "way out" will occur more quickly. You know which temptations are the strongest for you, and you can decide ahead of time how to handle them, with the wisdom and power that My Spirit gives you.

I've also seen My people enter into tempting situations with their eyes wide open, knowing they should run the other way. They're obviously not being led by the Spirit. Let's say you're attracted to a man at work, and you know the attraction is mutual. You're both married, but you each find one excuse after another to work late, leaving the two of you alone in the building. I can assure you that the Spirit did not lead you into that situation. You need to *flee*, and flee quickly.[4] And never get in that situation again.

While you're standing guard to avoid that big temptation in your life, whatever it may be, don't forget those that are so subtle you barely notice them. Those women who are living a decent life, serving other people, and striving to set a good example for others are especially vulnerable to two particularly insidious sins: pride and judging others. You may not even be aware that these sins are encroaching on your life. Being "good" without relying on My Spirit for a healthy dose of humility is the perfect setup for pride, and comparing your "goodness" with that of other people places you in an ideal position to start judging others by their behavior. Remember that any goodness you have comes from Me,[5] and the moment you're tempted to claim that goodness for yourself, recognize that for the sin it is.

Here's the thing—how you respond to temptation proves the strength of your faith and the depth of your love. Each time you resist temptation, you demonstrate how much you're relying on the Spirit, how highly you regard My love for you, and how much you love Me. But remember—it's not over if you give in to sin. Turn back to Me, turn away from the sin, and know that you are forgiven.[6] My grace, My unmerited favor on your life, will be all you need to get your life back on track.[7]

JESUS

Do you recall what happened right after My cousin John baptized Me? My Father had just placed His seal of approval on Me and the ministry that would soon begin, and then the Spirit led Me to the desert so that I would be tempted, or, in reality, tested. That's essentially what all of your temptations are; they're tests to determine your strength and commitment to following Me.

While I was in the desert, I fasted for forty days to prepare Myself for the onslaught to come. I knew I would not need physical strength to fight off this kind of attack; I would need the spiritual strength that came from focusing on My Father instead of on My physical needs and desires. Soon enough, the Enemy came, offering Me those things that he thought would turn Me away from God and toward him.

First, he tested Me to see if I would use My power to turn stones into bread and thereby satisfy My hunger. But I didn't go for the bait; I quoted Scripture and told him the Word of God was far more essential to life than mere bread was.

Second, he tried to get Me to jump off the top of the temple to prove that God's angels would save Me before I hit the ground. I again quoted Scripture and told him not to test God.

Third, he took Me to a mountaintop and told Me that I could have power over all the area before Me, as far as the eye could see, if only I would bow down and worship him. Again I quoted Scripture, telling him that God alone was worthy of worship.[8]

Did you detect the pattern in My responses to him? Instead of showing off the power I had at that point, I used the Word of God to respond to the temptations. Paul went so far as to call God's Word the "sword of the Spirit,"[9] a powerful weapon for cutting off the Enemy before he can hurt you.

And don't forget prayer. I made a point of including the matter of temptation in the model prayer I gave to My disciples, the one you call the Lord's Prayer.[10] The night before I died, I made another point of mentioning temptation, warning My disciples to stay on guard and continue to pray so they wouldn't fall into the temptation I knew would come their way.[11]

Temptation serves its purpose, if only to get you to rely more and more on God. The purpose of My temptation was not only to prove Me worthy of

My ministry but also to enable Me to share in your experience as a human being who is frequently subjected to temptation. I faced temptation and overcame it, and by that I showed you how you could do the same so you could then approach God with confidence and a clear conscience.[12]

GOD

One other thing. People use the saying "I'm only human!" to excuse their sin. Imagine how that sounds to Me. I sent My Son to die on the cross and My Spirit to live inside you so you could partake of My divine nature.[13] Yes, you are human, and as such you will fail at times. But My Spirit gives you the power to transcend your human nature, to live on a higher plane above the baseness of human depravity. You are human, but you are also My child, with all that I have and all that I am made available to you. Tell Me you've sinned, and we can deal with that together. Just don't tell Me that you're "only human," as if that absolves you of guilt. It doesn't.

Now imagine that you're defending your family from an actual physical attack. The enemy is at the door of your house, about to break it down. You've been at this fight for many hours, and you're exhausted. You have the weapons you need to fight off the attackers along with an unlimited stockpile of ammunition. But you're tired. "I'm only human!" you say as you wander off to the bedroom, leaving your family to fend for themselves.

Do you see My point? I've given you everything you need to fight temptation: My Spirit, My Word, My wisdom, My strength, My power. All you have to do is to call on Me and use what I've given you. With that, you can be a conqueror   in fact, more than a conqueror![14] I will never abandon you or leave you stranded without hope.

3
Why should we trust You?

Admit it. There are times when God and the things He does—or the things He allows—just don't make sense to you. You wonder why He allows your funny, kind, compassionate friend to die in a violent car crash and lets a hardened criminal avoid prison on a technicality. It's hard to trust a God who at times seems so, well, capricious.

The Bible and every one of God's followers tell you that you can trust Him. Still, you're not convinced. You want proof, some kind of guarantee that if you put your faith and trust in Him, He won't let you down. Enough people have done that already; it's too painful to think that God might disappoint you too.

Q   **God, I have a major trust issue. I trusted my parents to take care of me; one walked out, and the other became clinically depressed. I trusted my first love, but he jilted me. Now my friends say I should trust You. I have one question: Why should I?**

GOD

The short answer is that I love you more than anyone ever has or ever will, and I will always have your best interests at heart. But I know that isn't enough for you when it comes to trust, and understandably so. You've been deeply wounded, and you're afraid to trust anyone ever again. So I'll start the long answer with an explanation of what trust is.

Trust is a sense of assurance that you can confide in and rely on a person based on his character and his record of accomplishment in making you feel safe, unafraid, and confident in your relationship. Trust builds over time and relies on experience rather than mere words. Actions count more than ever when it comes to trust.

Think about someone you *do* trust—your closest friend. How did you come to be such good friends? How did you come to trust her with the secrets and the dreams and the private thoughts you've shared with her? Did she introduce herself and immediately say, "Trust me"? No, she didn't. The trust you have in each other developed over time. You spent hours together, getting to know each other, at first sharing "safe" personal information, and little by little, you opened up and shared those things that you wanted only her to know. Over time, you discovered that she would do what she said she would do, be there when you needed her, and never betray the trust you had placed in her.

Think of our relationship in that way. Your trust has been shattered by many people, so I expect you to take it slow when it comes to trusting Me. That's fine; we have time. Begin by sharing your heart with Me, even if it means admitting that you have a problem with Me. I want you to be honest with Me, because genuine trust without honesty simply doesn't exist.

Talk to Me. That's what prayer is. Listen as well, but understand that My response may not come in the way you expect it to or at the time you want it to. I love you and want to have a relationship with you. You can ask whatever you like, but don't forget that I am God, and I determine the best way and the best time to answer your prayers. Some people mistakenly believe that because I have made so many promises to My people, they can demand that I fulfill them now. That's not trust; that's arrogance. And a loving relationship cannot be built on arrogant demands.

There are people in your life who claim they trusted Me but say that I failed them. They've walked away from Me and the wonderful life they could have had. What they didn't realize was that they "trusted" Me for things I never promised, things that would have caused a great deal of pain and heartache down the road, but they could not see that. Only I know what the future holds, and that's one of the many reasons why you need to trust Me with your future.

When you refuse to trust Me, however, you hurt yourself. You figure you can handle life all on your own, but by not seeking My help, you make things harder on yourself than you can imagine. You see one piece of the puzzle; I see the complete picture.[1] Let Me help you put the right pieces in the right places.

Be open to the idea of trusting Me completely. Begin reading the Bible, My love letter to My people, to discover the many times I proved My trust-worthiness and came through for even those who disobeyed Me.[2] I have a proven record, one that spans all of time.

Don't just read isolated Bible verses. They're valuable, of course, but they're also like puzzle pieces. They make more sense when you see the big picture. Here's an example of what I mean. My servant David wrote many psalms that expressed his deep trust in Me. In Psalm 52, he praised Me for the things I had done and publicly conveyed his trust in Me.[3] That's a lovely thought, and one that reminds people of My faithfulness. But when you realize what had just happened to David, you see the depth of his trust in Me. A servant had just told King Saul a lie about David that put his life in jeopardy and cost the lives of dozens of priests.[4] Still, David continued to trust in Me, and his trust seldom faltered.

Other people will let you down, and you will let down other people, but I will be the one constant in your life, the One you can trust with your life. You will always be safe and secure with Me.

JESUS

One thing you need to understand is that trusting God the Father does not mean that He will give you an easy life. No one knows that better than I do. When I lived on earth as a man, I hardly had it easy, even though the Father announced that He was well pleased with Me.[5] I had many faithful followers, but many more abandoned Me or betrayed Me, like Judas, one of the twelve trusted men with whom I had chosen to share My life and My deepest truths. I faced constant harassment from the religious leaders. Soon enough, the people rejected Me. And then I was branded a criminal, sentenced to die on a wooden cross. I was severely beaten, taunted, and tortured, and I felt as if My Father had abandoned Me right before I died.[6]

No, Mine was not an easy life. Nor was it easy for My mother.

MARY

One of the hardest things I've ever had to do was watch my beloved son die such a horrible death and still believe that I could trust God. How could I possibly trust Him now? He had chosen me to be the mother of His Son, and I was so humbled by that. I was also overjoyed, and I anticipated living a glorious existence in the shadow of my son—the Messiah! Little did I know the suffering I would have to endure many years later.

I sensed something horrible was about to happen—mothers just know these things. But when I heard that my boy had been sentenced to death, everything became a blur. There was chaos in the streets as Jesus was being led to the cross, and I could hardly get close enough to see Him. I rushed to Golgotha where I knew the criminals would be executed. My son, a criminal! And sentenced to die! Everyone knew about the excruciating pain that was suffered by those who were nailed to a cross; I couldn't bear to think of it. Surely God would intervene and spare my Jesus!

But then it happened. The cruel and sadistic Roman soldiers took great pleasure in seeing my son mocked and taunted and tormented, as if being nailed to the cross wasn't enough! I spent several agonizing hours near the cross with my sister, the wife of our friend Clopas, and Mary Magdalene, whose grief was nearly as great as my own. I could hardly look at Jesus, and I could hardly take my eyes off Him! Just before He died, He looked at me and spoke the last words He would ever say to me: "Dear woman, here is your son," pointing to His good friend and disciple, John. We both knew what He meant; John was to look after me and become like a son to me in Jesus' absence.[7]

I can't begin to express how painful that time was, that is, until God restored my son, and His, to life! Yes, trusting God until the moment I saw my son alive was difficult, but I never saw Jesus' faith waver, and if He could trust the Father, I could. And in the weeks that followed, I joined with others who truly believed my son was the Messiah, continuing to pray and worship and trust in God.[8]

4
How are we made in Your image?

The Bible says that people are made in the image of God, but to most people, this is a puzzling concept. They wonder how, if God is a Spirit, human beings could be made in His image. So complex is this issue that an entire theology—called imago Dei, *Latin for "image of God"—has been constructed around it.*

Theology aside, people, especially women, want to know what this means. Being told that they are made in the image of God poses a particular problem for women who have always heard God referred to in masculine terms. They want to know how they can reflect God's likeness when only masculine pronouns are used to refer to God.

Q **God, the issue of being made in Your image is confusing. We know God the Father, Jesus the Son, and the Holy Spirit, who as a Spirit is usually referred to as a male anyway. How can we women relate to that? Just how** *are* **we made in Your image?**

GOD

The concept you're referring to is mentioned in the very beginning of the Bible: "God said, 'Let us make human beings in our image, to be like ourselves. They will reign over the fish in the sea, the birds in the sky, the livestock, all the wild animals on the earth, and the small animals that scurry along the ground.' So God created human beings in his own image. In the image of God he created them; male and female he created them."[1]

Those of you who are familiar with that passage will notice the wording is a bit different from what you're used to. Many of your translators used masculine nouns and pronouns in that passage and throughout the Hebrew Bible in reference to Me. When I gave people free will, that extended to the development of their languages, and that resulted in some confusion. I'll forgo the linguistics lesson and assure you that I made both men and women in My image—because My image represents the wholeness and unity of male and female.

You want to know how women are made in My image? Well, first you have to erase from your mind any picture of a physical human body, and along with it all those physical features that make males men and females women. And get rid of whatever picture of Me you've been carrying around in your head; I'm not an old man with a long beard and a stern expression on My face! I am Spirit,[2] and that means you cannot see Me. So being made in My image does not mean resembling Me physically.

How do you reflect My likeness? Have I created a race of divine clones? No. You are made in My image, but you are not God, a fact that is lost on some who refuse to acknowledge My authority. If you look at some of My characteristics and then look at yours, you'll see the resemblance.

One of My characteristics is that I am a living God, not a statue formed from a substance like metal, wood, or stone.[3] I didn't create a world filled with robots; I created living, breathing human beings. I am a living Being, and you are living beings made in My image.

Another quality we have in common is the capacity to love. I not only love; I am love itself.[4] Jesus pointed out the relationship between My love for you and the love you are to exhibit when He said that the world would recognize My people by the love they have for one another.[5]

I also created you to reflect My holiness—and the first people did, for a while. I was delighted with My creation! Everything was perfect; Adam and Eve were the image of holiness. But when Adam sinned, everything changed.[6] The good news, of course, is that you can be restored to again reflect My righteousness and holiness.[7]

Along those same lines, I created My people with a moral nature even before they were fully aware of good and evil. Adam and Eve instinctively knew that disobeying Me was wrong, even before their eyes were opened to the reality of good and evil. You have those same instincts inside you; you know right from wrong, and in that you are also a likeness of Me.

Look at all the other ways you reflect My image: You are intelligent, rational, creative, knowledgeable. You are capable of governing yourselves, and you are capable of having dominion over the natural world.[8] You have free will, the ability to make your own decisions. You form relationships, and you are able to have fellowship with Me. In all these ways, you are made in My image.

But if you're still not sure what My image is and how you were created to reflect it, keep in mind that Jesus is the mirror image of Me. When you see Him, you see Me, and in Him you see how I intended My people to reflect My likeness.[9]

Jesus

When I was on earth I provided people with a visual representation of who God is. Even then, however, I wasn't simply a stand-in for God; I was, and am, God Himself.[10] When you give up your old life and make a commitment to start a new life with Me, your new goal in life is to become like Me, to become Christlike. There is no better way to reflect the image of God.

If you want to become like Me, there is no better starting point than obedience. When I was on earth, I had given up all the authority I had in heaven and submitted My will to the will of the Father. In My case, that meant being obedient to the point of extreme suffering and death. In your case, it may mean being obedient to the point of feeling uneasy when you step out of your comfort zone and serve God in a radical new way.

Serving others, by the way, defined My ministry. God the Father made you to serve others as well. Those of you who are already involved in ministry to others know how draining and demanding it can be. I often tried to escape the crowds and get away by Myself, and on several occasions, I succeeded. The need was great, and because I carried within Me the compassion of God the Father, I couldn't abandon those who had placed their faith in Me. Serving others will help you become more Christlike, but be prepared—it will be both exhausting and among the most rewarding things you'll ever do. You will be acting in obedience to the Father, reflecting His love and compassion for those you serve.

Then there is forgiveness. Every time you forgive someone who has offended you—especially someone who really doesn't deserve your mercy—you are showing the world who God the Father is. Forgiveness is something only God could think up. If God had not invented forgiveness, you can rest assured that humans never would have. Forgiveness is a quality and an action that runs in direct opposition to normal human nature. Forgiveness is a supernatural, divine dimension of life that reveals the glory of God every time you activate it. My ability to forgive the soldiers who brutalized Me on the day of My death,[11] for example, could come only from a divine source.

If you want to know what it means to be created in the image of God, you need look no further than the example I gave you when I was on earth. Look at My actions, not My gender. Imitate the way I lived, the way I cared about people, the way I endured both the persecution and the foolishness that surrounded Me wherever I went. Love others, serve others, and have compassion on others. Be kind. Be forgiving. Be generous with your time, your money, and your possessions. Love the things of God, not the things of the world. *That's* what it means to be created in God's image—to live the life I lived when I came to earth and lived among My people.

5
How can Your Spirit live in us?

Perhaps because the term Holy Spirit *lacks the strong masculine connection that "Father" and "Son" have, women for the most part readily respond to teachings about who the Spirit is and how the Spirit works in a person's life. Even so, the idea of the Spirit living "inside" people—often referred to as the "indwelling" of the Holy Spirit—can be a puzzling concept.*

Once the "how" is understood, curiosity gives rise to a slew of "why" and "what" questions: why God sent the Holy Spirit in the first place, what the Spirit does in the lives of God's people that is so unique, and why living a life led by the Spirit is so important.

Q **God, we know You sent the Holy Spirit to be with Christ's followers after He returned to heaven. That's fine until we get to the part about the Spirit living in us—that's just so, well, personal. We know You are everywhere, but how can Your Spirit live *in* us?**

GOD

Consider for a moment the nature of a newborn baby. From the very first day, the baby in some way resembles both her parents. She has her father's nose or her mother's eyes. She carries the genetic qualities unique to each parent, and anyone who looks at her can see the physical characteristics that are specific to each of her parent's families. As she matures, the resemblance becomes even more striking, so much so that a complete stranger may see the family resemblance even after the child has become an adult.

On a spiritual level, when a person becomes a new creation by choosing to follow Me, My Spirit takes up residence in her. That's called being "born of the Spirit." In physical birth, your unique DNA contains physical family characteristics; when you're born of the Spirit, your spiritual nature takes on the characteristics of My family through the Spirit living within you.

It's important for you to understand that My Spirit lives within you, because the Holy Spirit is your assurance that you belong to Me[1] and your guarantee that My promises are meant for you.[2] That assurance also enables you to bring your old nature under the Spirit's control so you can be free from the power that sin once held over you.[3]

Here's another way of looking at it. Because My Spirit now lives inside you, your body has become the Spirit's home. And because the Spirit is holy, your body has become a sacred place in which the Spirit dwells.[4] Now you have a holy Being living inside a holy dwelling. What do you think that means for your life? In part, it means that everything you need to live a holy life is living inside you. Don't be thrown off by the word *holy*, by the way. Yes, when it refers to Me it implies spiritual perfection. When it is applied to My people, it simply means that your life is dedicated to worshipping and serving Me. Unfortunately, your culture has so misused the term that some people think holy women float through life with their palms pressed together in prayer, wearing a dreamy, saintly smile at all times, and thinking and speaking of nothing but Me.

Let Me tell you what a holy woman might really look like. She looks like a young mother dressed in jeans and a sweatshirt pushing a cart full of kids and groceries and thinking about her next stop on the list of errands to run. She might look like a divorced, middle-aged woman sitting in a cubicle intently studying a computer screen filled with insurance liability statistics. Or she might look like an exhausted widow scurrying from one table to another at the restaurant where she works, trying to forget the still-raw grief she feels over her husband's sudden death. If My Spirit lives within them, then these are holy women doing holy work. Their lives are still dedicated to worshipping and serving Me, no matter what else they may be engaged in.

There are people in your life who keep encouraging you to discover for yourself the experience of living a Spirit-led life, but you're confused about that as well. In their excitement and enthusiasm over this new adventure they're experiencing, sometimes My people don't always explain things very well—they just want you to join in their excitement, but they never really tell you what it involves.

One thing Spirit-led living doesn't involve is stopping to consult with the Spirit before you take your next step. Spirit-led living involves becoming so in tune with My Spirit that your thoughts and actions will begin to fall in line with My will—what I want for your life, what I know is the best way for you to live, and the best way you can serve Me and My people. If you truly want to live by the Spirit, don't look to your friend's life and follow her pattern; My Spirit knows your gifts, your talents, and your strengths and will use those—not your friend's—to bring glory to My name and help to My people. Let her work in the soup kitchen all she likes, but if that's not what the Spirit is leading you to do, stay away from the ladle.

And speaking of ladles, don't think that because you're a woman, your area of service is confined to hospitality. It may be your area now, but all too often some women—even those who have been taught how to discover their spiritual gifts and talents—assume that because they're comfortable in the kitchen, that's where I expect them to stay. Discovering your true gift—teaching or counseling, perhaps—and not just one you're familiar with, is an area where you can rely on the Spirit's guidance.[5]

My Spirit doesn't just reveal your gift to you and leave you on your own to figure out how to use it. No, the Spirit is ready to teach you what you need to know,[6] grant you the wisdom you need for the task at hand,[7] and even give you the words to say[8] as you minister to others. Can you see now why your friends have been encouraging you to live by the Spirit? Everything that I am is at your disposal when you have My Spirit living inside you.

Remember this too. My Spirit will help you when you don't know how to pray about a situation, or when you're too grieved over something in your own life to even get the words out.[9] When you begin living your life in harmony with the Spirit, you'll discover even more things that the Spirit helps you with, such as telling other people about Me, giving you control over sin and temptation, and empowering you to live a life of love, joy, peace, and faithfulness.

JESUS

Those qualities—love, joy, peace, faithfulness, and others—are evidence that you have replaced your sinful desires with a desire to follow Me.[10] Spiritually, when you make that commitment, it's as if you died—your old self, that is—and a whole new you has sprung to life.

Many of you are familiar with an encounter I had with a man named Nicodemus. He was a Pharisee and a member of the Sanhedrin, the ruling Jewish council. He was in the thick of the religious leadership at that time, and his colleagues were among my severest critics. He came to Me under cover of darkness one night—he knew what it would cost him if he had been seen associating with Me—and told Me what I already suspected. His words confirmed that at least some of the Pharisees, hypocrites that they were, knew where My power came from; he acknowledged that God was the power behind the miracles I performed.[11]

My response? I told him that only those who were born again could be part of the kingdom of God. Not surprisingly, he took that literally and asked how a person could reenter a woman's womb and be born a second time.

I answered him again, pointing out that humans give birth to humans, but the Spirit gives birth to spirit.[12]

Nicodemus still didn't get it. But because you have the Holy Spirit residing in you, you can understand this much better than he did. Your first birth is a physical one; a physical woman gives birth to a physical child. But in your second birth—when you come into full relationship with Me—the Holy Spirit gives birth to a whole new spirit in you. The water I spoke of symbolizes the cleansing and purification that take place at that moment, the moment when your old desires and your old sinful nature are crucified, or put to death. You so closely identify with Me that the symbol of crucifixion is not an exaggeration; some of My followers even visualize their old self and their old habits nailed to a cross—gone forever.

That's great news! Your old self no longer counts; it's dead and gone. In its place, the Holy Spirit gives life,[13] life as only God Himself, the Creator of life, can give.

6

Who's controlling our lives—You or us?

The matter of control is one of the trickiest problems in a person's relationship with God. The Bible says God is sovereign and in control of people's lives. When people come into a personal relationship with God, they're told that they have to turn over control of their lives to Him.

At the same time, followers of Jesus are told that their new life is one that's characterized by freedom. To make the matter more perplexing, the Bible says they've always had free will, whether in their old lives or their new ones. If God is really in control, they don't see how they ever had the freedom to run their own lives the way they wanted to.

Q **God, we believe that You are the all-powerful Lord of everything that exists. But You've also made it clear that we are free to make our own decisions, including whether or not to follow You. So which is it? Who's controlling our lives—You or us?**

GOD

Let's start with a basic understanding of how and where I operate and how and where you operate. You are well aware that I exist in a dimension you can't see and can't understand; it's a spiritual dimension in which there is no time and there are no spatial restrictions. I am everywhere at once. Don't worry—I don't expect you to fully comprehend that.

By contrast, you live in a dimension regulated by time and constrained by space. You can be in only one place at one time, despite your best efforts to be everywhere at once. You can't be in Tucson and Rome in the same moment. The limitations of time and space in the earthly dimension won't permit that.

Does that mean because I exist outside time and space, I can control a great many things that limit you and that you have no control over? Yes. Does that mean you have no control over your life, since I'm pulling the strings? No. What it means is that we both have control.

Earlier you asked how people were made in My image. One of the factors I pointed out was your ability to make decisions. That ability would be meaningless if I made all the decisions for you, and it wouldn't exactly help with your growth and maturity. But here's what you need to understand about that: I could make all those decisions for you if I wanted to.[1] I created everything in heaven and on earth, including those things you can see and those things you can't see. And I created everything for Myself,[2] including you. So, yes, I have the power to control every step of your life and every minute of your day—while you're brushing your teeth in the morning, attending an afternoon meeting at work, watching the late news on television, and everything in between. But I don't do that, for many reasons, the most important of which is that I created you to be in relationship with Me, not to do My bidding every second of the day. If I wanted robots, I would have built robots. I left that task to human beings.

Let Me give you an example of the kind of control I have over the circumstances of your life. If you were hospitalized, you, or a loved one if you're incapacitated, would want to be the one to make a decision about whether to opt for surgery, try medications first, or go with another form of treatment that also shows promise. So far, so good. You're the one in control. You opt for surgery, but during the procedure a complication arises that you cannot control; it's outside the realm of possibility for you to sense the problem while you're sedated, bring yourself to full consciousness, and have the necessary skill to correct the problem. Because it's outside your realm of possibility doesn't mean that it's outside Mine. This is exactly the kind of situation in which I delight to take over the reins. My Spirit intervenes by giving supernatural wisdom to the surgeon or someone on the surgical team, and the complication is simplified. It's your life, but I took control—and when you awaken, you'll be glad I did.

Intervening on your behalf is evidence of My love for you, not of any desire on My part to dominate you. Do I want you to turn to Me and allow Me to direct your steps? Yes, but even then, I wouldn't expect you to want Me to micromanage your life. But to help you make the big decisions and keep you from making major mistakes? Yes, you would welcome that. My prophet Jeremiah sought that kind of help from Me, expressing his request in this way: "I know, GOD, that mere mortals can't run their own lives, that men and women don't have what it takes to take charge of life. So correct us, GOD, as you see best."[3]

There's wisdom in Jeremiah's request beyond the words he used. In asking for My help, he humbled himself and acknowledged his need for My guidance. He knew that even though he had the freedom to continue living life the way he chose, it was much better to seek the assistance of the One who gave him that life.

Here's the way I want you to look at My involvement in your life. You have before you a life of endless possibilities, and you have the freedom to decide which of those possibilities you choose to pursue. I won't stop you from pursuing your number one choice—but if I know that you'll be unhappy or in danger as a result of that decision, I will warn you and even intervene if the situation warrants it. Remember, I have your best interests at heart.[4]

That control is rooted in the love I have for you. Total domination—controlling your life against your will—has no place in a loving relationship. Loving involvement and welcome guidance do. If you will let Me, if you will welcome My help in determining which of those infinite possibilities are right for you, I have promised to direct your paths and lead you in the way you should go.[5] I'll keep My eye on you and guide you continually.[6]

Here are a few more points I want you to consider as you continue to think about the relationship between My sovereignty—My supreme power over all that is and all that ever will be—and your free will.

First, if you truly believed that I had absolute control over your life, would you even consider worshipping Me? I want My people to willingly worship Me[7] and glorify Me,[8] not resent Me for running roughshod over them. Furthermore, if you believed I was running your life, what motivation would you have to even get up in the morning? I want My people to live life to the fullest, not go through life on autopilot because they think every aspect of their lives is set in stone.

Second, do you or anyone else you know live as if I'm completely running the show? People live by what they believe, and those few people who live as if I do exert total control are not living their lives to the fullest. No, people tend to exercise the freedom I have given them. You, for example, are already living in accordance with the answer I just gave to your own question. You exercise your free will, but you still call on Me for help and guidance and expect Me to intervene when things go awry. You are able to show Me that you trust Me, and I am able to prove My trustworthiness to you.

We both have control. The way we exercise it, in cooperation and harmony with each other, serves to strengthen the loving relationship we both want to maintain.

7

Why don't You prevent disasters from happening?

Natural disasters, especially those involving a large loss of life, nearly always provoke questions about the role of God. People want to know where God was, why He didn't intervene, and whether He had the power to prevent the disaster in the first place. And sometimes, the debate turns into a challenge to the very existence of God.

Because women tend to be so compassionate, human tragedy strikes them especially hard. Their hearts break for the innocent lives that were lost and the grieving survivors who often feel betrayed by God or nature or whatever else they may believe in. They want to know how God could allow such heartache to exist in the world He created.

Q **God, most of the time we believe You love us. But then tens of thousands of people die in an earthquake or a tsunami or a similar disaster, and we're not so sure anymore. If You have the power to create the universe, why don't You prevent disasters from happening?**

GOD

You cannot begin to comprehend how much it grieves Me when My people suffer because of a natural disaster in the world that I created. I hear every voice that cries out to Me, every agonizing moan and terrified shriek, and every last breath that a victim takes. I see every crushed and bloody and broken body, every tearstained and panic-stricken face, and every exhausted but determined rescue worker.

I see everything that happens in the world. I see the suffering, and I have compassion on victims whose pain seems to know no limits.[1] I hear everything as well, both the prayers and the curses that are uttered against Me.

You ask why I don't prevent disasters from happening. You won't like My answer, because it will never satisfy your need to make sense of tragedy. That's why you asked the question in the first place; you want an answer that will help you understand a world in which the unpredictable can suddenly reduce entire cities and towns and villages to piles of rubble.

Let Me first say that to assume I willingly chose not to prevent a natural disaster is to conclude that I either don't have the power or I don't have the concern to do so. Both are mistaken conclusions.

Here is why disasters happen: You live in a "fallen world," the term many religious people use to describe the condition of the world since sin entered. The sin of Adam and Eve didn't just infect humanity; it left its mark on the natural world as well.[2] Neither the people nor the world itself displays the perfection of My original creation. Just as human nature doesn't operate according to My original plan, neither does the physical world operate under the natural law I initially established.

The truth of the matter is that my gift to humanity, the freedom to choose, became its curse. In choosing disobedience, human beings established a sinful pattern that has affected the entire world. Contrary to what I hear so many people say—including religious leaders, who should know better—natural disasters are not My way of punishing people for the evil in the world. Natural disasters are instead the logical result of the evil in the world. If humanity hadn't rejected Me, the world would have remained in its original condition of perfection.

The ability to reverse the negative effects of sinful behavior on the natural world lies in the hands of those who choose to indulge in sinful behavior. And I'm not referring to the superficial behavior that so many self-righteous people say they'd never fall into, behavior like drunkenness or promiscuity or drug use. I'm referring to the sin that is at the root of all sinfulness: the sin of rejecting Me, denying who I am, and willfully disregarding everything I've ever said and done. All other sins are just symptoms of the underlying disease that's eating away at humanity like quickly spreading terminal cancer.

As I do with every other negative factor in your lives, I use the aftermath of natural disasters to serve My ultimate purpose for humanity—to bring people back into alignment with the way I created them to be. When disaster strikes, many people turn to Me for help, comfort, and wisdom, or they rail at Me for not preventing the tragedy. Either way, people are suddenly communicating with Me and thinking about Me, often for the first time in a long time. Those who have the courage to do so begin to think deeply about My active participation in the world in which they live.

Here's something those deep thinkers might want to ponder: No one ever asks Me how many disasters I have prevented. You have no idea how much worse your world would be if I hadn't stretched out My hand to stay potential disasters. Imagine, also, what would happen if I were to remove all the goodness that still exists in Creation, if I let people have full rein over the world. My involvement in the world, which you imply is insufficient, keeps the world from descending into complete chaos.[3]

Jesus

Repent has become a highly unfashionable word, but it describes how you can help in the process of restoring the world and humanity to their ideal conditions.

Let Me tell you a story, one of My favorite activities. During the time of My ministry on earth, Pilate, who could be ruthless, had some people from Galilee murdered, and then he compounded the tragedy by mixing the blood of the victims with the blood of the animal sacrifices on the altar. Certain people tried to bait Me into saying that those people were subjected to Pilate's actions because of their sins, but I didn't take the bait.[4]

I reminded them instead of another tragedy that had recently occurred in Siloam, just south of the main part of Jerusalem. A tower had collapsed, killing eighteen people. Were those people guiltier of sin than anyone else? No. I made the point that regardless of whether a tragedy is intentional, as in the Galileans' deaths, or accidental, as at Siloam, it has no connection with the sins of the specific people who died. It's just the natural order of things in a fallen world. But tragedy does have a connection with the overall sinful nature of the world, which disrupts the natural order, which is why I ended the conversation using the word that few people use anymore: *repent*. Unless they repented, I told them, they, too, would die.[5]

That word, *repent*, has been the subject of so many cartoons—you know the ones, usually showing someone who supposedly looks like Me holding a picket sign bearing the warning "Repent!"—that its meaning has become distorted and diluted. But repentance is a critical step in your relationship with Me and in humanity's restoration to its original condition. Those who heard Me use the word in the first century—Jews and Gentiles alike—knew its full meaning. Repentance involves not just confession and remorse but also turning away from the sin.

Until people turn away from the sin of rejecting God and refusing to live according to God's laws, which are not burdensome but life-giving, humanity will continue to suffer the natural consequences of their sin. Too many people live in a way that seems perfectly fine to them but violates God's laws.[6]

The good news, however, is that We have not abandoned you. Nothing—absolutely nothing in all of creation, no hardship, no disaster, nothing—can separate you from My love.[7] Furthermore, you have no need to fear the catastrophes that are sure to come, because God will always be with you.[8] You can look forward to a future time when the sufferings of this dark world[9] will cease and God will live among His people again, drying every tear from their eyes and putting an end to everything that causes grief and pain.[10]

The Word that gives life was from the begin-ning, and this is the one our message is about. Our ears have heard, our own eyes have seen, and our hands touched this Word. The one who gives life appeared! We saw it happen, and we are witnesses to what we have seen. Now we are telling you about this eternal life that was with the Father and appeared to us. We are telling you what we have seen and heard, so that you may share in this life with us. And we share in it with the Father and with his Son Jesus Christ. We are writing to tell you these things, because this makes us truly happy.

1 John 1:1–4 CEV

JESUS

> *Though He lived more than two thousand years ago, Jesus is considered the greatest person in history. His followers believed him to be both fully God and fully human while He was on earth.*

8.   Jesus, are You really God's Son? 49

9.   Why did You come to earth anyway? 53

10.   Why was a virgin birth necessary? 57

11.   Did You physically rise from the dead? 61

12.   Did You experience human emotions on earth? 65

13.   Is it true that You never sinned? 69

14.   Did You really die to save everyone? 73

8
Jesus, are You really God's Son?

No one in history has been investigated more than Jesus Christ. Ever since He appeared on the scene in first-century Palestine, Jesus has been the subject of intense scrutiny and study by people from all walks of life, all trying to determine if He was prophet, teacher, spiritual guide, failed politician, madman, charlatan, the Son of God, or some combination of those identities.

What people believe about Jesus determines their future. If they believe He truly is the Son of God—and understand what that means for them personally—that belief will lead them to God. If they deny that He is God's Son, their pathway will lead them away from God.

Q **Jesus, there's been a lot of talk in recent years about who You are—and we don't mean just in religious circles. The talk throughout the media is mostly about new archaeological evidence that allegedly casts some doubt on Your identity. So tell us—are You really God's Son?**

JESUS

Yes, I am. But since I know that such a simple but truthful answer is not likely to satisfy anyone, I'll offer substantial evidence to support that answer.

We have a lot of ground to cover here, so let's start with what My enemies said about Me. These were the people who were trying to undermine My ministry. But they were also among the most learned men in Palestine at that time, and they understood that I was claiming to be the Son of God.

One of the most telling incidents occurred after I raised My friend Lazarus from the dead. He had been dead for four days, and there was understandable concern that the stench would be overwhelming. I prayed and then commanded Lazarus to come out of the tomb in which his body had been placed. He came out, still wrapped in his grave clothes but as alive as anyone who was present at the event that day.

That demonstration of God's power shook the religious leaders to the core. They quickly called a meeting to decide what to do about Me; they were afraid that if I continued to perform miracles like that, everybody would believe I truly was sent by God—and that would threaten their power. What was most significant about their discussion was that they never disputed the miracle itself. Deep down, many of them knew what that meant. Even though there would be counterfeit signs and wonders,[1] they knew that only God could perform true miracles.[2]

On many occasions, the Jewish leaders challenged the things I said because they knew the Scriptures and because I referred to Myself in terms that were used exclusively for God. This incensed them, especially when they realized they couldn't refute any of the miracles I performed, failed to trip Me up with what they thought were difficult questions, and saw how many people were following Me. Had I not been who I said I was, they would not have felt as threatened as they did.

You have the testimony of My followers. Some did not fully understand who I was until after the resurrection, but others recognized Me as the Son of God during My earthly ministry. Most of you have heard that I once walked on water, which has become one of your culture's ways of referring to people who seemingly can do no wrong; but it originated with Me, the One who actually never did do any wrong. Others of you are familiar with the incident in which Peter tried to join Me and did fine until he got scared. I rescued him, of course, and after we reached the boat My disciples were on, the others began to worship Me and said, "Truly you are the Son of God."[3] They were Jews, and they knew what they were doing and saying. They worshipped Me as God and identified Me with God.

Peter later expressed his faith in Me as the Son of God when I asked My disciples a simple question: Who do people say that I am? They gave varying answers, and then I asked who they said that I was. Peter answered, "You're the Christ, the Messiah, the Son of the living God."[4] It was clear that God had revealed this to him. And even though he had some problems after I was arrested and denied knowing Me,[5] he regained his footing and some years later boldly referred to Me as "God and Savior Jesus Christ"[6] in a letter that was circulated among the churches.

Many others recognized Me as the Son of God and openly said so. Among those was Martha, Lazarus's sister, who once told Me that she truly believed I was the Son of God.[7] The Roman soldiers who were guarding Me at the cross became terrified when an earthquake struck at the moment of My death and cried out, "Surely He was the Son of God!"[8] And then there is the well-known incident with Thomas after I was resurrected, when he touched the scars on My body, realized that I wasn't just an apparition, and blurted out, "My Lord and my God!"[9]

Paul, of course, wrote many letters in which he affirmed My deity. And remember, he used to persecute My followers! But once he recognized Me as God, there was no turning back for him and no use trying to get him to stop writing. His letters to the churches at Rome, Corinth, Galatia, Ephesus, Philippi, Colossae, and Thessalonica and to Timothy, Titus, and Philemon are replete with references to Me as God.

Now look at what I said about Myself during My ministry. I called Myself "I AM," which was the ancient Israelites' name for God, and that nearly got Me stoned. The Jewish leaders considered that the greatest form of blasphemy,[10] as they did when the high priest asked Me if I was the Messiah and I answered yes, and as I faced another stoning when I said, "I and the Father are one . . . I am the Father and the Father is in Me."[11]

And then there are the things I did, like forgive sins, promise eternal life to those who believed in Me, turn water into wine, calm the sea, heal the sick, restore sight to the blind, cast out demons, raise the dead, and feed the multitudes with a few fish and some loaves of bread.

Yes, I really am God's Son.

GOD

I attest to that! For centuries, My Spirit led My prophets to tell the Hebrew nation about the coming of the Messiah, the Savior whose blood would be shed to pay the penalty for their sins. My plan all along was to visit My people in the form of My Son, whom they would call Jesus. My servant John rightly referred to Him as the Word, and made it clear that Jesus and I are One and the same—Jesus is simply Me in the flesh.[12]

Many of you are familiar with the account of Jesus' baptism. As you recall, as soon as Jesus emerged from the water, I sent My Spirit to Him in the form of a dove. And then My voice thundered from the heavens declaring Jesus to be My Son.[13] What a glorious moment that was. I placed My seal of approval on Jesus, and He was then ready to begin to fulfill the purpose for which He was sent to earth.

Jesus mentioned using the term "I AM" to refer to Himself, but that wasn't the only time He was referred to by names that were used exclusively to refer to Me. In the book of Revelation, one of My angels called Jesus the "Lord of lords and King of kings," and Jesus called Himself "the Alpha and the Omega,"[14] and I fully endorse the use of those terms to refer to both of Us.

There's so much more evidence that Jesus is My Son, but evidence alone won't convince you. You need to investigate the evidence, of course, but in the end it will be your heart and not your head that will need convincing. *Faith* is the operative word here. If I were to provide people with ironclad proof that Jesus is My Son, they would still find a way to dispute it. Believing in Me—believing in Jesus—takes faith, the evidence of things you can't see.

9
Why did You come to earth anyway?

Once a woman has settled the question of whether or not Jesus was the Son of God, more questions arise. If He was the Son of God, there had to be a significant reason why He came to earth. It's not as if God needed a spy—He knows everything already. He didn't come for the benefit of God the Father but rather for the benefit of the people.

Now the question concerns what that benefit was—or what those benefits were. If He came just to convey God's wisdom and perform miracles, that's fine, but it's hardly life changing. There had to be something more, a bigger reason why the Creator would personally visit His creation.

Q **It's hard enough for us to imagine giving up whatever little luxuries we have in life to live and work among the poor, but leaving the glory of heaven to live and work among mere humanity—well, to us that's incomprehensible. So, Jesus—why did You come to earth, anyway?**

JESUS

I can sum up My reasons for coming to earth in two words: *forgiveness* and *reconciliation*. Naturally, there's more to it than that, including many reasons that fit into those two categories. But in the grand scheme of things, I came to forgive people of their sins and reconcile them to God the Father, from whom they were estranged because of their sinful nature. Because I came to you, you can now have joy-filled fellowship with the Father.[1]

In that process, I gave God's people eternal life—a never-ending existence in the presence of the Father after they've passed on from their earthly lives[2]—by destroying the works of the evil one.[3] The judgment they once feared has been eliminated, completely abolished.[4]

I performed many works and proclaimed the gospel. Once when I was in

Nazareth, where I spent most of My life, I stunned the crowd by first reading a passage from the prophet Isaiah about an anointed one who would bring good news to the poor and then by saying that I was the Anointed One whom Isaiah had referred to.[5] Those words perfectly described My message to God's people, the good news that they could be set free and see things clearly for the first time. This is what the kingdom of God brings to people, and this is what I preached for three years. This is the abundant life I promised God's people.[6]

The Jewish leaders, however, just didn't get it. They accused Me of everything they could think of, including destroying the teachings of the prophets who came before Me. Nothing could be further from the truth. Early on, I told My followers that I had come not to abolish the prophetic teachings but to fulfill them.[7] That, of course, didn't make the religious leaders any happier, but I hadn't come to earth for their pleasure. I came, as I told the crowd that day, to fulfill the Scriptures. The leaders' arrogance had helped create the oppressive conditions God's people were living under. I came to serve God's people and show them how to serve others,[8] a concept that was foreign to the Jewish leaders at that time.

The Jewish people were expecting the Messiah to come as a political ruler, a king, and not as a servant. It was not surprising that many of them did not acknowledge Me as the Messiah. I wasn't what they had been looking for. What they didn't realize was that I am a King, just not the kind they expected. As I told Pilate, the Roman ruler who pronounced My death sentence, "My kingdom is not of this world." He didn't understand that, of course, and asked Me point-blank, "Are You a king then?" I answered that he was right in calling Me a king and that I had come to the world to declare God's truth.[9] As I told him shortly before My crucifixion, I came into the world to establish the kingdom of God.

GOD

Jesus is My gift to the world. I loved the world so much that I sent Him, My one and only Son, so that My people would be spared the punishment of sin and live with Me throughout eternity.[10] I wanted our relationship to be restored, and by sending My Son to die on the cross, I made a way for people to be forgiven of their sins and return to Me. Nothing that happened to Jesus was a surprise to Me; I knew He would be killed, and I had planned all along to allow that to happen but then to raise Him back to life.[11]

From the earliest time, I had required the Israelites to sacrifice animals to make amends for their sin. But that simply covered their sin rather than remove it completely, and the effect was temporary. To make the forgiveness for sins permanent, I went to earth as a human being, in the form of Jesus, and became the sacrifice that would result in once-and-for-all forgiveness. It is Jesus' blood that sets you free from the punishment sin would otherwise require.[12]

No matter what you have done, Jesus has paid the price for your sin and bought your forgiveness. We can now be reconciled and enjoy a loving relationship. That was why I sent Him to earth, and He accomplished that mission.

MARY

It was clear from the moment the angel Gabriel visited me—and what a moment that was!—that I would be giving birth to Israel's long-promised Messiah. That much I understood, but I didn't know how this could happen since I was a virgin. Then Gabriel explained that my pregnancy would be a miracle of the Holy Spirit, fulfilling the words of the prophet Isaiah.[13]

There was then no question of what my son's purpose in life would be—or so I thought. I thought Jesus would free the Jewish people from the oppressive Jewish rule and restore the ideal life we once had in the garden of Eden. After all, that's what Gabriel implied when he told me that my son, who would be called the Son of the Most High, would sit on the throne of David and reign over the kingdom of God forever.[14]

Imagine my surprise when I realized that the kingdom Jesus spoke of was not an earthly domain but a heavenly one—and not only that, but Gentiles would also be a part of this kingdom! This was not what I expected, but it just goes to show you what a magnificent and awesome God we Jews had been serving for so long. He was simply too generous with His grace to exclude non-Jews from the restoration of the perfect world He created.

ANNA

Oh, what a time that was! Many, many years earlier I had been widowed soon after I was married. Instead of finding my security in another marriage, which was the only option most women had, I went to the temple in Jerusalem and never left. I spent the rest of my life fasting and praying and serving God.

And then one day, a couple came to the temple to dedicate their infant son. I entered the area where they were talking with Simeon, who, like me, was eagerly anticipating the arrival of the Messiah. The minute I walked in, I knew who the baby was. This infant, the one they called Jesus, was the Messiah! That could mean only one thing: We Jews were about to be released from Roman rule! It didn't matter to me that I probably wouldn't live to see this child become the king of Israel—I was certain that's what would happen when He came of age. I still told every devout Jew I knew that the long-awaited Messiah had come.[15]

10
Why was a virgin birth necessary?

In a scientific age, some miracles are harder to believe than others. One that has been a stumbling block for countless people is the virgin birth, the teaching that Mary, who was a virgin, conceived the baby Jesus without the involvement of a man. Even young children in their first sex education talk know that's not possible. Even in an age of artificial insemination and test-tube babies, the males of the species participate at some point in the conception process.

That leaves many people wondering what the big deal is; surely Jesus could have been the product of a loving relationship between a man and a woman without needing some miracle in which the man was replaced by a spirit.

Q

God, we're women. And nobody knows more about conception, gestation, and birth than we do, except, of course, You. We acknowledge that. But we still don't understand why we have to believe that Jesus was conceived in some supernatural way. We want to know: Why was a virgin birth necessary?

GOD

My daughters, I know how much some of you struggle with believing that My Son was conceived by the Holy Spirit and born to a virgin. You're troubled by the questions you have deep within your own spirit, and you're intimidated by people who challenge your intelligence for believing such an unscientific and primitive concept. To you, a virgin birth is a biological impossibility, and that's that. Some of you have never given much thought to the virgin birth as a supernatural possibility.

Many others of you, however, readily accept the supernatural conception of Jesus for this reason: You fully believe in My miracles and My power to override the laws of nature. To you, there is no distinction between healing a broken leg and parting the Red Sea or turning water into wine and having a virgin give birth. You know that your intelligence is not compromised by acknowledging My authority over all of life.

So it's to the first group of women, those who struggle with miracles, that I'm specifically directing My answer, though those of you in the second group will better appreciate the miracle of the virgin birth once you understand why Jesus had to be born that way.

First, a history lesson. As you are aware, Adam and Eve introduced sin to the world back in the garden of Eden. I placed the responsibility for that sin on Adam,[1] so it was through Adam that sin was passed on to future generations, as was physical death,[2] which was not part of My original plan for humanity.

I sent My Son to earth to reverse the effects of Adam's sin, and so My Son had to be born without a sin nature. To ensure the purity of His lineage, He had to be born to a woman who was sexually pure in the sense that she had never had intercourse. To be born as My Son, He had to be conceived by the Holy Spirit. The union of the Holy Spirit and the Virgin Mary produced the only sinless person who ever lived, Jesus Christ.

Furthermore, because I wanted My people to experience Me in a way they could relate to, Jesus had to be human—God with skin and flesh and bones. That required human participation, hence the need for a human being to give birth to Him in the way that all humans are born. I chose Mary to be the one to give birth to My Son. The union of the Virgin Mary and the Holy Spirit produced the only fully human, fully divine person who ever lived, Jesus Christ.

In choosing to send My Son to first-century Palestine, I also chose to ensure that His unusual conception and birth conformed to the social and legal constructs of that time. Let's say, for example, a young man named Nathan was the son of a man named Jesse. Nathan would also be known as the son of Jesse, which would give him the legal right to act on his father's behalf. No one would question Nathan's authority to conduct business, make decisions, or speak on behalf of his father, Jesse.

Can you see how this relates to Jesus? As the Son of God, My Son, He had complete authority to act and speak on My behalf. As the Son of man, a name He was also known by, He had the authority to speak on behalf of all humanity.

Now for those of you scientifically minded women who need more evidence, consider this: The longest account of the circumstances surrounding Jesus' conception and birth was written by Luke, a first-century physician. By that time in history, physicians attended medical school and knew a great deal about human anatomy and medical treatment. But because technology and medical knowledge have advanced dramatically in your lifetime, you look on ancient medical knowledge as primitive and insufficient. Physicians in the first century were more knowledgeable than you think. In fact, the first reference book on gynecology and obstetrics was written two thousand years before Jesus lived on earth.

And keep this in mind: People have always known where babies come from.

MARY

The first thing I said to the angel Gabriel when he told me I would give birth to Jesus was this: "How will this be, since I am a virgin?"[3] I was first astonished by Gabriel's presence and then by what he said. I was engaged to be married to a man named Joseph, and to be told I would have a child, when Joseph and I had never had sex, well, that was just too much. Then Gabriel briefly explained that the Holy Spirit would "overshadow" me, and I would conceive this child.

Gabriel knew how incredulous I was, so he reminded me that my cousin Elizabeth, who was barren and past childbearing age, was now six months pregnant. "Nothing is impossible with God," he said. That did it. "I am the Lord's servant," I said. "May it be to me as you have said."[4]

I couldn't wait to tell Elizabeth, but before I could share my good news with her, the Holy Spirit revealed to her that I was carrying God's Son in my womb! She sensed it the minute she saw me and told me that the baby she was carrying had leaped for joy in *her* womb.[5] If anyone still has doubts about my virginity, believe me, Elizabeth would not have responded with such joy if she believed for one second that Joseph, or any other man, had had anything to do with this.

I couldn't contain my joy. I burst into a song of praise to God, glorifying Him and rejoicing in Him for the favor He had shown to me. I wasn't anyone special, but He had singled me out and had done such a great thing for me. I could hardly stop praising Him![6]

During this time, Joseph had a difficult decision to make. When he found out I was pregnant, he decided to break off our engagement and allow me to leave the area quietly so I wouldn't face public humiliation. But after an angel appeared to him in a dream and told him what Gabriel had told me, Joseph believed God and changed his mind about ending our relationship. Instead, we were married as planned.[7]

Part of what the angel told Joseph was that all of this was happening to fulfill a prophecy given by Isaiah about seven hundred years earlier. Isaiah had written that a virgin would give birth to a son called Immanuel and that this would be a sign directly from God.[8] I was the virgin Isaiah wrote about. Everything that happened was a sign from God. And in case you're wondering, I didn't disobey God when I named Jesus. Jesus was called by many titles and was known by many descriptive phrases during His life, and one of them was Immanuel, which means "God is with us."

II

Did You physically rise from the dead?

Belief in the physical resurrection of Jesus is another problem area for some people. Numerous theories have been posed in an attempt to explain away the resurrection, theories such as the suggestion that Jesus merely fainted, that He didn't really die but just hid out for three days to make it look as if He rose from the dead.

Women today who struggle with the concept of Jesus' bodily resurrection would do well to consider the eyewitness accounts of people who saw Jesus die and then saw Him after He came back to life—especially since many of those eyewitnesses were also women. Their accounts of this life-changing event rang true in the first century and still ring true today.

Q

Lord, here's another area where people can be so condescending, calling us foolish for believing that Jesus' resurrection really happened. You told us to expect this kind of treatment, but it would help if we could back up our belief with something tangible. Did You physically rise from the dead?

Jesus

Crime-solving shows are particularly popular right now, so for the sake of those skeptics among you, let's take a look at the evidence that I not only came back from the dead but also that I came back in bodily form.

First, there are the eyewitness accounts of people who saw Me and even touched Me after the resurrection. Among those was My friend Thomas, the Thomas in the popular phrase "doubting Thomas," which many people use to describe someone who needs to have tangible evidence before he'll believe in something.

Let's begin with a little background. On the day of My resurrection, My disciples were huddled together behind locked doors, still afraid that the authorities were going to arrest them because of their association with Me. I dropped in on them for a little visit—you can only imagine their shock!—showed them My scars, and assured them that I was in fact very much alive.

Thomas wasn't with them at the time, however, and when they told him about My resurrection, he said he wouldn't believe it unless he saw the scars with his own eyes.[1] For the next week, he stubbornly refused to believe the others, despite the jubilation that had broken out among them. My disciples had gotten together again, and this time Thomas was there. I suddenly appeared among them, walked straight up to Thomas, and told him to touch My hands and My side.[2] He believed.

Look next at all the other times I appeared to people in the flesh. I even ate with them, which was further proof that I had a physical body. I know that one of your favorite accounts of My post-resurrection life involves a bit of a walk I took from Jerusalem to Emmaus with two of My disciples, who were despondent over My death. I joined them on the road. They didn't recognize Me and started telling Me about the events surrounding My death and the discovery of the empty tomb earlier that same day.

As we walked, I began to teach them about the prophecies that Jesus had fulfilled, and how Jesus'—My—death and resurrection were necessary. It wasn't until we stopped for the night and I blessed the evening meal that their eyes were opened and they recognized Me. They believed.[3]

Later, I appeared again to some of My disciples and even made breakfast for them.[4] More than five hundred of My followers saw Me at another time, as did My half brother James, who had been a skeptic at one time;[5] and several others.[6] In My resurrected state, I continued teaching My disciples[7] and encouraged them to spread the good news about the love of God.[8]

The most compelling evidence is the changed lives that resulted from My resurrection, starting with those first frightened disciples who suddenly found faith and the boldness to proclaim the truth of who I am to all the known world at that time. Many of them gave up everything they had to obey Me and tell others about Me. My servant Stephen gave his life for refusing to back down and stop telling people that I was God.[9] They wouldn't have done that for a mirage or a myth.

The conversion of Paul was one of the most dramatic among all My followers. Paul was a brilliant man, but he was also as zealous as they come. That was fine once he began following Me, but before that, it was all he could do to keep from persecuting every single person who believed in Me. It was time to reveal Myself to him and convince him that I am indeed God. As Saul—that was his name before he became My follower—traveled down the road one day after My resurrection, I put on a bit of a light show for him, which threw him to the ground and took away his sight for several days.

"Saul! Saul! Why are you persecuting me?" I asked him. He asked who I was, as if he didn't know. "I am Jesus, the one you are persecuting! Now get up and go into the city, and you will be told what you must do." After that dramatic display of My power, he instantly obeyed, began meeting with some of My disciples, who were understandably hesitant to believe that his conversion was real, suffered relentless physical abuse from the Jewish leaders because he had become My follower, and became one of the most significant articulators of My message. He believed.[10]

Finally, there's the not-so-insignificant fact that women were the first eyewitnesses to My resurrection. During the time I lived on earth, women were held in low esteem by both the Romans who governed Palestine and the Jewish men who lived there. That's one reason why I find it amusing that some skeptics insist that My resurrection was an elaborate hoax by My disciples. If that were the case, why would they record the fact that women were the ones who discovered the empty tomb? Men didn't trust women's testimony in court, so who would believe their word on a matter like the disappearance of My body? No one would. Some of My own disciples had trouble believing them on the actual day of My resurrection.

Mary Magdalene

You cannot imagine the confusion and chaos of that day. I was so distraught I could hardly think straight. I remember walking to Jesus' tomb with several other women, but when we got there we saw the most amazing thing happen. An earthquake struck as an angel came down from heaven and rolled away the huge boulder that had been placed at the entrance to the tomb. The angel was terrifying but radiant, and the Roman guards just about died of fright. Then the angel told us not to be afraid, that Jesus had risen from the dead and would meet His disciples in Galilee.[11]

Well, we rushed to tell some of Jesus' disciples, who thought we were talking nonsense and didn't believe us until they saw for themselves,[12] and then who did we run into but Jesus Himself! There He was, waiting for us on the road. Oh, we ran to Him and fell at His feet and began worshipping Him. Then He told us not to be afraid but to tell His disciples to go straight to Galilee, that He would meet them there.[13]

Did Jesus physically rise from the dead? Yes! I know He did, because I was there, and I grabbed onto His feet when I fell down before Him that day. He was no spirit or apparition or figment of my imagination. He was as alive as He had been before the crucifixion.

12

Did You experience human emotions on earth?

The gospel writers are credited with presenting four accurate and well-rounded accounts of the life of Christ. But whether due to the translators or preconceived ideas about Jesus, people who usually have no problem understanding who Jesus is or what His mission was realize that the Gospels sometimes present a rather serious and stoic picture of Him. Although the last three years of His life were full to overflowing with activity and people and ministry and controversy, somehow Jesus Himself seems almost devoid of emotion.

Some people chalk that up to the fact that He is God, and surely God could never feel sad or lonely, for example. But they forget that He was also human.

Q **Jesus, we know You were human when You lived on earth, but how human were You? Since You're also God, You would have had power over feelings like rejection and frustration, but maybe You chose not to use it. Did You experience normal human emotions while You were on earth?**

JESUS

If you recall from our conversation about whether I really am the Son of God, I was fully God and fully human when I lived on earth. In choosing to be fully human, I wanted to experience life as you experience it, with all the joys and frustrations you live with every day. That means I also chose to experience the full range of human emotions. If you read the Gospels carefully, you'll discover many occasions when My emotions were evident to others.

Let's look at some of the emotions I experienced.

Love. This one should be obvious to anyone familiar with My life and ministry. Part of My purpose was to reveal the love of God to others, so I spoke about love a great deal. As we've already discussed, I would never ask people to do something I'm not willing to do, so when I told My followers to love their enemies, you can be confident that I was loving My enemies all along. I also showed people how to love God by demonstrating My love for the Father every time I obeyed Him,[1] and I reminded people that the source of My love for them was the Father's love.[2]

I know that some people—not many, but enough—have problems with the occasional mentions in the Gospels of individuals that I appeared to love more than others. I can understand why they would be upset that God might love one person more than another. But keep in mind that when I was on earth I spent a great deal of time in the company of a limited number of people. Yes, the crowds often followed Me, but I also managed to spend private time with a number of close friends, some who were part of the original Twelve and some who were not.

In that second group was one family that as a human being I was especially fond of: Mary and Martha and their brother, Lazarus. When Lazarus died, despite the power I had as God, as a man I was overcome with emotion. Mary and Martha knew how much I loved him. When they sent word to Me that he was sick, they didn't even have to use his name. They simply said, "Lord, the one you love is sick."[3] That was one occasion when I wept openly. Even My critics could see My love for him.[4] And yes, this is the same Lazarus I raised from the dead. I didn't use My power to avoid feeling sorrow, but I did use it to comfort two grieving friends by bringing their brother back to life.

You're also familiar with the disciple I loved. This was another situation where My special affection for one individual was evident. That person was My disciple John. He didn't want to draw attention to My fondness for him by making a big deal out of it, so frequently in his account of My life, he simply referred to the "disciple whom Jesus loved."[5] I loved and trusted him so much that as I was dying on the cross, I placed My mother's care into his hands.[6] The cross was My ultimate expression of love. As I told My followers, "There is no greater love than to lay down one's life for one's friends."[7]

Compassion. Sometimes I was so tired—yes, I did get tired—that I just wanted to go off by Myself and get some rest. But then I'd look around and see so much need that I couldn't walk away from the crowds. The gospel writers often made note of My compassion, the deep understanding I had for the suffering of others, and My desire to alleviate their suffering. There were times when I thought My heart would break for them.[8] That was the real motivation for healing people, not to show off My power but to ease the suffering of God's people.[9]

On one occasion, the crowds had been following Me for three days, and we were in a deserted location. I realized the people had run out of food. I had to either send them away and run the risk that some would collapse from hunger, or forgo My need for rest and provide food for them. We fed more than four thousand people that day and had food left over, even though we had started out with only seven loaves of bread and a few small fish.[10] Another time, My disciples and I were heading for an isolated place where we could take a break after ministering all day. But the crowds figured out where we were going and got there before we did. That time, I sensed their deep need for a shepherd, a leader who would care for them and protect them. So I just kept ministering to them well into the evening.[11]

Frustration. Even the Son of man felt frustrated at times. You can see this throughout the Gospels too. Sometimes it was exasperating trying to get My disciples to understand My teachings. One day was particularly challenging. First, some of the Pharisees tried to trip Me up once again by asking Me to provide on command a sign from heaven. I recall letting out a deep sigh and making it clear that I wasn't going to play their games.[12] Later that same day, My disciples were worried because they had forgotten to bring bread for us to eat, just us, not the masses. Now I had just fed more than four thousand people with only seven loaves and a few fish. And they were worried that we wouldn't have enough to eat. "Do you still not get it?" I asked.[13] Once you start looking for signs of frustration in My words and actions, you'll find more examples throughout the Gospels.

Anger. I experienced anger and plenty of it. As God, I could not allow the merchants and loan sharks to turn the temple, the most sacred place in all of Palestine, into a shopping center. Once when I arrived in Jerusalem for the Feast of the Passover, I saw the temple area teeming with what you now call consumerism. So I took godly action: I turned over the loan sharks' tables and told the merchants to get out. This was the temple![14] And then there was My ongoing anger at the arrogant religious leaders and the burdens they placed on God's people. Their hearts were so hard that it was impossible for them to hear God's message of love and forgiveness.

Sorrow. Distress. Grief. Disappointment. Read those sections of the Gospels that describe My last meal with My disciples, My agonizing night in the Garden of Gethsemane, and My crucifixion. You'll discover many human emotions you may have thought I never experienced. I was troubled that one of My disciples would betray Me and disappointed when those who accompanied Me to the garden couldn't stay awake after I asked them to keep watch with Me. I was deeply grieved over what I knew was coming and even asked the Father to spare Me if it was at all possible. But it wasn't, and I knew it. This was what I had come to do, to give My life as a sacrifice for others, and I had to see it through to the point of death.[15]

Joy. Let's end on a positive emotion. I rejoiced over every person who turned away from his or her old life and chose to follow Me. I imparted My joy to them, wanting them to experience it to the fullest.[16] Don't forget also that I thoroughly enjoyed Myself at the many dinner parties and other celebrations I was invited to. I socialized with people of all types, and for that I was called a "gluttonous man and a drunkard, a friend of tax collectors and sinners!"[17]

Did I experience normal human emotions? I certainly did. Being fully God did not exempt Me from being fully human.

13
Is it true that You never sinned?

Believing that Jesus was "fully human, fully God" is one thing, but believing that He never sinned—never had a single sinful thought or committed a single sinful action—is a stretch for most people, especially women who have a finely tuned awareness of their own sinfulness. How can anyone be fully human and not sin? It just doesn't seem possible.

What is possible, however, is that Jesus' unique nature was customized by the Father to distinguish Him from humanity in that one area, and, at the same time, enable Him to experience the power of temptation just as people do. Even so, people still have trouble understanding His sinless human nature.

Q **Jesus, if we tried to recall our sins from just one day, it would take all night—and we'd still have to deal with the sinful thoughts we had while we were recounting our daytime sins. So tell us—is it true that You never sinned?**

JESUS

I understand how difficult this is for you. I'm fully aware of the pervasiveness of sin, the wide-ranging types of sins, how easy it is to fall into sin, how hard it is to avoid sin—all of it. I came to earth to release you from the power of sin, but as long as you live on earth, you will be exposed to sin and you will sin. With My help, though, you can keep at bay the power that sin has over you.

It is true that I lived a sinless life on earth. That was possible because I did not inherit Adam's sin nature from an earthly father[1]—one of the reasons why it was necessary for Me to be conceived by the Holy Spirit. I received My divine nature from the Spirit and My human nature from Mary. When Gabriel appeared to Mary, she questioned how she could have a child since she was a virgin. Gabriel told her that the Holy Spirit would come upon her and her child would be the holy Son of God.[2] From the very beginning, I was declared holy, sinless, and righteous in every way.

I was tempted in every way, just as you are. But I never gave in to the temptation and so remained sinless.[3] And like you, I was tempted by Satan, who tried to find a weak spot in My human nature; he knew better than to tempt My divine nature. As he well knew, God cannot be tempted, and the Father never tempts anyone to do evil.[4]

Then there's the matter of My holiness. I existed as holy God before I came to earth, and I will exist as holy God throughout eternity. My holiness didn't vanish during the years I lived as a man. My basic divine nature is immutable and never changes.[5] My holiness, My spiritual and moral perfection, accompanied Me to earth and back. It cannot be separated from who I am.

Some of you also wonder what Paul meant when he wrote that I became sin itself so you could be declared righteous.[6] It's true that on the cross I took upon Myself all the sins of all people, past, present, and future.[7] That means I suffered the punishment you deserved.[8] But I Myself did not sin. There's an important distinction in that, because if I had sinned, I would have received the same punishment you would have received—eternal separation from God. But as God, I could not sin and could not be separated from Myself.

If I had committed a single sinful act, I would not have been qualified to sacrifice Myself on your behalf, because such a sacrifice required the blood of an animal without spot or blemish. I became such a sacrificial lamb by virtue of the fact that I had never sinned.[9]

Not even the religious leaders of the day could come up with any evidence of sin on My part until they conjured up a bogus charge of blasphemy. They didn't like Me, mainly because I exposed them for who they were—hypocritical sinners themselves. They couldn't see that God had sent Me; if they had, they would have loved Me, which is what I told them. They couldn't see because they didn't want to see; they couldn't handle the fact that God had come to earth and called them on their punishing treatment of the Jews. In fact, I told them that they were the offspring of the evil one, a murderer who fills the world with lies, and everything they did was simply to please him. But when I came telling the truth, they wanted nothing to do with Me. I challenged them to come up with a single sin I'd committed, just one sinful word or deed they could pin on Me. They couldn't do it because I didn't commit a sin.

Now for a little review. The original state of humanity was sinlessness. Adam and Eve did not know sin until they gave in to the temptations of Satan. They lived in a world of purity. They themselves were pure, and everything in them and around them reflected the purity of God. Did I exist before Adam and Eve were alive? Of course. I am eternal. I existed before the creation of humanity. In coming to earth, I wanted to come in the form of humanity before sin entered the world. You know what sinful humanity looks like; you needed to see a representation of sinless humanity.

When I took on human flesh, nothing about Me changed but My form and the direct way I related to My people. It isn't as if I became a whole other being when I took human form. My Spirit, in all its glory and holiness and the distinctions that make Me God, remained. I am the same yesterday, today, and forever.[10]

Consider what some of the New Testament writers wrote about My holiness, My coming to earth in human form, and My taking on the sins of the world for the sake of God's people. The apostle Paul, who clearly taught that I was sinless, wrote that I redeemed people from the curse of the law by becoming a curse in humanity's place.[11] Through that act, he wrote in a letter to a follower of Mine named Titus, I purified those who would eagerly follow Me and want to do what was right.[12]

My friend John rightly taught that because I lived a sinless life and sacrificed that life on the cross for you, you now have the right to be called children of God. Others may not see you in that way—some may even ridicule you for making that claim—but those people are blind to who I am and what the Bible says about My work on earth. As John expressed it, you have the "glistening purity" of My life to follow as a model for your own lives as children of God. He called sin "a major disruption of God's order." That's putting it perfectly. If I had come in the form of man after sin entered the world, I would have created a major disruption in the order I established! By following My life as a pattern for your own, you can put an end to the ongoing practice of sin.[13]

My disciple Peter wrote this:

"This is the kind of life you've been invited into, the kind of life Christ lived. He suffered everything that came his way so you would know that it could be done, and also know how to do it, step-by-step. He never did one thing wrong, not once said anything amiss. They called him every name in the book and he said nothing back. He suffered in silence, content to let God set things right. He used his servant body to carry our sins to the Cross so we could be rid of sin, free to live the right way. His wounds became your healing. You were lost sheep with no idea who you were or where you were going. Now you're named and kept for good by the Shepherd of your souls."[14]

14
Did You really die to save everyone?

The question about whom Jesus died for has been debated since shortly after the resurrection. Entire denominations were founded on a particular belief about who will be saved—who will enjoy an eternity with God—and who will not.

Even within a single denomination, there can be significant disagreement over this subject, with some people claiming with absolute certainty that they know exactly where the dividing line is between the "saved" and the "lost," in their terminology. Meanwhile, others in the same denomination may admit they aren't so sure where that line is, or even if there is a line. To add to the confusion, people with radically different views can find Bible verses to support each of those views.

Q **Jesus, some people believe that if we don't say a specific prayer in just the right way, after we die we will be separated from God, condemned to eternal damnation. Others say that everyone will spend an eternity with God. Did You really die to save everyone?**

JESUS

Nearly everyone who has read the New Testament is familiar with the verse known as John 3:16. Those are the words I spoke to Nicodemus, a Pharisee, in describing for him the immense love of God, a love that would sacrifice the life of His own Son so that people could spend eternity with Him.[1] The Father loves the world—the entire world—far more than you can imagine in your life on earth. He wants everyone to have everlasting life, starting here on earth and continuing throughout eternity. Everlasting life is simply your life with God from now on.

God the Father loved the world so much that He sent Me and gave Me over to death by crucifixion so that those who believe in Me—God—would not have to "perish," which means to die. Now I know what you're thinking;

73

everyone has to die, right? Yes, but just as you can experience two births, natural and spiritual, you can also experience two deaths. In both birth and death, the second choice is really up to you. You can choose to be born spiritually by being reborn into a life with God. If you choose not to, then you've essentially made the choice to experience spiritual death as well as natural death—spiritual death meaning an existence apart from God and all that is good and holy throughout the afterlife.

Bear in mind that God the Father did not send Me into the world to point My finger at anyone and condemn him or her for not following Me. He sent Me into the world to point My finger at all people and lovingly beckon them to follow Me into an eternal existence in the presence of their loving Father. But you see—and you know this by just looking at many of the people you're known in your life—there are people who really don't want to have anything to do with God. They love evil.[2] There's no denying this, because some of them flaunt their sinful ways, and those who try to hide their sin are seldom successful at hiding it from others and never successful at hiding it from God.[3]

What I offered when I was on earth, and what I am offering now, is *life*—an abundant, rich, joyful life of freedom on earth[4] and bountiful surprises in the life to come.[5] No one has ever seen, heard, or even imagined all that the Father has in store for those who take Him up on this offer of life.[6] But the Father won't force you to accept that offer; it's really an invitation that's yours to accept or reject. Think of Me as standing on the porch of your house and knocking on the door. You can open the door and invite Me in; you can open the door, hear My offer, and say, "No thanks"; or you can ignore Me completely.[7] I won't barge in. The Father gave you free will for a reason, and you get to exercise it even in this situation.

GOD

Some people have so distorted My words and My promises that other people get the impression I'm an unfair judge who spends My time looking for evil in people so I can condemn them for their sin. They make it seem as if I take perverse pleasure in spiritual death. I don't. I take no pleasure in the fact that some have made the choice to live without Me. I want everyone to turn to Me and have a life with Me now and in the future.[8]

Some of you have wondered why it seems to be taking Me so long to make good on My promises of a better life to come, a time when pain, suffering, and sorrow will die away.[9] You need to understand that for the most part, time is of no concern to Me since I live in eternity. One day or a thousand years; it's all the same to Me. But time is of great importance to Me in this one respect: I want to give the world time to turn to Me and choose the life I've offered.[10] Does that sound like love or condemnation? I'm lavishly expressing My love through My kindness, tolerance, and patience so people will choose Me over evil.[11]

This is why I so often urge My people to pray and tell others about the life they have with Me. I want people to know the truth, that I sent Jesus at just the right time to reconcile everyone to Me; He gave His life to do that.[12] Those who recognize that, who see the love inherent in that and acknowledge that Jesus is My Son, can rest in the assurance that My Spirit is in them.[13] They are My people, and they have confidence that they will spend eternity with Me because they have experienced My love, which eliminates any fear of what will come after death. They know that where My love is, there is no punishment.[14]

Jesus

The next time you're reading the Gospels, make note of all the occasions in which I spoke of God's love and salvation being for everyone. No one was excluded from reaping the benefits of My sacrifice on the cross. I am the Savior of the world,[15] the Lamb of God who takes away the sin of the world—the entire world.[16] I "tasted death" for *everyone*; I gave Myself as a ransom for *all*.[17]

And I commanded My disciples to go into the entire world, be My witnesses, and make disciples and baptize people from every ethnic group.[18] If My sacrifice didn't apply to everyone who ever lived, then I would have told My disciples which people they should go to and which they should forget about. But I didn't do that. I told them to take the message of God's love to everyone everywhere.

Here's what you need to remember. I paid with My life so that everyone who ever lived would have the opportunity to have everlasting life with God in the future, and so that those who are alive now or who are yet to be born would have the opportunity to begin that everlasting life while they're on earth and then continue enjoying God's presence throughout eternity. That opportunity did not come cheaply. I paid dearly for it, and I rejoice over making that payment, as should you. I would sacrifice My life for you all over again if I had to.

But I don't have to. What I did, I did once and for all. That's it. It's over. The penalty for sin has been paid. Whether you choose to acknowledge that and live in the joy and freedom that life with God brings, well, that's entirely up to you. My servant Paul stated this truth clearly: "If you confess with your mouth that Jesus is Lord and believe in your heart that God raised him from the dead, you will be saved. For it is by believing in your heart that you are made right with God, and it is by confessing with your mouth that you are saved."[19] The decision is yours.

*Since childhood, you have known the Holy
Scriptures that are able to make you wise
enough to have faith in Christ Jesus and be
saved. Everything in the Scriptures is God's
Word. All of it is useful for teaching and
helping people and for correcting them and
showing them how to live. The Scriptures
train God's servants to do all
kinds of good deeds.*

2 Timothy 3:15–17 CEV

THE BIBLE

Many women grew up with the Bible but now aren't sure what to think of it. They want to know whether the Bible relates to their lives today—and if so, how.

15. Who actually wrote the Bible? 81

16. Must we obey everything in the Bible? 85

17. Did all those miracles really happen? 89

18. Which biblical promises apply to us today? 93

19. How can the Bible still be relevant? 97

20. What can Bible women teach us? 101

Who actually wrote the Bible?

For centuries, scholars and laypeople alike have examined the authorship of the Bible, often in an attempt to validate or discredit its authenticity. But seldom has there been such widespread speculation about the books of the Bible as there is today. Pop culture phenomena like The Da Vinci Code *have only added to the confusion.*

For women in particular, the cultural discussion about the role of Mary Magdalene in the life of Jesus has led to concern, and in some cases anger, that writings by and about women may have been omitted from the Bible by men who wanted to downplay the power women exerted in Christ's ministry and the early church.

Q **For years, many of us have taken the Bible for granted without realizing it. But now, there's so much talk about it—about which books were included and why—that we know it's time we ask You this: Who actually wrote the Bible?**

GOD

Those of you who are familiar with the content of the Bible know that ultimately, I am the One who wrote the Bible. Does that mean I took pen in hand and wrote the words on scrolls of papyrus? No. But it does mean that through the work of My Holy Spirit, I conveyed My thoughts, My warnings, My desires, and, most of all, My love to those who did actually write the words down.

I made sure My people understood all that by prompting certain writers to emphasize the Holy Spirit's involvement. Paul in particular was careful to attribute the inspiration behind his writings to the Holy Spirit.[1] Even my hotheaded friend Peter attributed Scripture to Me: In what you know as his second letter, he reminded his readers that none of the biblical prophets spoke for themselves but rather spoke for Me through the prompting of the Holy Spirit.[2]

Remember, also, that those prophets and other biblical writers lived over a span of sixteen hundred years. Imagine the writings of forty authors, produced between now and the end of the twenty-second century, being compiled into a book that is cohesive and consistent in its message. That's not likely to happen, is it? Neither is it likely that the Bible would convey a cohesive and consistent message unless there was a single author behind all the writings. There was, of course. I was the single author, and through the inspiration and power of My Holy Spirit, My Word was understood, expressed, and preserved by My people.

JESUS

As many people have pointed out, I was careful to quote the Jewish Scriptures when I was on earth. I knew they were from God. In fact, very few people in the Jewish community at that time doubted that the Scriptures were from God. But I wanted to make sure they always remembered that, and so I not only quoted the Scriptures but also explained how the ancient prophecies had been fulfilled and were continuing to be fulfilled.[3]

On one occasion in particular, I spent a great deal of time with two of My followers explaining to them how I was the fulfillment of so many prophecies, dating all the way back to the time of Moses.[4] The thing is, I kept them from recognizing Me, and I didn't tell them I was Jesus. This was after I had been crucified, and they had no idea I had been brought back to life. So we walked along from Jerusalem to Emmaus, which was about seven miles away. They were talking about the crucifixion the whole time, and I was explaining prophecy to them.

By the time we reached Emmaus, it was late, and they insisted I stay with them. We sat down to eat, and as soon as I broke the bread and thanked My Father for it, they recognized Me. That was a memorable moment for everyone. They not only recognized Me physically, but they also recognized the truth in what I had been speaking to them about as we walked.[5]

GOD

Some people in your time have referred to the Bible as My love letter to My people. That is a perfect description of the Scriptures. But you have to bear in mind that the love I have for you is not the sentimental kind of romantic feeling that so many people mistake for true love. If that were the case, My love letter to you would be very different from the Bible; it would speak only of the warm affection I have for you and lead you to believe that you are perfect in every way. If you have ever received such a letter, you knew the person who sent it wasn't being honest with you. No human being is perfect in every way.

My love for you is much deeper than that. Instead of flattering you with dishonest descriptions of your flawlessness, I showed you the reality of imperfect human nature, provided you with a way to overcome that nature— My Son's death on the cross and eventual resurrection—and offered you the promise of a joyful, abundant life on earth and an eternity with Me in the life to come. Now that's a love letter, one that expresses a love so profound that you can only catch glimpses of it while you are on earth. I promise you this: The best is yet to come.

PRISCILLA

As one of the earliest followers of Jesus after He ascended into heaven, I can tell you that we clearly heard the message of God's love in the letters of Paul that circulated among the churches in the Mediterranean region. In a letter that was addressed to the church in Rome, he wrote that he was convinced that nothing—not even death—could separate people from God's love.[6]

Aquila and I were actually good friends with Paul, and as Jews, we were well aware of how frequently he quoted from the Jewish Scriptures in his writings. He knew them to be the Word of God and wanted to ensure that the followers of Christ did the same.

GOD

Paul's letters are also a part of Scripture, which brings up the question of who decided which writings were Scripture and which were not. The short answer is that I did. I guided My people in the process of discerning which writings were truly inspired by My Holy Spirit. I'll elaborate on how that process unfolded.

About four hundred years before I sent Jesus to earth, a council of rabbis convened to determine how the Hebrew Scriptures should be arranged. They and other rabbis had long known which books comprise My Word. the Law, the history books, what you call the poetry or wisdom books, and the books of the prophets. But at this council, they arranged the books and placed their official seal of approval on them.

Several hundred years later, a group of Jewish scholars translated the Scriptures into Greek and rearranged the order of the books into the sequence found in what you call the Old Testament today. This translation, called the Septuagint, is the one My Son quoted from when He was on earth.

After Jesus died, some of His early followers began writing down accounts of His life and His teachings, the books you call the Gospels. One of the gospel writers, Luke, also wrote an account of the early church in the book called Acts or Acts of the Apostles. And then, as the news about Jesus began to spread, His followers began writing letters to others throughout the Mediterranean who also believed in Him, as Priscilla mentioned.

As happens with humans, certain teachers began spreading false messages about Jesus. In some cases, that was a result of a misunderstanding, and people like Priscilla and Aquila would gently correct them.[7] But others wanted to capitalize on Jesus' fame, and they purposely began teaching things that simply weren't true.

Eventually, the church leaders knew they had to put an end to the false teachings. They convened a council to discern which writings were from Me and which were not. Their task was not that difficult, because most of the churches had already determined that twenty-seven specific writings conveyed My truth. Still, they sought the guidance of the Holy Spirit, and the Spirit led them to discern that those twenty-seven books were truly from Me. They became the expression of a new relationship I had with My people through the work of Jesus on the cross. You know those twenty-seven writings as the New Testament.

16
Must we obey everything in the Bible?

The Bible contains harsh laws that seem impossible to obey. The Old Testament sometimes portrays God as a vengeful deity who exacts brutal punishment on His enemies and expects His people to do the same. It's difficult for women today to reconcile that image of God with the loving image presented in the New Testament and determine where the line is drawn between "an eye for an eye" and "turn the other cheek."

It isn't as simple as drawing the line between the two Testaments. The Ten Commandments are in the Old Testament, and most people of faith agree that they still apply. Christ's followers want and need to know which laws they're expected to obey.

Q **If the Bible is the inspired Word of God, does that mean we have to obey everything in it? If so, we'd be stoning adulterers and committing genocide against entire nations. That's obviously not the case, but where *do* we draw the line in obeying Your commands?**

GOD

Before I answer your question, I want to assure you and women everywhere that faith is not a matter of strict obedience to a long list of laws. Well-meaning people often think that following Me means compiling a list of biblical laws and making sure they follow each one. Other people, equally well meaning, mistakenly believe that if they adhere to a personal code of good and proper behavior, that shows their faith in Me.

People have tried to redefine faith ever since I clearly spelled out the only definition that counts more than two thousand years ago.

Faith involves following My Son, Jesus. A component of faith is obedience, which means following the guidance of the Holy Spirit and those biblical principles that are consistent with the new covenant, or agreement, I made with My people when My Son died on the cross. I had made previous covenants with My people, of course, such as those I made with Noah both before and after the Flood,[1] with Abraham,[2] and with Israel, when Moses served as the mediator.[3] The Israelites were never able to be completely obedient to the laws that accompanied those covenants. But with this new covenant, I also made new promises, and the fulfillment of those promises is what enables you to obey My Spirit and My Word.

What are those promises? I promised to give you a new nature,[4] a nature that would want to live a life pleasing to Me. But wanting to obey and actually being obedient are not the same thing, so I sent the Holy Spirit to give you the power to obey Me.[5] I also promised to continue to forgive your sins so that you could always be in right relationship with Me.[6] And I promised you eternal life, relationship with Me that will never end. Together, those promises provide both the means and the motivation for you to be obedient to My Word and to Me.

Now to your question. Instead of worrying about where to draw the line in obeying My laws, think in terms of which laws are consistent with the new covenant. Some people, by the way, take that to mean only the commands expressed in the New Testament are relevant in your time. However, you'll find commands that are consistent with the new covenant throughout the Jewish Scriptures. Before I continue this part of the discussion, I'm going to have Jesus respond to your question, because while He was on earth He had a great deal to say about obedience to My commands.

JESUS

It was clear to Me that I had been sent to earth to fulfill the law—meaning the law of Moses contained in the first five books of the Bible—and the words of the prophets contained in the rest of the Jewish Scriptures. What does that mean? It means that I fulfilled the requirements of every Old Testament law,[7] right down to sacrificing My life, so people would no longer be under the burden of the laws that were difficult or impossible to keep, as well as some of the others I fulfilled directly, such as animal sacrifice. However, the underlying principles contained in other Old Testament laws still apply, even today.

In fact, part of My mission involved *transforming* some of the older laws. In what you call the Sermon on the Mount, I quoted several passages from the law of Moses. In commenting on the law of retribution—"an eye for an eye," which demanded that wrongdoers sacrifice something equal to what they had taken from someone else—I told the people not to resist those who hurt them.[8]

I went on to quote what some people mistakenly believed was part of the Law: "Love your neighbor and hate your enemy." No, I told them, you are to "love your enemies and pray for those who persecute you."[9] Love was the foundation for everything I did and said; I had come to earth as the embodiment of God's love, and love, more than any other quality, characterized My ministry. When the Pharisees tried to trip Me up by asking me a theological question—which of the commandments was the greatest?—I answered with love: "'You must love the LORD your God with all your heart, all your soul, and all your mind.' This is the first and greatest commandment. A second is equally important: 'Love your neighbor as yourself.' The entire law and all the demands of the prophets are based on these two commandments."[10]

That is to be your guiding principle in determining which commandments must be obeyed. Does the commandment reflect your love of God and love for your neighbor? If so, then yes, it is a commandment to be obeyed. If not, then it is a commandment I fulfilled so you wouldn't have to be burdened by it.

GOD

Remember also that obeying these commandments is not something you should ever need to do grudgingly, because My only reason for issuing them is to benefit you. Forgiving others, for example, releases you from the burden of carrying offenses and thereby allows you to put situations to rest that would otherwise haunt you throughout your life. Repenting—turning away from sin—restores your relationship with Me and empowers you to live according to the law of love, which clearly benefits you.

Let's look at some of the commandments in the Old Testament, starting with the Ten Commandments, the laws I gave to My servant Moses on Mount Sinai. When you apply the principle of love to those ten laws, as Jesus just said to do, you can see that obeying the commandments is simply a matter of loving Me. The way you show your love is by placing Me first, avoiding idols, honoring My name, and dedicating your time to Me. And you show it by loving others, honoring your parents, refusing to commit murder, adultery, or theft, and avoiding dishonesty and wanting what others have.

These commandments apply to Christians today because they are consistent with the teachings of the new covenant.

Here are some other Old Testament laws, all from Leviticus 19, that you can test by using the principle of love for Me and for other people to determine which still apply today:

* Don't show partiality to either the poor or the wealthy. *Love for others applies.*
* Don't wear clothing made of two different types of material. *Love does not apply.*
* Don't cut the hair at the side of your head or the edge of your beard. *Love does not apply.*
* Don't tattoo your body. *Love does not apply.*
* Don't give your daughter over to prostitution. *Love for others applies.*
* Don't mistreat people from other countries. *Love for others applies.*
* Don't reap the entire harvest from your field, but leave some produce for the poor to glean. *Love for others applies.*

That last commandment is an example of a law that had a literal meaning in the time and culture in which it was given. It also contains a universal principle that applies today in a nonagrarian, consumer culture: Whatever you produce or consume, leave something for those less fortunate.

Love is what creates the line of demarcation between what I want you to obey and what no longer applies. The Holy Spirit will *always* move you in the direction of love. My Spirit will guide you to do and say those things that bring freedom, light, and joy to your own life and the lives of others. Those things also reflect your love for Me. Love Me, love others; every commandment that applies today embodies those two elements.

17

Did all those miracles really happen?

The parting of the Red Sea. Jesus walking on the water. Jesus turning water into wine. Those are just a few of the biblical miracles most people are familiar with, and they're just a few of the many that involve water. Is it possible that natural law could be suspended and even overridden in order for these supernatural events to take place? It's often difficult for twenty-first-century minds to believe that something so unscientific could occur.

What's more, those who do believe, or would like to believe, in the biblical miracles are frequently ridiculed for taking these stories seriously. Skeptics chide women for believing in what they call fairy tales and challenge them to explain the science behind the stories.

Q

God, we need to know if the miracles in the Bible really happened. It's so hard to respond to people when they make fun of us for believing in the supernatural events described in the Bible. Were the miracles for real?

GOD

I once told My people through the prophet Isaiah to remember not only all that I had done for them in the past but also that My nature is unique and I alone could alert them to the things to come.[1] My people needed to be reminded that I am all-powerful and that I can and will do whatever I please. Ever since, people have continued to need that reminder.

Those who truly believe in Me, however, should have no problem believing in the miracles recorded in the Bible. They know that I am the Creator of the universe and all that it contains. I created natural law, and I can transcend natural law. I created humanity. If a miracle will help the very people I created, I will perform it. Nothing is impossible for Me.[2]

Do you realize how easy it was for Me to give My people a solid footing on dry land as they crossed the Red Sea? I created that body of water, and

I dried it up so they could escape the oppression they had known in Egypt. That miracle, which for Me was a simple suspension of natural law, not only allowed them to flee in safety but also gave them an assurance of My presence with them and My love and concern for them. All the biblical miracles served a similar purpose: to strengthen the faith of My people by showing them My power and My love for them.

A woman's view of the miracles in the Bible says a great deal about her view of Me. Those people who mock the miracles believe in a powerless god or they believe in no god at all. They certainly don't believe in Me, nor do they know Me at all. Those who believe the miracles know Me, believe in Me, and understand My nature.

JESUS

When I was on earth, I became known as a miracle worker because of all the supernatural events that characterized My ministry. I was able to perform those miracles because the power of God was in Me, and I understood that power far superseded natural law. I had no problem walking on water[3] because I knew My Father had created water and could change its attributes to suit His purposes, just as He could change water to wine[4] to inaugurate My ministry.

What you call the miracle of the loaves and fishes was for Me simply a matter of knowing the power of God. Here's what happened. I had just learned that My cousin John—the one you call John the Baptist—had been killed, and I wanted to be alone for a while. But a large crowd of people followed Me to a remote area, and by the time I finished ministering to them, it was getting late. My followers wanted Me to send the people away, but some had come from a distance and needed to eat before they began the long walk home.

All we had on hand were five loaves of bread and two fish, and we had thousands of mouths to feed. But I knew the power of God. Five loaves of bread and two fish placed in God's hands could be, and were, transformed into a feast for the multitude.[5] If that sounds impossible, remember that it's only *humanly* impossible—and God is not human.

Look around you. Things that were seemingly impossible earlier in your life have now come to pass, such things as technological breakthroughs and advances. If humans can do the seemingly impossible, how much more do you think God can do? He is able to do immeasurably more than you can imagine.[6]

SARAH

I'm ashamed to admit that I was among those who had a hard time believing that God could do more than I imagined. God had promised Abraham, my husband, that he would be the father of many nations. But that meant he had to be a father biologically, and I was unable to conceive. In our culture, however, it was a wife's duty to give her husband a son, an heir, and if she couldn't, she had to give her husband over to a woman who could. Because I disbelieved God's promises and His ability to work a miracle, I took matters into my own hands and insisted that my husband, Abraham, have sex with my servant Hagar in hopes that she would bear him a son. She did, and that caused nothing but grief.

More than a decade later—by this time, I was ninety and my husband was ninety-nine—the Lord told us that I would give birth to a son the following year. And do you know what I did? I laughed. I actually scoffed at this message from God. I was old and worn out, and I couldn't imagine conceiving a child at that age. It seems I hadn't yet learned that God could do immeasurably more than I imagined He could do. God pointed out my inappropriate reaction to Abraham, asking him, "Is anything too difficult for the Lord?" I tried to lie my way out of it, but the Lord let me know that He heard me laugh.[7] I was mortified.

But a year later, the miracle occurred: I gave birth to a son. We named him Isaac, which means "laughter" in Hebrew. No longer was I laughing in derision; I was laughing for joy. Imagine. This was a miracle indeed. I was long past childbearing age, but God changed the natural order of things so I could conceive.

GOD

For Sarah and Abraham, the birth of Isaac was the great miracle of their lives. But I did not give them a son merely to prove that I could do such a great thing. Isaac's birth deepened their faith in Me and set in motion a much larger plan for My people, a plan that would culminate in the death and resurrection of Jesus.

Many people are blind to the reasons why I override natural law, which makes it even more difficult for them to believe that the miracles happened. The plagues I brought down upon Egypt are a good example of that.[8] In your time, many people consider them part of an entertaining story without realizing the stubbornness of Pharaoh's heart. Pharaoh had a steely resolve that could be broken only by a dramatic display of My power and might—and My own resolve, which far surpassed his. My people needed to be free of his oppression, and I made life miserable for him and the Egyptians until he relented and set the Israelites free.

Some people wonder how important it is to believe that the miracles in the Bible actually happened. To them I say this: Your understanding of who I am will be diminished to the extent that you doubt the miracles. If you believe that I am who I say I am—that I am the all-powerful Creator of the universe who would and could move heaven and earth to show you My love—then believing that I can heal the sick and raise the dead and make heavy metal float[9] should be your normal response.

18
Which biblical promises apply to us today?

In many Bibles, a list of God's promises follows the New Testament. It can be comforting for a woman to scan the list and find a biblical promise that relates to a problem in her life. A woman who feels worn out, for example, may find great comfort in Jesus' promise to give rest to the weary,[1] while a woman who is tempted to enter into a wrong relationship finds the promise that God will help her overcome temptation[2] a tremendous help at a critical moment.

Still, it's not always clear which promises apply to all God's people and which apply only to people in the Bible. Women need to know which promises they can count on.

Q

God, Your Word is filled with so many promises. In fact, there are so many that it almost seems too wonderful to believe that they are all meant for women who are alive today. Is it really possible that all those promises apply to us?

GOD

This is a great question. It allows Me to offer reassurance to those who genuinely want to follow Me and reap the many benefits of believing that I will do what I've said I will do. Let Me guide you into an understanding of My promises so you will know which ones apply to you, the women of today.

Take, for example, the promises I made to the first followers of Christ, the early church. They were those people—Jew and Gentile alike—who believed that Jesus was My Son and who wanted to follow His example. They considered Jesus to be the model for their lives, and He was the focus of their devotion and adoration. They worshipped Him and obeyed His commands.

So what about those promises, the ones I made to the early church? Do you think they apply to you? Of course they do. Women of today who believe in Jesus, follow Him, worship Him, and obey Him can take any promise made to the early believers and apply it to their own lives. You can ask for wisdom, and I will grant it to you generously.[3] Because I am faithful, I have promised to protect you from the evil forces in the world.[4] Those are just two such promises.

Some of My promises, in both the Hebrew Scriptures and the writings that came after Jesus' time on earth, come with a condition attached. For example, My servant James wrote this: "Humble yourselves before the Lord, and he will lift you up in honor."[5] I love to see humility in My people, and I promise to honor those who humble themselves in My presence. Do you think I would do the same for an arrogant person? You can be assured that I would not. This is a promise with a condition; to receive the promise of honor, you must meet the condition of humility.

JESUS

The promises I made to the people living in first-century Palestine also apply to women today. Like the women—and the men—of that time, you can ask for anything in My name, and I will do it.[6] If you treat your enemies well, you will receive a great reward.[7] Whoever follows Me will have the light of life.[8]

Many of the promises I made also came with conditions attached. Some of the conditions were a matter of common sense, however. During My final meal with My disciples before My crucifixion, I spoke to them about the things that were to come. I promised them, among other things, that the Father would send the Holy Spirit to them, and that the Spirit would be their counselor and teacher, One who would help them remember all My teachings.[9]

Common sense should tell you that in order to experience that promise working in your life, you need to be listening to the Holy Spirit, willing to learn from the Spirit, and willing to follow the Spirit's guidance. So that's another example of a promise that comes with a condition.

GOD

That's an important point and one often overlooked. Many people take Our words and use them to suit their own purposes. They want to see the promise fulfilled in their lives, but they don't want to live in a way that honors Me or honors other people. Jesus, another example from Your ministry is the time You told the people to first seek My kingdom and My righteousness and then they would receive "all these things," which in context meant nourishment and clothing.[10]

Some people ignore the first part and misinterpret the second part because it suits their needs better. They give lip service to Me, thinking that simply by going to church, for example, they're seeking My kingdom and My righteousness. Then they expect Me to bless them with much more than their basic needs. My promises don't work that way, and neither do I. For millennia, people have been trying to force Me to bless them by quoting My words, but that won't work today any better than it did thousands of years ago.

Here's what they don't understand: I love My people and want to bless them. But I will not encourage anyone to continue living a diminished life, a joyless existence that comes with placing a higher priority on material things than on serving the people I love and serving Me. I will fulfill My promises only when the conditions are met, but none of my conditions are that burdensome. Seeking My kingdom and My righteousness is hardly asking too much.

Back to My promises. Let Me give you some examples of biblical promises that do not apply to you today. I promised David that his son Solomon would become king after him and that Solomon would build My temple. I made that promise to a specific person at a specific time about a specific event. It may seem obvious to you that such a promise would not apply to anyone in your place and time, but I have seen people who profess to know Me use that promise to justify a building program for their church.

Some promises I made to specific people do contain universal principles that apply to all My people. The covenants I made with Israel and the promise to love them forever despite their continual disobedience apply to those who follow Jesus as well. Many believers in Jesus have found a great deal of comfort in the promises I made to Israel, and they are right in their understanding that the underlying principle also applies to them.

If you're still unsure which promises apply to you today, remember the element of consistency. Is the promise consistent with those things that I've clearly promised to the church? Keep in mind the element of specificity. Was the promise made to a specific person in a specific context? And learn to pay close attention to the language the Holy Spirit used in conveying the promises to those who wrote them down. Words like *all, whoever*, and *anyone* indicate that the promise likely applies to you, as in this passage: "Here I am! I stand at the door and knock. If anyone hears my voice and opens the door, I will come in and eat with him, and he with me."[11] When Jesus was speaking with a woman at a well in Samaria, He told her that she could drink from a well of living water. But He clearly indicated that the living water was available to anyone, not just her. Look at what He said: "No one who drinks the water I give will ever be thirsty again. The water I give is like a flowing fountain that gives eternal life."[12] The word *whoever* extends the promise beyond that one woman.

What you, the women of today, should keep first and foremost in your minds is that there are far more promises in the Bible that apply to you than do not, and that as long as you are seeking Me and living for Me, those promises will be fulfilled in your life.

19
How can the Bible still be relevant?

Women have many resources available today to help them navigate their way through life. They need those resources because their roles as women have changed dramatically in recent decades, and they're trying to sort through all those changes. It's helpful to know how other women handle similar challenges. Women buy self-help books, watch talk shows geared toward women, visit women's Web sites, and read the blogs of women who share their interests.

Friends or relatives, however, may keep encouraging them to read the Bible. They say that biblical wisdom applies to women today. But it's hard to understand how a book written so long ago—when women had limited responsibilities and even fewer rights—could possibly help today.

Q **God, how can an ancient book be relevant to today's women? Thousands of years ago, women led lives that were so different from ours. How can the Bible help us deal with all the things we have to handle in our everyday lives?**

GOD

Let Me rephrase the question in a way that will provide a better foundation for the answer. Ask Me this: "God, since You live in eternity and outside of time, is it possible that You prompted the Bible authors to write some things that would be relevant in every time and place?" My answer to that would be a resounding yes. Because I am the ultimate author of the Bible, it is unlike any other book, and to treat it is an archaic document that has no bearing on the lives of women in the twenty-first century is to miss its eternal quality.[1]

Many excellent resources are available to you today, and many of them draw on the wisdom I communicated to My people for thousands of years, wisdom they recorded in the pages of the Bible. Women and men writing today are able to convey My truth and My wisdom using contemporary stories and other helpful means. When you read the Bible, the Holy Spirit reveals its truth and wisdom to you,[2] and for that reason, you would be wise to place a priority on reading the Bible and discovering for yourself the time-liness and timelessness of its message.

When Jesus lived on earth, the Jewish people could have asked a question similar to yours. The last books included in the Hebrew Scriptures were writ-ten four hundred years earlier, and they could have asked if a book written so long before had anything to say to Jews living under the oppressive rule of a Roman government. But despite their religious shortcomings, the religious leaders of Jesus' time had high regard for My Word and knew that the wisdom contained in the Scriptures was just as relevant for the Jewish people in their day as it was for the people who lived when it was originally written.

JESUS

Many people don't realize how often I quoted from what is now known as the Old Testament when I was on earth. In fact, I quoted the Scriptures so often when I taught in the temple that it astounded the Jewish leaders, who thought I was simply the uneducated son of a carpenter named Joseph. But I carried within Me the eternal wisdom of God,[3] so quoting Scripture was part of My nature. Like the writers today who often use stories to teach about God, I did the same thing in My time. I told stories about God that were rel-evant in that time and place.

GOD

Do you realize how many stories about women are actually in the Bible? Do you recognize the similarities between the lives of the women in the Bible and your own? Take the life of Sarah, for example. Women who know her story think of her only as a woman who miraculously conceived a baby when she was long past her years of fertility. She was that woman, but she was also a woman who experienced many things that twenty-first-century women have to face.

One example is Abraham and Sarah's move from their homeland. Sarah had to leave everything that was familiar to her—her home, her family, the land that she knew. She and Abraham didn't even know where they were going; they simply had to trust Me and follow Me where I led them. The details are different, but many women today find their lives similarly uprooted. They have to leave behind things they love and give them comfort whenever they relocate for a job or for a military posting. The feeling of displacement is universal. You've felt that too.

By reading Sarah's story, you can understand the importance of placing what I want for you above what you want for yourself. If Abraham and Sarah hadn't obeyed Me—no matter how much it hurt or how unclear the plan was—they wouldn't have been a part of My unseen plan to bring hope to the world through Jesus.[4] You can still learn from that.

Like Sarah, most of the women whose names made it into the Bible are remembered primarily for one thing. Imagine what Eve felt when that one thing was being the woman who introduced sin into the world. You could easily dismiss Eve as someone you can't identify with—after all, no matter what you've done, it can't be as bad as what Eve did, right? If you do that, though, you miss a large part of her story, the part that has to do with My mercy, My kindness, and My compassion.

After Adam and Eve disobeyed Me, it was clear they immediately regretted it. The experience was a horrible one for them.

EVE

We suddenly realized that we were naked, and we were ashamed of that. Why would we feel that way? We had always been naked, so it didn't make sense. The best way to explain it is that we felt exposed. Our nudity was almost like a symbol. We realized God could see our blatant disobedience, and we were afraid.

We quickly put together some clothes made out of leaves so that our nakedness, our transparent disobedience, wouldn't be so obvious. And we hid, or we tried to hide, from God. He knew where we were, of course, and He confronted us about what we had done. And He punished us severely,[5] which was only to be expected. We'd had it all, and we botched it by disobeying Him. But do you know what He did next? He looked at the way we had tried to cover our bodies, and He made new clothes for us, much better than the ones we had thrown together. And He gave us an opportunity to experience family life,[6] something He could have taken from us and given to another more deserving couple of His own creation. But He didn't. He was merciful to us, even after what we had done.

GOD

If you look at that part of Eve's story, you can glean a great deal of wisdom from it. First, you can see that disobedience can have serious consequences. And the shame that often follows disobedience? I am willing to cover that, just as I did their nakedness. I did that to show My kindness, compassion, and mercy. I will extend mercy to anyone who turns away from disobedience and decides it's better to live My way.

MARTHA

God is amazingly kind, patient, and forgiving. He certainly proved that to me when my brother, Lazarus, died. My sister, Mary, and I had sent word to Jesus that Lazarus was very ill. We knew how much He loved Lazarus—all three of us, really—and we expected Him to come right away. But He didn't come for another two days.

When I finally heard that He was coming, I ran out to meet Him. But the first thing I blurted out was so rude. I actually scolded Him for not coming sooner. I immediately caught myself and tried to make it better, telling Him I knew that even though Lazarus was dead, God would answer any prayer Jesus prayed. Jesus didn't berate me for that. Instead, He spoke words of reassurance.[7]

GOD

Throughout history, women—and men—have reacted in a similar way. They express their frustration with Me, and even though they try to backtrack, they can't take back the words they've spoken. But I am kind and compassionate. My mercy applies to you today, just as it did to the women in the Bible.

20

What can Bible women teach us?

Everything that's written in the Bible is there for a purpose—for women and men alike. Women can learn a great deal from the stories of female leaders in the Bible, but they can also learn a lot from the male leaders in the Bible. Some people read the stories in the Bible and simply think of them as interesting tales with little relevance to their lives because of cultural differences.

But it is wise to read biblical stories with the understanding that they weren't included just because they were interesting. They were included because the principles embedded in them have eternal value.

Q **Some of us are in positions of responsibility, but the few women in the Bible who were in authority were actually national leaders—hardly on the same level that we're on. How can we learn anything from the Bible's female leaders?**

GOD

Many of the accounts of historical events in the Bible are a source of wisdom and instruction, so it's essential that you look beyond the story itself and discover the larger principles that you can apply to your lives today. What appears to be a short and fairly straightforward story about Deborah, a female judge who led an army to victory, is actually an account that reveals the importance of conveying a message I've given and seeing to it that it is followed. That principle applies to women today regardless of the scope of their authority and responsibilities.

As the queen of Persia, Esther would appear to be a leader, but her leadership was not on the same level as other female leaders' in the Bible. In later times and other areas, some queens had real power, much more than she had, but not in Persia in 480 BC. Her husband, King Ahasuerus, had tremendous power, and his wives—first a woman named Vashti and then Esther—served as queen according to his whims and pleasure,[1] as was the custom in that time and place. Esther wasn't a leader as you think of one today, but she did have power. It just wasn't political power. Her power came from her wisdom and courage in a situation that could have cost her life.

This is what you can learn from her story. First, she came from humble beginnings. She was orphaned at an early age and brought up by an older cousin named Mordecai.[2] Second, she was a Jew, a minority in the Persian culture. Because she had grown up in Persia, very few people knew she was Jewish,[3] but she knew, and she saw how other Jews were treated.

People considered Esther beautiful, and that earned her a place in the king's harem and, a year later, a place on the throne. Later on, she and Mordecai had no doubt that I had put her in that position for one purpose— to influence the king and save the lives of the Jewish people.[4] That's a long story and one you can read about in the book of Esther in the Bible. But here's the main point: I can take an ordinary woman and use whatever gifts I have given her for My own purposes. One of My gifts to Esther was her beauty, but I had also given her many other gifts, including the ability to use My wisdom in a crisis. That was the important one.

Another female leader was Deborah, and she actually was a national leader. She served the nation of Israel at a time when judges ruled the country in place of kings. The Jews thought of their judges as "deliverers," delivering decisions in court and in some cases delivering My people from oppression or threat of oppression. She was also a prophet, giving My messages to My people. And she was a military leader responsible for a significant victory of the Israelites over the Canaanites.[5]

That may sound daunting to you and other women whose leadership roles are limited to a smaller sphere of influence. But that doesn't mean your influence is limited. You may never know the extent of the impact your decisions can have. In Deborah's case, she told Barak, the army commander, that I had promised the Israelites victory if they would go to battle against the Canaanites. She believed that I would accomplish what I said I would do.

Barak, however, was hesitant; he wasn't as confident that the Israelites could defeat the Canaanites, so Deborah had to remind him of My promise.[6] He agreed to go into battle, but only if Deborah accompanied him. As I had promised, the Israelites won the battle, and that had a significant impact on their faith and history.

What you can learn from Deborah's story is that you should always speak what I tell you to speak.[7] If Deborah had failed to deliver My message to Barak, the army would have been defeated. She had to continue to convince Barak to follow My command.[8]

You may be reluctant to be persistent, but when I give you a message to deliver, you need to have the confidence to deliver it and keep on delivering it. You have the power to have an impact on your culture just as Deborah did. If you would trust Me and understand that you have more power than you can see, you wouldn't hesitate to give voice to what I say to you.

Another woman is often overlooked when it comes to leadership. Although Moses held the position of highest power among the Israelites, his older sister, Miriam, and their brother, Aaron, also served as leaders during the time when I brought My people out of Egypt. At a time when Pharaoh had ordered that all the male babies born to Hebrew women be killed, Miriam helped save Moses' life. After their mother hid the infant Moses in a basket and placed it in the Nile River, Miriam watched discreetly until an Egyptian princess found him. Miriam then offered to find a Hebrew woman to nurse him. It took great courage for such a young Hebrew girl to approach an Egyptian princess and make that offer. The princess didn't know it, but the nursing Hebrew woman was Moses' and Miriam's own mother.

I later showed My power by allowing My people to escape from the tyranny of the Egyptians and cross the Red Sea unharmed. Miriam led the women, who had been frightened just a short time earlier, in dance and in a song of praise and thanksgiving to Me for the miraculous deliverance they had experienced.

Miriam was both a prophet and a leader, and though she made mistakes and suffered for them, she was still highly regarded among the Israelites. The story of how she led the people into a time of joyful celebration can serve as a reminder to you to stop and rejoice over the great things I have done in your life. The Israelites knew that despite the victory I had given them over the Egyptians, they had a long journey ahead of them to reach the land I had promised to give them. But Miriam did the wise thing; she brought the women together in a spirit of utter delight and gratitude, offering them an opportunity to take a break and enjoy themselves after years of toil and oppression.

Women today need to remember not only to take time to celebrate when I have intervened on their behalf but also to bring other women along with them. You have an opportunity to be an influence on the women in your life—and the men as well—even when it comes to celebrating and singing and dancing and experiencing joy in My presence. David expressed what My presence meant to him as "fullness of joy."[9] You can experience that "fullness of joy," and you can share it all with others by leading them in joyous celebration in My presence.

God has also given each of us different gifts to use. If we can prophesy, we should do it according to the amount of faith we have. If we can serve others, we should serve. If we can teach, we should teach. If we can encourage others, we should encourage them. If we can give, we should be generous. If we are leaders, we should do our best. If we are good to others, we should do it cheerfully.

Romans 12:6–8 CEV

LIFE

> *God gave the gift of life to the first humans and all who would come after them. Understanding the purpose of life makes all the difference in how people use this gift.*

21. Is there a purpose to life?.. 109

22. How do we know what You want? 113

23. Can we ever be free of guilt? 117

24. Jesus, what does following You involve?.......................... 121

25. God, do You really forgive and forget?............................. 125

26. Do we have to go to church?... 129

27. What about women in ministry? 133

28. How can we do it all?... 137

29. How can we stop worrying so much?................................ 141

30. Is it possible to find genuine peace? 145

31. How can we share our faith inoffensively?....................... 149

21

Is there a purpose to life?

Philosophers, theologians, and laypeople have pondered the mean-
ing of life for millennia. Most atheists consider life to be an accident;
Life with a capital "L" has no significant purpose, though individual
lives may have a limited purpose, such as providing for a family.
Many who do believe in God consider life's purpose to be doing
good, treating other people well, and generally not making things
worse than they are.

But the Christian view of life is unique, and it's one that bears inves-
tigating, especially by women who feel that their lives consist of
little more than the routine of taking care of others. They need to
discover God's purpose for human life and their lives in particular.

Q **God, as women we have no shortage of reasons why**
we're alive. We're the ultimate caregivers, tending to
the needs of others, and life-givers, ensuring the
future of the human race by giving birth. But there
must be something more, some bigger purpose to
life. If so, what is it?

GOD

Does it feel strange to ask Me if there's a purpose to life? It should,
because if you believe I exist—and you do, since you directed your question
to Me—then you must believe I created you and all of life with a purpose in
mind. Let's agree that there is something more, some bigger purpose to life,
and look at what it is.

You need to understand why I created you in the first place. I am com
plete in Myself and have no need for anything outside Myself. I created you
not out of a need for companionship but for the simple pleasure of knowing
you and having you get to know Me. In short, I created you because I wanted
to.[1] I'm not some impersonal ball of energy but rather a personal Being who
derives pleasure from being in relationship with you and everyone else I
created.

My purpose in creating you gives your life purpose because I created you to have a relationship with Me. Enjoying the fellowship we share is part of your purpose. Without that relationship, the lives of many people are meaningless. My servant Asaph discovered that at a time when he began to feel envious of people who had no relationship with Me but seemed to have everything else a person would want in life—prosperity, good health, power, a life of ease. But as he described it, he suddenly awoke as if he had been dreaming and realized that I was all he wanted and needed. "Whom have I in heaven but you?" he asked Me. "I desire you more than anything on earth."[2]

When you reach the point of desiring Me more than anything on earth, you are in a position to be conformed to the image of Christ,[3] another purpose for your life. Becoming Christlike occurs as you allow the Holy Spirit to transform your thoughts and actions and bring them into line with the kind of life I want you to live. As Paul wrote to the Roman church, My Spirit will transform you by changing the way you think.[4] To the church at Corinth, he wrote that My followers reflect My glory by being transformed into My image.[5]

What does it actually mean to become like Christ? To you, that may seem like an overwhelming challenge. Paul, however, understood what it meant, and he provided numerous examples of becoming like Christ for the early followers of Jesus—and for you. As Paul explained it, becoming Christlike meant understanding your true identity as a child of God and allowing yourself to become transformed into the human being that Jesus modeled for you when He was on earth.[6] Jesus was the perfect example of My original intention in creating people.

In a letter to the Philippian church, Paul encouraged believers to become like Christ by being tenderhearted and compassionate, loving one another, working toward unity, becoming selfless and humble, and looking out for the interests of others.[7] This he defined as having the same attitude Jesus had when He was on earth. "Work hard to show the results of your salvation, obeying God with deep reverence and fear. For God is working in you, giving you the desire and the power to do what pleases him," he reminded the Philippians.[8]

Jesus

Remember, too, that an important part of your purpose in life is to tell other people about Me and show them how they can also become like

Me in thought, word, and deed. That's what it means to "make disciples," which was My final command to My followers when I was on earth. They clearly knew what I meant by that because they had lived it for three years. Becoming My disciple meant much more than learning about Me and what I taught about God; it meant spending time with Me, getting to know Me on a personal level, and imitating the way I lived until it genuinely became the way they lived.

Early on in My ministry, I chose twelve ordinary men to come alongside Me as I ministered to the ordinary people of Israel. In doing so, I demonstrated that becoming one of My followers did not require vast knowledge of the Jewish Scriptures or religious tradition. It required only a soft heart toward God, a willingness to follow My teachings, and the tiniest measure of faith in Me, faith the size of a small seed. I didn't expect My followers to understand everything I taught right away; I knew that small seed needed time to grow.

I also demonstrated God's concern for the "lost sheep of Israel"—those people who had been severely oppressed by both the Roman government and the religious leaders of their time, as well as those whom society had shunned or forgotten, such as prostitutes, lepers, and the disabled. I walked among them, stopped and ministered to individuals, and wasn't afraid to mingle with people whom the Pharisees looked down on.

Here's one of the keys to why My ministry was effective and how it differed from what My disciples and the people had known in the past: I became their friend. Though there was an intensity and sense of urgency to My ministry, I took the time to socialize with My followers, My potential followers, and even My critics. In fact, some of My most important teaching occurred when I shared a meal with others.[9]

I want you to follow that pattern as you make disciples. Encourage them to learn about Me, of course, but also encourage them to spend time with Me. Become their friend. Share meals with them. Take advantage of those wonderful teaching moments that arise in the course of normal conversation, as I did when I was on earth. God the Father sent the Holy Spirit to help you know what to say as you tell others about Me.[10]

Women are often daunted by the rest of that command to My disciples, the part about making disciples "of all nations." With so many responsibilities at home, and with the mistaken impression that I was speaking only to My male disciples, women don't see how I can expect them to take off for the far reaches of the world and transform entire nations. I don't expect you to do that. So while it may seem as if I wanted My followers to make disciples of every country, My command was to make disciples of every ethnic group—in other words, everyone. I wanted to be sure My followers understood that My message was for every person on earth.

GOD

Look again at the purpose of life, and in particular, the purpose your life has. Your purpose includes being in a relationship with Me and enjoying the fellowship we share and becoming more Christlike, which involves loving and serving others and loving and obeying Me. This is in addition to everything else I mentioned as an attribute of Christ and making disciples of all groups of people. As you can see, your life has deep meaning. Only those who don't know Me suffer from lack of purpose. You can help them by pointing them in My direction.

22

How do we know what You want?

It isn't difficult for women to know what God wants when there is a choice between something they know is right (such as giving to the church) and something they know is wrong (such as stealing from the church). But some choices are not black-and-white, good-or-bad decisions. Jesus told Martha that Mary chose the "one essential thing," staying in God's presence. But it isn't always clear where God's presence is.

Few women have the luxury of spending their time trying to figure out where God wants them to be and what God wants them to do. Even if they had the time, that process can be overwhelming and confusing.

Q

God, how do we live in Your presence and do what You want us to do? Are there any rules or instructions that could provide a shortcut to figuring all this out?

GOD

Paul, one of the early followers of Jesus, once wrote a letter to Jesus' followers who were living in Rome. He was going to be visiting them, and he wanted to make sure they understood the things that Jesus said while He was on earth. He also wanted to tell them some of the things that I had personally taught him about how to have a relationship with Me and how to know what I want My followers to do. Paul did a beautiful job of conveying My thoughts. He told the Romans to take their ordinary, everyday lives and present them as an offering to Me, becoming immersed in My life rather than being immersed in the life of the culture around them, and then they would know My will for their lives.[1]

A woman who offers her daily life to Me cares little about society's expectations of who she should be and what she should do. Her sense of identity is found in Me and not in the culture around her.

Priscilla was one of the early female followers of Jesus who discovered the truth in what Paul wrote. She was in Rome when Paul's letter arrived. In fact, he mentioned her in it. That letter had such a profound effect on the believers throughout the area that many of them memorized passages from it.[2] Paul encouraged the believers to give their lives to Me as an offering and emphasized that if they fixed their attention on Me, they would be transformed—changed from the inside out.[3] Once that transformation took place, they would be so conformed to My way of thinking that they would simply know what I wanted them to do.

PRISCILLA

The idea that we could be transformed, or as some interpreted it, that our minds could be renewed, was a radical one for us. It didn't occur to people in that place and time that we could change so dramatically. You were born into a certain position in life, and that determined the course of your life. My husband, Aquila, was a tentmaker,[4] and that meant he would live the life of a tentmaker. But then we started hearing about this Man named Jesus who was transforming people's lives, and suddenly our lives were transformed as well. Aquila was still a tentmaker, but he no longer thought of himself simply in terms of what he did for a living.[5] Instead, he thought of himself in relationship to God, something that, as a Jew, he had understood. But then, as a follower of Jesus, he didn't merely understand that relationship; he actually lived it.

GOD

Ruth was another one of My followers who fully understood the tension between doing what I wanted her to do and doing what others expected of her. She lived many hundreds of years before Paul wrote about living transformed lives immersed in Me, and she grew up in Moab, a pagan culture that worshipped idols. Despite all the signs I had given them,[6] many Moabites knew nothing about My truth—and many of those who did know ignored Me in favor of their idols.[7]

Then a Jewish couple, Elimelech and Naomi, moved to Moab where Ruth lived, when a famine forced them to leave Judah.[8] The Moabites and Israelites were sworn enemies, however. Ruth married one of Elimelech and Naomi's sons, and another Moabite, Orpah, married their other son. After all three men died, the women had some decisions to make. Naomi knew what she had to do. Since the famine was over, she knew she had to return to Elimelech's family in Judah. She urged Orpah and Ruth to stay in Moab, which the Moabites expected them to do. They were not Jews, and they were therefore under no obligation to follow Naomi. Orpah ended up staying in Moab, although at first she set out for Judah with Ruth and Naomi.

For Ruth, that's when the tension between following Me and following cultural obligations rose to the surface. In the years she had spent with her extended Jewish family, she had come to know a great deal about Me. Ruth knew what I wanted her to do. She was to follow Naomi. Naomi's people would become her people, and I would become her God.[9] So even though Ruth and Naomi knew nothing about the concept of radically transformed lives, they knew what I wanted. If you read the writings from Ruth's time,[10] you can tell that the people, or at least the leaders, were well aware of what it meant to follow Me, even though some of them willfully did whatever they wanted.

Today, you have many advantages that the women of the Bible did not have. You have both the Hebrew Scriptures and the New Testament—the entire Bible. In addition, you have the example of Jesus, who provided the ultimate pattern for how I want My people to live. Finally, you have the Holy Spirit living inside you to guide you and help you determine what I want you to do.

In the Bible, you will find a great deal of instruction about how I want you to live, as well as wisdom that provides the principles you need to make difficult decisions. Take the final chapter of the book of Hebrews as an example. In Hebrews 13, you'll discover that I want you to treat strangers and prisoners with kindness, hold marriage in high honor, have a healthy relationship with money, imitate the faith of those who taught you about Me, be careful whom you learn from, praise Me and be thankful, joyfully obey your leaders, pray for others, and much more just in that one chapter.

With the example of Jesus, you have a model for godly living. Look at how He related to the people He encountered, and be an imitator of His life and His conduct. Simply having the same depth of love and compassion for others that He had will answer many of the questions you have about what I want from you. He was gentle when a situation required gentleness, and He was confrontational when power, greed, and corruption required confrontation. He resisted temptation, He pointed people to Me, and He told people about My kingdom and the freedom they could have by living in My kingdom even during their earthly lives. As you read the gospel accounts of Jesus' life, you'll find the pattern for living a life that is pleasing to Me.

Finally, you have prayer and the guidance of My Holy Spirit. When you find yourself in a situation in which you need to decide between two seemingly right choices, for example, ask Me what you should do, and rely on My Holy Spirit living inside you to guide you and help you make the right decision. I have not left you on your own. I've given you the Bible, My Son, and My Holy Spirit to show you what I want. In following the wisdom you glean from the Bible, the model Jesus provided for you, and the leading of the Spirit, you'll discover the life I've wanted you to be living all along.

23
Can we ever be free of guilt?

For reasons that psychologists and theologians continue to analyze, women are particularly vulnerable to feelings of guilt. Some women, even followers of Christ, can go through their entire lives weighed down by an oppressive burden of guilt that God never intended them to carry. They cannot imagine a life free of this burden.

As many other women will attest, it is possible to live a life free of guilt. But believing that isn't always easy; it's much easier for some women to slip back into the habit of blaming themselves when things go wrong or failing to believe they are forgiven for things they're guilty of doing. They need to deal with the issue of guilt once and for all.

Q **God, sometimes we women feel as if everything is our fault. Those of us who are mothers blame ourselves if our children don't turn out "right," but even those who aren't mothers find plenty to feel guilty about. Is there any hope that we can ever be free of guilt?**

GOD

You're actually talking about two separate issues: guilt itself and feeling guilty unnecessarily. Let's talk first about guilt. Those of you who are in a deeply committed relationship with Christ, have confessed your sins, and have sought My forgiveness are already free of guilt. My love for you is so deep, so wide, and so infinite that I've forgiven you completely. It's as if you never sinned.

I know human nature, and that means I know how hard it is for some of you to fully accept that. Many of you come into a relationship with Me and believe that you are fully forgiven and fully cleansed from your sin—for a while. Then, gradually, the truth of that becomes more than you can possibly believe. Doubt creeps in, and you wonder if it's all true after all.

Some of you even start to doubt that I have forgiven you for specific sins. You sort them out in your mind and decide that, yes, you can believe that I forgave you for being mean to your parents when you were a child, but no, you cannot believe that I could ever forgive you for cheating on your husband. You need to come to grips with the reality that it's all over, completely erased, thrown into the depths of the sea, never to be brought up again.[1]

Some women have an entirely different problem with guilt. They have no problem believing I have forgiven them for the sins they committed when they were estranged from Me, but they feel that it's much harder for Me to forgive the sins they committed after they came into relationship with Me. It's as if they picture Me debating the situation: *Hmm, in the past I've forgiven her for lying to everyone she ever met, mocking Me every chance she got, and embezzling thousands of dollars from her employer, but today she took home a pen from work without asking permission. I don't know. I just don't know if I should forgive her for that now that she's a follower of My Son. I'll have to think long and hard about that.*

I understand the logic behind that kind of thinking—those women believe that now that they have the Holy Spirit, they should have power over sin and be more accountable for it. What they need to understand is that My love trumps logic every time. What appears to be logical in the earthly dimension is not necessarily a reality in My kingdom.

When you confess your sins, you can be certain that I will be faithful in forgiving them.[2] That's My nature, and to deny you forgiveness would be to act in opposition to My nature. It would perpetuate the rift in our relationship that the sin caused. Let Me be clear once again: I love you. I forgive you. Now let's enjoy our relationship.

The second issue, that of feeling guilty long after you've been forgiven, is one that you yourselves perpetuate in casual conversation. You confess to feeling guilty about so many superficial things: The house is a mess, you forgot to return a phone call at work, you put a dent in the car. When you apply the word *guilty* to things like that, it isn't surprising that you harbor feelings of guilt about the actual sins in your life you've confessed and should be done with.

Holding on to guilt is symptomatic of believing that you have to do something more to stop feeling guilty. Confession isn't enough for you; you need to suffer. You punish yourself by reliving your sin repeatedly in your mind until you've tortured yourself enough to accept My forgiveness. You never seem to arrive at that point, however. You think you have to keep working to earn My forgiveness through your suffering.

Let Me remind you that My Son suffered for sin so you wouldn't have to.

Let Me also remind you that you can do nothing to earn My forgiveness. Nothing. Suffering and torturing yourself with feelings of guilt have no place in My kingdom. Am I not greater than your feelings?[3] My grace is perfectly adequate to meet your needs and release you from the burden of a guilty conscience;[4] My grace allows you to walk in the freedom I promised you. Paul expressed it this way to the church in Rome: "Sin is no longer your master, for you no longer live under the requirements of the law. Instead, you live under the freedom of God's grace."[5]

JESUS

Let me remind you of an incident that occurred when I was on earth. I had been talking to My disciples about how to handle a situation in which one of My followers offended another one. I began by telling them to go to the offending person and try to resolve the problem in private, and then I gave them some more detailed instructions. Peter, who was always one to challenge Me, asked Me how many times he would be required to forgive another follower who sinned against him. He suggested that seven times might be the upper limit for extending forgiveness.

It was obvious that he had simply pulled that number out of thin air, so I responded by doing the same. Peter always needed to know that I was on to him when He tried to trip Me up. So I played a little math game with him and told him he needed to forgive "seventy times seven" times—490 times, to be precise. But of course, precision in such a situation would be foolish. Did I expect Peter, or anyone else, to keep score so they could suddenly stop forgiving on the 491st occasion? No. My point, which Peter knew full well, was that My followers are to forgive one another an infinite number of times.[6]

What does that have to do with either your genuine guilt or your perpetual feelings of guilt? Look at it this way. Would My Father ever ask you to do something He is unwilling to do? No. That would also be contrary to His nature. If He expects you to forgive countless offenses, then He will do the same. Notice, too, that in My response to Peter, I made no distinction between offenses I expected My followers to forgive and offenses they didn't need to forgive. The Father makes no such distinction either; He forgives every type of offense.

As to your feelings of guilt, My response to Peter applies to those as well. One of the reasons you can't get rid of those haunting feelings of guilt is that you just can't bring yourself to forgive yourself. But that's as much of an offense to the Father as is an unwillingness to forgive others. He has forgiven your sins. He expects others to forgive you for anything you've done to hurt them. Don't you think He expects you to forgive yourself? Your feelings of guilt are an affront to Him—and they certainly are an affront to My death on the cross. Your guilty feelings are robbing you of the freedom My death bought for you, and they're keeping you from serving Me completely. Nothing more is needed but for you to embrace the total forgiveness that you already have.

24
Jesus, what does following You involve?

From the moment they come into a genuine relationship with God, women understand that such a relationship involves following Jesus Christ. That sounds nice and religious, and most women have no problem agreeing that it's a very good idea. But when it comes right down to it, when it comes to following Jesus in action and not just in word, they realize they haven't a clue what that actually involves.

What often happens is that women take their cues from one another, thinking that other women know how to follow Christ. And what results is a default approach—a one-size-fits-all form of obedience that ruins any opportunity to live the kind of spiritual adventure Jesus has for them.

Q **Jesus, I want to follow You—I really do. But it gets confusing when I read what You said about denying myself, picking up my cross, giving up everything, and hating my family. I don't see anybody else doing that. So what does it mean to follow You?**

JESUS

One of the best ways you can discover what it means to follow Me is to read the four gospels and see how My disciples followed Me when I was on earth. They weren't perfect, and they didn't always follow Me perfectly, but in a big-picture way, you can learn a lot from their example. The original twelve disciples left their routines behind and willingly accompanied Me as I ministered throughout Palestine. They listened carefully as I taught them about the kingdom of God. They didn't understand everything I said, but they did ask questions. For the most part, they honored Me and recognized Me as having been sent by God, even if they all didn't comprehend that I was God Himself. Some, like Peter and Andrew, certainly understood My identity and said as much.[1]

Over the centuries, I've heard people express regret that they didn't know Me when I was on earth and claim that they would have known I was God. Even though My followers on earth were able to travel with Me and spend hours alone with Me, they didn't have the advantages you have today. You can read what I taught about the kingdom, ask Me questions about things you don't understand, and honor Me as they did, but you also have the entire body of Scripture to help you understand what it means that I am the Son of God. Remember, many of My followers were no longer alive by the time My theologian friend Paul, under the guidance of the Holy Spirit, wrote the letters that cleared up some false teachings about Me and helped My followers understand the new covenant God had made with them. You have the benefit of his wisdom and teachings, and the teachings of other New Testament writers, which is something My earliest followers did not have.

Now to the specifics of what it means to follow Me since I am no longer on earth and you can't literally walk in My shadow. First, you need to be fully convinced that I am who I say I am—God Himself. If you don't believe that, then you'd might as well give up the effort, not because I'd condemn you, but—especially if your mind is closed to the possibility that I actually might be God—because you'd be embarking on a journey that is doomed to failure. Sure, you can live by some of My teachings and have a pretty decent life, but truly following Me means a wholehearted commitment to Me, to obey My teachings and My leading. To make such a commitment to a mere human teacher would be unwise at best; if you consider Me simply a human teacher, then you'll likely abandon Me when I ask you to do difficult things. And I will ask you to do difficult things, not to make your life miserable but to help you mature and become more like Me.

Following Me, then, means much more than reading about Me and modeling your life after Mine. It means giving yourself over to Me to be transformed. You need to be willing to have your beliefs, thoughts, values, actions, and words begin to fall into line with everything I taught and every-thing that I am. Notice that I didn't say you have to work at this, strive to do everything right, and worry that you haven't gotten it all right. This transfor-mation will take place on its own, without your even realizing it, as you live your life in cooperation with the Holy Spirit.

Let Me be even more specific and tell you what I once told a large group of My followers. I emphasized that they were followers and that I was their leader. They would follow My example in all things, even in suffering. I didn't avoid suffering, and I didn't avoid self-sacrifice. Following Me involves both suffering and self-sacrifice, but it's worth it because, as I told them that day, when you give yourself completely to Me, you have nothing worthwhile to lose and everything worthwhile to gain.[2]

I want you to get a clear image of what it means to deny yourself and pick up your cross in order to follow Me. Denying yourself means letting Me take the lead, letting Me steer you in the way you should go, and sacrificing your own desires and your need to do and have whatever you want. It means moving away from self-centered living and toward God-centered living. It means living your life in tune with My Spirit.

The cross is a symbol of My suffering, so taking up your cross means accepting and even embracing whatever suffering comes your way as a result of serving Me. That suffering can mean anything from the disapproval of your friends and family to death at the hands of terrorists whose hatred of Me has turned violent. I'm not telling you that to frighten you; I'm telling you that because you need to understand the cost of what is known as "discipleship"—following Me no matter what price you have to pay.[3]

I know what you're thinking: *What on earth is in it for me? Suffering? Disapproval? Death? That doesn't sound at all appealing!* Let's look at the payoff. Not only do you get to spend eternity with Me—there's no suffering there, I promise!—but life on earth is so much better when you live it My way. Remember, I once lived as you live, on solid ground. I know the hardship and difficulties life can bring, and I know there's a better way to live in this world than most people have discovered. Living My way isn't all sacrifice and suffering; living My way is also goodness, joy, and peace.[4] Following Me is like an adventure.[5] If you let Me, I'll shake up your dull and boring routines and give you the kind of life you've only dreamed of before.

You see, denying yourself—becoming God-centered—also means getting rid of those things that plague you: fears, insecurities, worries, struggles, shame, anger, hatred, resentment, hostility, regrets, and so much more. What you get in return is love, forgiveness, compassion, hope, confidence, patience, courage, trust, strength, wisdom, and, again, so much more. The trade-off is overwhelmingly weighted in your favor.

As for that part of the question about hating your family, let me say that your own language borrowed from the Greek a word that explains the strategy I was using when I made that statement—*hyperbole*. That means using exaggeration to intensify the meaning of your words. And that's what I was doing. I wanted My words to have an impact and be memorable at the same time. I used the same device when I spoke about a camel going through the eye of a needle[6] and a log in a person's eye.[7]

On one particular occasion, a large crowd was following Me, and I turned and told them, "If anyone comes to Me and does not hate his father and mother, wife and children, brothers and sisters, yes, and his own life also, he cannot be My disciple. And whoever does not bear his cross and come after Me cannot be My disciple."[8]

Those of you who know Me and know the message of love that I preached understand that I am not telling you literally to hate your family and your own life any more than I am telling you to carry a wooden cross on which you will be crucified. I used exaggeration for effect so that the people who were clamoring after Me would understand that My ministry was no sideshow. If they wanted to truly follow Me, and not just follow Me around, they had to make a serious, life-changing commitment to Me. That meant loving Me more than their families, their lives, and their comfort.

Become God-centered rather than self-centered. Embrace whatever hardship results from your commitment to Me. Obey My commands by living in harmony with the Holy Spirit. Prepare for a life far more exhilarating than anything you could imagine. That's what it means to follow Me.

25
God, do You really forgive and forget?

For many women, accepting God's forgiveness comes readily. They have experienced forgiveness on a deep level in their own lives because their compassionate nature compels them to forgive others. But that's not true for all women; those with an unforgiving nature have an especially difficult time understanding the forgiveness God offers.

Believing that God will forget their sins is another matter entirely. Plagued by the awareness of their sinful nature, the fear that God will remind them of their sins when they meet Him face-to-face after they die, and their own inability to forget even those wrongdoings that they have forgiven, some women find it impossible to grasp the concept that God will forget their sins.

Q **God, I've done so many horrible things in my life, things I can't forgive myself for doing. I've broken many of Your commandments, and the memories of those sins haunt me day and night. I need to know— do You really forgive and forget my sins?**

GOD

What sins? I have already forgotten those you confessed to Me. Believing that I will forget your sins comes down to believing what is written in My Word. Do you believe what the Bible says? Then you should have no trouble believing that I have forgiven and forgotten your sins.

The Holy Spirit prompted Isaiah to tell My people, after they had repeatedly sinned against Me, that I would erase their sins and purposely forget them.[1] If you know the history of the Israelites, you know the struggles I had with them. They would obey Me for a time and then go right back to worshipping other gods or sinning against Me in other ways. But I assured them, through Isaiah, that I would blot out their sins so completely that I would essentially forget them.

Forgetting your sins means that I will never bring them up to you again. If you're afraid I will recite a long list of your sins when you meet Me in heaven, rest assured that I will not do that. The joy we will experience in that moment will be evidence enough that your sins are long gone and so far removed from that picture it will be as if they never existed. Look forward to the joy of that moment and the eternity to follow. Don't allow fear to mar your vision of our reunion with each other. Your sin is no more. That's the end of it.

At the same time that Isaiah lived, I continued to plead with the nation of Israel to return to Me through the writings of My prophet Micah. "What have I done to you?" I asked the Israelites. "How have I burdened you? Answer me."[2] Through Micah, I showed Israel the glory that was to come, the future that would be theirs if they would turn to Me. And then Micah responded by calling out to Me and providing the nation with a picture of who I am and how extensive My forgiveness is. He reminded the people of My compassion and eternal love, and gave them an image of Me casting their sins into the depths of the sea.[3]

My servant David once used a striking image to illustrate just how much I love My people and just how far away their sins are: "As high as the heavens are above the earth, so great is His lovingkindness toward those who fear Him. As far as the east is from the west, so far has He removed our transgressions from us."[4] Yes, David was right. My lovingkindness reaches to the heavens and knows no bounds. In another place, David described My lovingkindness as being even better than life![5]

But if that isn't enough to convince you of My mercy, my compassionate concern for your distress and the action I take to alleviate it, David went on to use a different geographical image to show how far I have removed your sins from you. He said that your sins are as far away as the east is from the west. Think about that: You can board a plane that starts flying east, but can you determine when it reaches "west"? No. It never does. The same is true if you're flying west; you can't possibly determine when you reach "east." David understood the significance of what he wrote. He was underscoring the impossibility of ever finding those sins again.

Here's another declaration of My promise to forget the sins of My people. Through My prophet Jeremiah, I assured the Israelites of a new covenant that I would make with them, one that would be placed so deep within them that they would have no doubt that I am their God and they are My people. Their certainty about Me would be so far-reaching that they would have no need to tell others about Me; everyone would know Me already. I then told them this: "I will forgive their wickedness, and I will never again remember their sins."[6]

If you believe My Word—and if you have placed your trust in Me—you can believe that I have forgotten your sins.

JESUS

When I died on the cross, I did so to pay the debt for all your sins, past, present, and future. That's what forgiveness is—the payment of a debt. *Forgiveness* is the word your culture uses to describe a debt that has been paid in full; you say that the debt has been forgiven. If that's the case, does a creditor continue to hound you for payment? Does a creditor ever send you another bill to remind you of what you once owed? No, not unless the creditor made a mistake. But God the Father does not make mistakes. When He sent Me to die on the cross to pay the penalty for your sins—to pay that debt in full—your sins and your debts were completely forgiven.

To those who feel that they owed no debt to begin with, I would point out the many places in the Bible where God made it clear that everyone has sinned.[7] Every human being has sinned, and every human being needs to be forgiven of that sin. And because sin is ultimately an act of rebellion against God, whether the person committing sin sees it that way or not, only God can forgive sin. The good news is that I came to earth in human form to make sure all your sins would be forgiven. A second bit of good news is that God wants to forgive your sins.[8]

It's a mistake to think of God the Father in the same way you think of your earthly father—or any other human being, for that matter. It's especially damaging to think of God the Father in human terms when it comes to forgiveness. You've heard people in your life say something like this: "I'll forgive you this time, but if you ever do that again . . . !" Then, they follow up with a threat of some sort. God the Father is not like that. His forgiveness is endless. He wants you to turn away from sin, of course, but His forgiveness of your sin at the very moment you seek it is complete and final.

THE TOWN HARLOT

I will never forget the night Jesus forgave my sins—or the words He uttered to those who condemned me. Jesus was dining at the home of a Pharisee, and normally I would never have set foot in such a place, but when I heard Jesus was there, I had to go. He'd had such an impact on my life. I had a bottle of expensive perfume that I'd reserved for a special occasion, and, to me, there was no more special occasion than this.

I sat at Jesus' feet and began crying uncontrollably. I had enough presence of mind, however, to see that my tears had drenched His feet. I quickly let down my hair and started drying His feet with it, and then I anointed His feet with the perfume. The Pharisee knew I was a prostitute and figured that if Jesus was the prophet everyone believed Him to be, He would also know who I was and would not allow me to touch Him.

Not only did Jesus know the kind of woman I was, but He also knew what the Pharisee was thinking. He confronted the Pharisee in a subtle way by telling the brief story of two men who owed a banker different amounts of money. When both men confessed that they could not pay the debt, the banker forgave both loans. Jesus asked the Pharisee, who was blind to the trap Jesus had set for him, which of the two debtors would be more grateful. The Pharisee rightly assumed that the one who owed the most money would be more grateful.

Then Jesus spoke those words about me. Me! "Do you see this woman? I came to your home; you provided no water for my feet, but she rained tears on my feet and dried them with her hair. You gave me no greeting, but from the time I arrived she hasn't quit kissing my feet. You provided nothing for freshening up, but she has soothed my feet with perfume. Impressive, isn't it? She was forgiven many, many sins, and so she is very, very grateful. If the forgiveness is minimal, the gratitude is minimal."[9]

Even more astonishing, He spoke to me: "I forgive your sins . . . Your faith has saved you. Go in peace."[10]

I know what the dinner guests were thinking: *Who does He think He is? What makes Him think He can forgive her sins?* But Jesus ignored them. He gave all His attention to me. He wanted to assure me that my sins were indeed forgiven. I was assured, believe me. I had faith in Him. He rewarded my faith by giving me a gift that I never believed I was worthy to receive—the gift of God's forgiveness.[11]

26
Do we have to go to church?

The word church *can be loaded with emotional baggage. While many people have found great comfort and joy in their church experiences, others have encountered difficulties that had a lasting effect. And the word evokes countless different images: One person may visualize a particular sacred building, another may see the Sunday school room of their childhood, and yet another may envision a group of warm and loving people worshipping God together.*

Many women are naturally drawn to the church experience. Their love of God coupled with the opportunity to share that love in community gives them reason enough to become actively involved in the life of a local church. But that involvement is seldom problem-free.

Q **God, some of us enjoy church, but others think it's boring. And sometimes newcomers feel like they don't fit in because they don't know the ropes. We don't want to sound like whining children, but could You please settle this—do we have to go to church?**

GOD

I want to start by making sure you understand what *church* is, and I'll do that by clarifying what it isn't. Over time, the word has come to describe any building where followers of Christ meet to worship Me. It has also come to mean a worship service. So when people speak of "going to church," they mean either going to a sacred Christian building or going to a worship service. But that's not what the church is in its pure form.

The church is the family of people who believe that Jesus is My Son and who have committed their lives to Him. My servant Paul referred to this family as a "body," which is why you've heard some of Jesus' followers talk about the "body of Christ." They're not referring to Jesus' physical body, the one He inhabited when He lived on earth, but rather to a spiritual body that you can't see with your physical eyes—a "body" formed by the unity of those who follow Christ. Some of your theologians have described it as a mystical union, a fellowship that cannot be detected with the five senses—sight, sound, smell, taste, and touch. That has helped many people understand Paul's use of the word *body*.

Understanding that meaning of the word, then, you can understand why the concept of "going to church" was a foreign one to the early followers of Christ. They considered themselves the church, the body of Christ. When they got together as Christians—no matter where they were—they formed the church. Also foreign to them was the idea of a church building. They met in one another's homes and shared their lives on a daily basis.

Once Christians began to meet in special buildings set aside exclusively for that purpose, people began calling those buildings churches, and from there it became common to talk about going to church.

So, in terms of your cultural understanding of the term, do you have to go to church—to a specific building set aside to worship Me? No. You can search the Bible from the first to the last page and never find a single instance where I command My people to "go to church." If you are a committed follower of Christ, however, this fact is inescapable: You are a part of the church, the body of Christ. Whenever you get together with other followers of Christ, your group, however small, is the church, and together you help form the larger body of Christ.

Let's look a little deeper at the image of the body of Christ, in particular at the way Paul described it in a letter to the church—the body of Christ—in Corinth. He explained that each follower of Christ served a specific function in the church, much the same way that an arm or a leg serves a specific function in a physical body. Without all the parts working together, a physical body cannot function to its optimum capability. The same is true of the body of Christ, which means that each person contributes to the optimal functioning of the church. Other followers of Christ need the gifts and talents—the specific functions—I've given you.

The idea of not using those gifts to help the body of Christ would also have been a foreign one to the early church. The followers of Christ regularly met not only to worship Me but also to take care of one another, ministering to their fellow Christians' physical and spiritual needs and offering prayer for one another and protection from those who were intent on persecuting Jesus' followers. The notion of going it alone in an environment that was hostile to the followers of Christ was the exception, not the rule.

JESUS

At the time I came to earth, the Jewish understanding was that God dwelled in the deep recesses of the temple, the Holy of Holies, which was accessible only to certain people at certain times. I disabused the people of that notion when I told them, "The kingdom of God is within you." They were suddenly aware that even the lowliest people living on the streets, begging for a mere morsel of food, had access to God right where they were.

This released people not only from the idea that God was available only at a certain place but also from the law, which established who could enter the Holy of Holies and who could not. Their newfound liberation paved the way for the formation of the church, My body, an organism pulsating with the life-giving blood of the sacrifice I made on the cross.

In that body, My early followers discovered the joy of spending time with kindred spirits and worshipping Me in their presence. Did they agree on everything? Certainly not. Were there serious conflicts? There certainly were. But for the most part, that didn't stop them from getting together and sharing their lives with each other. In each other, they found strength,[1] protection,[2] accountability,[3] encouragement,[4] and an opportunity to pray for one another and confess their sins to one another[5]—actions they considered essential to their personal growth and their close relationship with God. Many people came to know Me because they saw the love My people had for one another, a love that was so selfless and sacrificial that it couldn't be explained away as simple human emotion; it had a depth and quality that people recognized as having its source in Me.

Paul understood another important purpose for My followers to get together, to continue hearing the good news I shared when I was on earth.[6] My followers knew they were supposed to preach the gospel, but that also meant reinforcing the message of the gospel to the church. As God gave further wisdom to My followers, they taught the others what God had revealed to them. Educated and literate followers like Paul preached to the church as well as to those who didn't know Me and wrote letters to churches throughout the Mediterranean, sharing God's newly revealed wisdom and clarifying some of the teachings with which they were already familiar.

Do you have to "go to church"? No. Church attendance is certainly not essential for your salvation. But do I want you to share your life with other people who believe in Me and follow Me? Absolutely. Getting together with other believers will help you in ways you can't imagine, and you will help them in ways you can't even see. Make an effort to find other believers who support one another by praying for each other and encouraging one another, who worship Me whenever they meet, and who study God's Word.

Find a group of people who aren't boring. Some people have managed to drain the excitement and wonder out of My life and My message while I was on earth, and they communicate the Israelites' history and the words of the prophets as if they were the dullest writings on earth. God's Spirit breathed life on those words, and to rob the words of that life is to rob them of the power of God's Spirit.

27
What about women in ministry?

The question about whether a woman can serve as the primary leader of a church is one that has caused great division in denominations and in individual congregations. And as is often the case, people on both sides of the issue can point to the Bible to support their position. That leaves the woman in the pew—and the woman who feels called to the pulpit—in a place of utter confusion.

Men are often confused as well. Even male pastors who oppose women in ministry sometimes allow women to teach from the pulpit, unsure whether they've violated a biblical principle in permitting them to do so. Men and women alike seek clarity on this issue.

Q **God, we look at the church listings in the paper, and we see women named as pastors of some churches. Yet elsewhere in the same paper, we read about the ongoing controversy of women's ordination. Are women allowed to preach?**

GOD

The controversy you speak of has to do with women having authority over men, such as a female pastor would have over the men in a congregation. Some churches also have restrictions on women standing in the pulpit—the "preaching" platform in those churches—and speaking about anything or even singing; most of these are churches that are especially careful to do everything according to their interpretation of what the Bible says.

As we discussed earlier, Priscilla, a leader in the fledgling church, corrected Apollos when she heard that he was preaching a different version of the good news than the one Jesus proclaimed when He was on earth. Leaders who say that women should not teach men seldom mention Priscilla's story or the fact that most churches routinely send women to the foreign mission field to teach women and men.

During one of the darkest times in Israel's history—and there were many—King Josiah needed someone to interpret the Book of the Law and explain what I wanted from the country, which had spent the previous five decades rebelling against him.[1] Hilkiah the high priest at the time knew where to turn.[2] My prophet Huldah had been faithful to Me throughout Israel's period of disbelief, and she knew My voice when I spoke. Huldah told Hilkiah to deliver to the king a message from Me: disaster would come upon Israel, but because Josiah had sought a word from Me, he would die before disaster struck.[3] Huldah's prophecy came true because it came from Me. I have used women to speak My truth in the past, I used them at the time of Christ and in the early church,[4] and I will continue to do so in the future.[5]

Jesus

One of the results of My ministry on earth was the shattering of the barrier between male and female, just as I broke the barriers between Jews and Gentiles and slaves and free persons.[6] I counted a number of women among my closest friends and my most faithful disciples, something that was unheard of in first-century Palestine.

It is in that context, and in the context of the entire Bible, that some of the troublesome passages about women in ministry need to be understood. If I have shattered the barrier between female and male, and if the Father granted the gift of prophecy to women and allowed them to express the prophecies they received from God to men, and if the Spirit gave women the freedom to convey a word of correction to men, then those difficult passages need to be interpreted in the context of that larger understanding of how God uses women in ministry.

Let's take one of the passages as an example, this one from Paul's first letter to Timothy. One of your translations expresses Paul's thought in this way: "I do not let women teach men or have authority over them. Let them listen quietly."[7] In light of what we've just discussed, this appears to be a contradiction. But the Bible is inspired by the Holy Spirit, so we know that no part of the Bible can contradict another part.

That means that the problem has to be in the interpretation. There's little room for interpretation in the passage about say, Priscilla, but there is room for interpretation in the passage from the letter to Timothy. I know the questions that passage has prompted: *Was Paul really writing under the inspiration of the Holy Spirit? After all, he wrote, "I do not let women . . ." Does*

134

that mean he was acting on his own and not obeying an order from God? Was he addressing a specific problem in a particular church?

If you take Paul's statement literally and make it a doctrinal stance for the church in the ages to come, then you must view the rest of the letter from that same perspective. However, those of you who abstain from alcohol are going to have a problem when you read this bit of advice to Timothy: "Stop drinking only water, and use a little wine because of your stomach and your frequent illnesses."[8]

Do you see the kind of problem that results when you rely on one verse—or even several verses—to develop your position on a particular issue? Make this a habit: When you come upon a puzzling passage in the Bible, or when you hear a teaching that doesn't sound quite right in light of what you know about God, start studying the "whole counsel of God"[9]— everything the Bible says about the matter. Let the Holy Spirit reveal to you the Father's purposes[10] in everything that is written in Scripture. The Spirit will bring to your mind those passages that relate to the problem you are studying and will guide you in using research materials to point you toward passages that are unfamiliar to you. Throughout this entire process, pray that the Spirit will illuminate the meaning of verses you don't understand. Pray that you will be open to whatever the Spirit has to say to you about the matter, and that you will use what you learn wisely. Use what you learn not to win an argument with those who believe differently than you do but rather to serve the body of Christ in a way that is honoring to God and to His "whole counsel."

LYDIA

There was never any question in my mind that God had called women to share the news about Jesus with others. I lived in Thyatira near Philippi, a Roman colony near the northern shore of the Aegean Sea, at the time Paul was traveling throughout the area. According to Luke, who was one of his traveling companions, one night Paul received a vision of a man in Macedonia, where Philippi was located, asking him to come and help the people there.[11]

Since Macedonia was not brimming with Jews, Paul and his companions had no synagogue to visit to find potential converts. But some other women and I went outside the city gates and met by the river to pray on the

Sabbath, even though we weren't Jewish. That's where Paul found us, and he began to tell us about Jesus.[12] I was already accustomed to worshipping the Jewish God, but I wasn't caught up in the teachings of the Pharisees as the Jews in Jerusalem were. As a result, I was able to respond readily and enthusiastically to what Paul said.[13]

My entire household came to believe in Jesus, and we were all baptized. Paul and his traveling companions came to stay in my home, which became the central meeting place for all the believers in the area.[14] If God had frowned on this—a woman's taking of the lead in establishing the church at Philippi—He certainly didn't show it. In fact, Philippi is the place where Paul and Silas were released from jail after an earthquake that not only rattled their jail cell and the chains that bound them but also the jailer, who became a believer when he realized that the power of God was behind the earthquake.[15]

28
How can we do it all?

Most women have one obligation piled on top of another. Their days are filled with responsibilities. Yet they are also expected to live the way Jesus did. Women live in constant tension between doing what God wants and doing what other people want.

Most women are so used to multitasking that they have fallen into a routine that requires dual responsibilities and activities at every point in their day. Some women can handle this with grace and ease, but many can't. It doesn't really matter, though, because most seem to be missing the abundant life. They feel they have to fulfill obligations to their friends, families, employers, and anyone else on their schedule, or they think they're letting God and everyone else down.

Q

God, You want us to follow Jesus' pattern for living, but life was a lot simpler when He was on earth. How can we imitate Jesus when our lives today are so full of obligations? Do You see the problem? How can we do it all?

GOD

Yes, I see the problem, but I also see each of you as individuals, with your own strengths, weaknesses, skills, and talents. Because I know human nature, you can be assured that if I haven't given you a specific talent, then I won't be "let down" when you resist trying to use a talent you don't have. But the bigger question is this: Who is loading these obligations on you? If I'm not doing it, then you are allowing others to dictate how you use your time and talents.

When My Son was on earth, He witnessed what you described. Let me tell you about one situation in particular. Jesus and His followers had just arrived in the village of Bethany and at the home of a family very dear to Him—Mary, Martha, and Lazarus, their brother. As soon as Jesus and His followers arrived at their house, Martha graciously welcomed them and began catering to them. She seemed to have everything under control, so Jesus began to talk to the others. Mary gave Him her complete attention. She sat at His feet and seemed aware of nothing but the words He spoke.[1]

Martha was bothered by the attention Mary was giving to Jesus. Martha interrupted His teaching, pointing out that Mary wasn't helping at all. Martha wanted Jesus to order Mary to help her.[2] But Mary was hungry for what Jesus had to say about Me, and it was important for her to stay and listen. What Martha didn't realize was that it was important for her, too, to hear what Jesus was saying.

JESUS

I had to make sure Martha understood that. "Martha, dear Martha," I said to her. "You're fussing far too much and getting yourself worked up over nothing."[3] In that society, at that time, there were certain rituals that a host was expected to perform when a guest arrived. But you see, Martha had already fulfilled those cultural obligations, and instead of joining us, joining Mary, she chose to bustle about in the kitchen. She made a choice. But so did Mary, and she made the better choice. She chose that one essential thing—staying in My presence. In those moments, she was living the abundant life.

Martha loved Me with all her heart and wanted to honor Me in the way that she thought was best. She grew up in a culture where honoring people meant "fussing" over them. That's what she knew to do—prepare a special meal, use the best of everything she had in the house, and make sure that My every need was met. But I taught her an important lesson that day: The burdensome expectations that are placed on you don't come from Me. My followers and I expected an offer of food and drink because that was common courtesy. But the lavish meal Martha was preparing? That was Martha choosing to show her love with an abundance of food rather than with her undivided attention.

GOD

Martha and Mary talked about this at length. Mary was so wrapped up in what Jesus was saying that she never gave a thought to what was going on around her—and certainly not to any cultural expectations. She knew Martha had met their immediate needs, so she felt free to sit at Jesus' feet and listen to Him. Mary was grateful to Martha, but she had no idea Martha was still running around and working in the kitchen. Mary was focused on Jesus.

Here's the point that you and all women in every era need to understand. Whenever cultural expectations conflict with what I want you to do, the "one essential thing" is to stay in My presence by being where I want you to be and doing what I want you to do.[4] I may want you to extend hospitality and participate in whatever event is going on. If that's the case, I'll give you the grace to do all that. But if I want you to do one or the other—giving your full attention to hospitality *or* giving your full attention to something else—then I'll give you the grace to do the former without resentment and the latter without guilt.[5]

You can see how the situation at Mary and Martha's that day isn't that different from your own life. I've seen how many women feel they have to do over and above what is required of them, and I've seen the conflicts that result between those women who feel they are carrying more than their share of the burden and other women who haven't the slightest awareness that there's even a burden to be carried.

Jesus

I once spoke to a large crowd of people about the burdensome obligations that had been placed on them. I was speaking specifically to those in the crowd who appeared tired and worn out. I welcomed them into My presence, assuring them that if they would only come away with Me, they could discover what it meant to take a real rest and then to really live. I invited them to pay attention to My life and the God-given grace that gave Me strength. I told them that being joined with Me would never be difficult or burdensome.[6] My words apply every bit as much to women today as they applied to the people in the crowd that day.

On another occasion, I told a story that has come to be known as the parable of the good Shepherd, in which I placed in stark contrast the behavior of the supposed shepherds of the Jews at that time—the scribes and Pharisees—and My own character and conduct in serving the people as the Good Shepherd. Not everyone understood this, but those who did knew that when I referred to the thieves and robbers, I was criticizing the religious leaders who had placed impossible burdens on the people by adding rituals and traditions that were not part of the covenant law God had given to the Israelites.

Because of those ungodly burdens, many Jews stopped trying to follow the law because no one could follow all the Pharisees' edicts, not even the Pharisees themselves. When I pointed out that sheep will not follow a stranger—and keep in mind that most of the people at that time were acquainted with the way sheep behaved—some began to understand that they were the sheep and the Pharisees were the thieves, robbers, and strangers. They realized I was the Good Shepherd, the One whose voice they recognized and trusted.

That's when I pointed out that the robbers—the Jewish leaders—had stolen their freedom to worship God, killed their motivation to serve God, and destroyed the hope that they could ever please God.[7] I wanted the people to know that by following Me, they would be free of the burdens that the religious leaders had placed on them. I wanted them to know that I would replace their burdensome lives with a life that was full to overflowing with God's blessings, a life more wonderful than they could possibly imagine.

This overflowing, wonderful, burden-free life is available to you today. You can fulfill your God-approved obligations and allow Me to introduce you to abundant living at the same time.[8]

29
How can we stop worrying so much?

Worry seems to be the middle name of many women. Those who have children are particularly susceptible to worrying, and that's understandable. Their nurturing nature inclines them toward protecting their young. But even women without children seem to find plenty to worry about. If it isn't finances, job insecurity, or the world situation, something else will come along to cause them undue concern.

Many worrying women would love to change their habit of fretting over every little thing. Some are familiar with passages in the Bible that tell them not to worry—and that causes them to worry that they're displeasing God! They need supernatural help to stop this all-too-natural cycle of worrying too much.

Q **God, we know that worry is an indication that we don't trust You, or so we've been told. But for some of us, worry seems to be written into our DNA; we can't seem to get rid of it no matter what we do. How can we stop worrying so much?**

GOD

Oh, My daughters, how I long for you to stop worrying the way you do! Our relationship is supposed to release you from the fears that lead to worry[1] and from the toll that worry takes on your physical and spiritual health.[2] Worry is a certain indication that you've taken matters into your own hands, chosen your own wisdom over Mine, and placed yourself in an unhealthy position.[3]

The burdens that many of you carry were meant to be shared, first with Me and then with the people in your life whom you're closest to. But some of you have been abandoned by those people, especially those of you who are single mothers and the father of your children is no longer a part of your life. Your worries never leave you, not even when you attempt to find peace when you sleep. You need to turn to Me and trust that I will replace your constant work and worry with the refreshing rest only I can give.[4]

How do you do that? Trust in Me throughout the day, seeking My wisdom and not relying on your own. Acknowledge My presence and believe that I will direct you in the way you should go.[5] Entrust your loved ones to Me; I will take care of your children[6] even as you teach them My ways.[7] Believe that I will provide for you and your loved ones,[8] but also learn to be content with what you have.[9]

One of the reasons why some of you worry so much is that you look at the circumstances in the world around you and think you are alone in facing the problems you see. You forget that I am your provision—I am your problem-solver as well as your provider—just as My beloved Israelites continually forgot that My provision was sufficient for them. At a time when the Israelites had once again wandered far away from Me, I told them through My prophet Isaiah that they did not need to seek, and would not find, satisfaction and provision in the world around them. I beckoned them to return to Me, where they would find the finest food and drink in abundance. There was no need for them to spend their money on those things that had little nutritional value.[10] In that situation, I was speaking of spiritual nutrition, and that's what I'm speaking of now. I will provide for you physically, but I will also provide for you spiritually, and you'll find your freedom from worry in My spiritual provision.

My servant David was among those who discovered that one of the keys to overcoming worry and anxiety was meditating on My Word and on who I am. Throughout the psalms that he wrote, he referred to Me by words that describe My attributes, words such as *rock, fortress,* and *place of refuge,*[11] characteristics of Me that give you the assurance you can trust Me to protect you. When you learn to meditate—to think deeply about Me as David did, you may find yourself breaking out into praise in the midst of your difficulties, just as he often did.[12]

Remember this: I am not a distant, far-off god; I am always with you, as close as the prayers you pray. When you find yourself worrying about something, anything, talk to Me about it. You can ask Me for help of any kind, and I will hear you. I don't want you to waste your life worrying; if you ask Me to help you overcome your tendency to worry, you can trust Me to answer that prayer.[13]

Jesus

Many of you feel you have much more to worry about than people did in ancient times. But I can assure you that people have experienced worry and anxiety throughout history. When I was on earth, the number of things people worried about was staggering. They not only worried about the necessities of life, but they worried about such things as incurable diseases and other types of afflictions, crime, and the whims of their Roman oppressors. That made the burdens placed on them by the Pharisees all the more heinous. The people had enough concerns in their lives; those who wanted to be good Jews didn't need the religious leaders making it impossible for them to be obedient as well.

It was so clear that the people were worrying about things like food and clothing, I specifically addressed the problem in what you know as the Sermon on the Mount. What I most wanted to convey was the pointlessness of worry. Living life to the fullest is much more important than worrying about what you will eat or drink or wear, or where any of that will come from. I pointed out how God the Father provides for the birds, which don't even have to store up food for the future,[14] and how He clothes the lilies of the field, whose apparel is much finer than even what Solomon wore.[15]

As I asked the crowd assembled that day, has all of your worrying given you the power to add even a single hour to your life?[16] No. Your worrying hasn't bought you anything of value. Furthermore, when you allow yourself to become anxious over these things, you're no better off than people who don't know the Father and don't have the slightest idea that they can trust Him to provide. Everything the Father has is at your disposal. All you need to do is focus your attention on God and His goodness,[17] and He'll give you everything you need. Stop worrying about tomorrow, and deal with today's concerns today[18] by believing that He loves you enough to make sure you and those you love are taken care of.

On another occasion, I had to reassure My own disciples, those who were closest to Me and had seen so much evidence of the Father's provision, that they didn't have to worry either. This was when I was sending them out to tell people about Me and to perform miracles in My name.[19] As I warned them that they wouldn't always be warmly received and in fact would likely be arrested, I had to tell them not to worry, that the Spirit would be with them and give them the words they should speak at the time.[20] I later had to warn them to guard their lives carefully to keep the anxieties and worries of life from robbing them of their awareness of what the Father was accomplishing in the world.[21] Worry was as much a problem among My disciples as it was among the general population at the time and as it is in your world today.

My disciples needed to be reminded of this just as you do: You already have everything you need to overcome worry and anxiety. You have the power of prayer and praise,[22] you have the power of the Holy Spirit,[23] and you have the assurance that your Father loves you and cares about you.[24] All of that is sufficient.

30
Is it possible to find genuine peace?

Women don't have to look very far to find evidence of strife in their lives. Conflicts abound in families, workplaces, schools, churches— in every institution and segment of society. And then there's conflict on the international stage. Peace seems to be fleeting at best and unattainable at worst.

And yet there are people who exude an inner peace despite the contention that swirls around them. It's easy to think that they're simply oblivious or deluded. In fact, it's a matter of self-preservation to believe they aren't quite right. To think otherwise would be to admit that inner peace is actually attainable, which in turn would mean that many people are approaching conflict the wrong way.

Q **Jesus once said that He was leaving us with His peace. But in the two thousand years since then, we haven't seen much evidence of that. Now we're not quite sure what He meant when He said that. God, is it possible, amid so much strife, to find genuine peace?**

GOD

It is indeed possible to find genuine peace on earth, and those of you who are seeking peace actually hold the key to bringing it about. That may come as a surprise to you, since most people expect someone else, whether it be a powerful leader on a global scale or an expert in conflict resolution on a more personal level, to put an end to strife and contention. But their efforts pale in comparison to what My people could do if they would take seriously a few short paragraphs from one of the apostle Paul's letters and apply its message to their lives.

You'll find Paul's instructions on how to experience My peace in his letter to the church at Philippi, a church he established years earlier. Word had reached him that there was an ongoing conflict between two women, Euodia and Syntyche, who had at one time worked side-by-side with him in telling people about God. He urged the two women to resolve their dispute, but then he went a step further and urged others in the church to help them out.[1]

Here's what Paul understood and what's so important about this passage: You cannot find genuine peace if you are at odds with the people in your life. Earlier, Paul had given specific instruction on how to imitate the humility Jesus showed when He gave up His position in heaven to serve humanity by coming to earth and sacrificing Himself for others. Those who are united with Christ, he wrote, show their love for Him by being of one mind, deferring to one another, and taking into consideration the interests of other people.[2] Euodia and Syntyche needed to learn that lesson.

Paul also understood that the conflict between those two women was affecting the entire church, and the Christians in Philippi needed to get involved and help conclude the matter peacefully. You recall our earlier discussion about the church as the body of Christ, how each Christian is a member of that body. Here was a case in which one part of the body was in conflict with another, and when that happens, the entire body suffers.[3] Paul wanted the suffering to end.

Paul then shifted the focus from the strife to another step in the cure: rejoicing in Me! He followed that up with a reminder that gentleness, a grace-filled demeanor, should be a visible attribute in a Christian's life, and specifically in the case at hand, an evidence of the peace that would come when the conflict at Philippi was put to rest.[4]

The next step in Paul's prescription for peace was to bring all your anxieties to Me in prayer, which we discussed when you asked about worry.[5] That, he said, would result in a peace that is nearly impossible for someone who has never experienced it to comprehend, but that peace will protect you and your faith in Christ.[6]

Paul's gift as a writer eloquently capped off everything that came before. He wrote that the way to dwell in that peace—to live in it day after day, regardless of the circumstances of your life—is to focus your mind on those things that are true, honorable, right, pure, lovely, of good repute, excellent, and praiseworthy.[7] To live in My peace, you must intentionally meditate on the qualities that are compatible with My nature and avoid dwelling on the opposite. When you put all that into practice, he wrote, then My peace would be with you.[8]

Paul was a master at communicating My message. His prescription for discovering genuine peace, My peace, is exactly what women today need.

Jesus

Let Me remind you of what My last days on earth were like. I had been staying in the countryside after eluding a crowd of Jews in Jerusalem who had threatened to stone Me. But when I heard that My friend Lazarus had died, I knew I had to return to his home in Bethany, which was just outside Jerusalem. It was risky to return to a place where so many people were intent on killing Me, but I knew the Father would bring glory to Himself by raising Lazarus from the dead.[9]

My disciples questioned My decision to travel to such a dangerous area, and they reminded Me of the stoning that was likely to result. Thomas finally spoke up but sounded resigned to a fatal outcome: "Let us also go, that we may die with Him."[10] No sooner had I returned to Bethany and raised Lazarus from the dead[11] than word of the miracle got back to the chief priests and Pharisees, who got together and plotted to kill Me, fearing that so many people would believe in Me that the Romans would be able to wrest power from the Jewish leadership.

Things intensified when the people heard that I would be going to Jerusalem for the Feast of the Passover, one of the major religious commemorations among the Jews. As I rode into the city on a donkey, the people lined My route, waved palm branches as I passed, and shouted out that I was the new King of Israel.[12]

Throughout that week, which led up to My crucifixion, the turmoil in Jerusalem was palpable, with both the Jewish and the Roman leadership fearing complete chaos. Some people wanted Me crowned as their king; others wanted Me killed for the religious crime of blasphemy; still others wanted Me out of the way so they could restore order in the city. Then there were people who didn't particularly care what happened but who spilled into the streets anyway just to see how all this was going to play out.

You can imagine what My disciples were thinking. The situation was even worse than they had anticipated and was about to get much, much worse. The night before I died on the cross, as I shared My last meal with My closest disciples, I exposed one of them, Judas, as My betrayer, foretold My death, and told an astonished Peter that before the night was out, he would deny he ever knew Me.

All this was too much for My followers; I could sense their bewilderment, disbelief, and deep anguish. My next words spoke of the very thing you seek and consider to be so elusive in your own lives: peace. Don't let your hearts be troubled by all this, I told them. Believe in God; believe in Me.[13]

How could I speak of peace at a time like that? How could I expect My disciples to experience any measure of peace under those circumstances? I could do so because of what I told them later that night, that when I left them, I would leave My peace with them, and My peace would overcome their troubled hearts.[14] What's more, I would send the Holy Spirit,[15] who would help them overcome the difficulties in their lives that would threaten to rob them of their peace.

Bear in mind that I warned them that trouble in the world and in their personal lives would continue, but I had overcome the world for them. As a result, they could still experience peace.[16] The way they accomplished this was by allowing My peace to have complete rein over their lives,[17] trusting Me, relying on Me, and never forgetting that I promised to give them peace.

31

How can we share our faith inoffensively?

Talking to others about God can be daunting for some people under the best of circumstances. But in a multicultural society in which people come from myriad religious and nonreligious backgrounds, simply mentioning God can be considered offensive and inappropriate.

That leaves followers of Christ in a difficult position because they want to help others discover the new life they can have if they become followers of Christ as well. What's more, before He ascended to heaven, the last thing Jesus told His disciples to do was to preach the good news about Him and lead other people to become His disciples. To obey Jesus' last words on earth, His followers need the freedom to talk about Him.

Q **Jesus, we don't want to offend anybody, but it seems as if we can't talk about You without running that risk. Sometimes we feel that we're bursting at the seams, wanting to tell people who are hurting that You are their answer. How can we share our faith inoffensively?**

JESUS

I've seen many of you in the United States and other Western countries struggle with this in recent years. It wasn't so long ago that you could mention My name, and while some people didn't respond well to it, not many people considered it offensive. But your society has changed, and now the mention of My name may provoke a great deal of animosity and could even cost you your job.

These changes have brought about division among My followers. Some defy the laws and workplace regulations, believing that no one has the right to take away their freedom to speak My name. Others believe they should comply with the policies of a company or public institution and find ways to lead people to the truth about Me without defying those policies.

But here's the real issue: Are you sharing your faith in love? I know how that sounds to the warriors among you, those who will fight to the death for the right to speak My name. It sounds weak and spineless. But remember that My love is strong, uncompromising, and sacrificial. My love is the kind that loves no matter what. There's nothing fragile about it.

Sharing your faith starts with love—having compassion for others, showing mercy to others, making sure your encounters with others are grace filled. That means taking into consideration everything you know about the person and understanding the pain in her life. You need the Holy Spirit's guidance in such situations because the Spirit can reveal things to you that will help you know how to proceed as well as how not to proceed. When a person is in pain, you don't want to add to it by saying the wrong thing or something that would offend her and cause her to shut you out of her life completely. Relying on the Spirit is critical in keeping the door open for the future.

Sometimes, however, when you speak the truth in love, it is painful to the other person. But if you do so under the guidance of the Holy Spirit, the pain that results is like the aftermath of surgery; in the end, the patient is healed, and that makes every painful moment worthwhile.

Relying on the Spirit also eliminates the likelihood that your friend will become suspicious that you have a certain agenda in mind for forging the friendship. If you're depending on the Holy Spirit to guide the relationship, any agenda you may have had becomes immaterial. You may think it's your job to bring your friend into a full relationship with Me, but the Holy Spirit may see your role as entirely different.

Can you see how depending on the Holy Spirit allows you to relax and enjoy the relationships you have with those who don't know Me yet? Instead of bursting at the seams with anxiety over whether or not you can say My name, you can let your joy burst forth and let the Spirit reveal to your friend who I am.

That kind of faith-sharing is nothing new. My followers have led others to Me like that in countries that have never had either the measure of religious freedom you used to have or the measure you still have today. You can learn a great deal about how to tell people about Me from My followers in countries where evangelizing—trying to get people to convert to Christianity—could get them imprisoned or killed.

It's wonderful that your relationship with Me means so much to you that you want to help other people have the same kind of relationship with Me. That's what I want My followers to do, and it's an indication that you've grasped a full understanding of what it means to follow Me. Be patient with yourself and with the unbelieving people in your life, however, as you seek to introduce them to Me.

Sharing your faith starts with genuine love. Are you kind? Do you resist being envious, boastful, proud, rude, or self-seeking? Do you likewise resist being easily angered or keeping score of wrongdoings? Do you despise evil and rejoice in the truth?[1] Answering yes to those questions is an indication that you understand the nature of genuine love. Let your loving attitude and the Holy Spirit guide your encounters with unbelievers.

GOD

Long before Jesus lived on earth, I told the prophet Isaiah that the Messiah would be the cornerstone of My kingdom, but He would also be a "stone of stumbling" and a "rock of offense"[2] to the Jews. Paul was among those who recognized the fulfillment of that prophecy in Jesus. That the truth about Jesus would become offensive to some people was no surprise to Me or to Paul once he became a follower of Jesus. It shouldn't be a surprise to those of you who are familiar with Paul's letter to the Romans, in which he quoted My words to Isaiah,[3] or his first letter to the church at Corinth, in which he described Jesus and His crucifixion as a stumbling block to the Jews.[4]

Also in that letter to the Corinthians, Paul emphasized that you are not to give offense to anyone. You are to do everything to My glory, including making your own interests secondary to the interests of those with whom you're sharing your faith.[5]

Paul further mentioned that in order to lead people to Me, he became familiar with different cultures, ways of living, and ways of thinking so he could speak to people about Me in ways they would understand.[6] He was one of the early church's most effective evangelists, those who shared the good news about Jesus. The methods he employed are worth using as a model for sharing your faith even in modern society.

One of the methods Paul used was to customize his message to his audience. On a visit to Athens, the birthplace of Greek philosophy, he used a philosophical approach to communicate the truth about Jesus. He was well aware that the Greek philosophers were curious about new ideas, so he mingled with them and talked with them in the marketplace where they met each day.[7] Though they did so derisively, soon enough they asked him to tell them more about the "foreign god" he kept talking about.[8]

Paul then made a brilliant move. Drawing from one of their cultural artifacts, Paul pointed out that he had seen a particular altar among the many in the city that exemplified the Athenians' interest in religion. This particular altar, he said, was dedicated to an unknown god, and he was there to reveal to them who this god was—Me.[9] In his speech, he even quoted some of their poets, creating another connection between his new teaching and the teachings with which they were already familiar.[10] He finished by telling them about Jesus' resurrection, which not surprisingly was an obstacle to some, and they continued to mock him. Others wanted to hear more, however, and some of those listening to him that day became followers of Christ.[11]

Paul made the most of every opportunity he had to tell others about Jesus. That's what I want you to do as well, making sure that you do so with grace, gentleness, and respect.[12] Treat unbelievers with the same measure of respect that Jesus did.[13]

By using the wisdom I've given you and following the Holy Spirit's leading, you can share with others the truth that leads to freedom[14] without compromising the message and without offending others in the way you present that truth. Your words, your attitude, and your purity—never compromising your values as you interact with people who have different values—will shine so brightly in a darkened world that people will clearly see Me as the God you serve.[15]

*This is the confidence that we have in Him,
that if we ask anything according to His will,
He hears us. And if we know that He hears us,
whatever we ask, we know that we have the
petitions that we have asked of Him.*

1 John 5:14–15 NKJV

PRAYER

Some women have a tough time praying. When things are going okay, there doesn't seem to be much reason to pray. And when things are rough, prayer isn't the first thing on their minds.

32. God, how can we know You're listening? 157

33. Do You hear everybody's prayers? 161

34. Why aren't some prayers answered? 165

35. Can prayer really make a difference? 169

36. Is there one right way to pray? 173

37. Should we pray about only major problems? 177

38. Is it okay to pray repetitious prayers? 181

32
God, how can we know You're listening?

Sometimes the act of praying feels like talking to a brick wall. The words seem to dissipate into thin air, with no voice, no echo resounding from the heavens to provide assurance that the words indeed reached the ears of God. The resulting silence is so far from golden that it feels leaden.

When women talk about the deep concerns of their lives, they need to know that someone is listening. Because so many of their words appear to go unheeded—such as those directed at their own disobedient children or a classroom of chattering teenagers—when they open their hearts and lives to God, they want to know that He's listening in a way no one else is.

Q **God, sometimes You seem so silent and so distant. Prayer is hard enough for some of us; we don't want the added burden of wondering if anyone "out there" is actually paying attention to our words or the wordless cries of our hearts. How can we know You're listening?**

GOD

Before I talk about prayer, you mentioned that sometimes I seem distant. I want to assure you that I am always with you—closer to you than you can imagine. Because I am Spirit, I am everywhere,[1] as near to you as your own spirit. The psalmists often wrote of My nearness, praising Me for drawing My people close to Me[2] and being near not only to the brokenhearted[3] but also to everyone who calls on Me.[4]

The psalmists, David in particular, also wrote with complete assurance that I heard their prayers. "Morning, noon, and night I cry out in my distress, and the LORD hears my voice,"[5] David wrote in one of his psalms; "The righteous cry out, and the LORD hears, and delivers them from all their troubles,"[6] he wrote in another psalm.

You can have that same assurance, just as you can be assured that, unlike humans, I make no distinction between *hearing* and *listening*. I see your frustration when it becomes clear that people aren't really listening to your words; they hear the words with their ears but not with their full attention. But I am never distracted the way humans are. My hearing is perfect. You can have confidence that when you come to Me in prayer, I hear you.[7]

I know that you, My daughters, want to feel My presence when you pray. You want an emotional encounter with Me, often because you've had such an experience with Me in the past. Those times when you've felt My presence or sensed I was moving in your life in a way that was almost tangible were precious times to you. But you need to trust Me and believe I am always with you, even during those dry periods when your prayers don't seem to be answered, nothing significant appears to be happening in your life, and you can't seem to find Me—you can't sense My presence—no matter how hard you try. It's in those times that your faith in Me has an opportunity to grow. But that will happen only when you stop relying on your feelings and begin to believe that My Word is true. I am always with you, I am nearer to you than you can even envision, and I am listening to your every prayer.

One of the ways you can have assurance that I am listening is to be in constant prayer,[8] which doesn't mean that you have to give up eating and sleeping and everything else in your life, but it does mean that you approach praying as an act of your will and not of your emotions. Maintain a prayer-like connection with Me throughout the day by keeping your heart and thoughts turned toward Me even though your conscious thoughts are on work or your family, for example. Also spend dedicated time in purposeful prayer, even when you don't feel like it. When you can do that, you will know that prayer for you is no longer dependent on your feelings; it has become something you do as an act of faith that shows you believe I'm listening.

Know that My silence is never an indication of My indifference toward you. When you learn to persevere and trust Me during the times when I seem remote and distant, you will have learned a lesson in trust that will carry you through the rest of your life.

Jesus

There's no better evidence that God hears people when they pray than the prayers I prayed while I was on earth. Remember, during My time on earth I was still God, but I had taken on the form and nature—minus the sin—of a human being. I prayed as a man, and when I prayed I did so because as God, I knew the Father heard My prayers.

When My disciples came to Me and asked Me to teach them to pray, I didn't hesitate to give them a model they could use to talk to the Father on their own. I showed them how simple prayer can be; there was no need for them to use religious-sounding words, thinking maybe that would impress the Father and make it more likely their words would be heard.

I gave this model: Pray to the Father, keeping in mind that He is a holy God and that His name should be kept holy. Express your desire for His kingdom to become apparent soon on earth. Ask Him to meet your daily needs and to forgive you of any wrongdoing, in the same way that you forgive others of their wrongdoing. Ask Him also to keep you from giving in to temptation.[9]

When I was on earth, many people had a difficult time believing that the Father sent Me and that He was the power behind the miracles I performed. I often retreated to a remote place so I could talk to the Father in private, but occasionally I prayed in public as well. One time in particular—the death of My good friend Lazarus—I prayed specifically for the benefit of those who were standing by waiting to see how I would handle the situation.

Lazarus and his sisters, Mary and Martha, were among My closest companions throughout My earthly ministry. I cried when I heard of his death, and while some of the Jews saw My great love for him in My tears, others questioned why, if I was so powerful, I had not prevented his death.[10] I knew then what I had to do.

I asked that the stone be removed from the entrance to his tomb. Martha, always the one to point out practical details, expressed her concern about the odor of Lazarus's decomposing body; I pointed out that she needed to have more faith in the Father.[11] Then I prayed aloud, for the sake of those who doubted Me: "Father, I thank You that You have heard Me. I knew that You always hear Me; but because of the people standing around I said it so that they would believe that You sent Me. [Then I cried out,] 'Lazarus, come forth.'"[12]

The sight of Lazarus emerging from the tomb was one that no one would soon forget—he walked out on his own strength, wrapped head to toe in his tightly bound grave clothes. The people were so astonished that I had to tell them to remove the cloth so Lazarus could walk and breathe.[13]

The Jewish leaders were so disturbed by this display of My power that they began to plot against Me in earnest.[14] They couldn't allow Me to continue offering undeniable proof that I was the long-awaited Messiah.

For those of you who remain unconvinced that the Father hears your prayers, you can have the confidence of knowing that the Holy Spirit inside you goes before the Father on your behalf even when you don't have the words to express what you want to pray about.[15] I can assure you, I am also there at the Father's side, going before Him on your behalf as you pray.[16]

33
Do You hear everybody's prayers?

Women sometimes wonder if they've committed a sin that would cause God to refuse to hear their prayers, which in turn causes them to speculate about just whose prayers God does hear—and whose He ignores. They want to know how they can make sure they're in the group whose prayers are heard.

Then there are questions about the prayers uttered by people of other faiths, whether God hears the prayers of Muslims, for example, or people who pray to a universal consciousness, which is their under-standing of who God is. It's difficult enough to imagine God hearing the simultaneous prayers of millions of people, let alone sorting out those worth hearing from those that aren't—if that's what He does.

Q **God, we've heard some preachers say that You hear only the prayers of "righteous" people, while some even say that You hear only the prayers of Christians. But what about everyone else? Are they wasting their time and breath? Do You hear everybody's prayers— or don't You?**

GOD

I hear everybody's prayers. If I didn't—if I refused to hear the prayers of truly evil individuals or entire groups of people whose religious beliefs are different from your own—I would never hear the cries of repentance or pleas for forgiveness that could be embedded in their prayers. That would mean that I have offered the gift of salvation to only a select group of individuals. But that's not the case. Salvation is available to everyone.

What you have heard your preachers say is based on a broad under-standing of the word *hear* that is much closer to the definition of *heed*, meaning to pay close attention to something and act on it. I hear all prayers but heed far fewer. I can hear an unconscionable person pray for the death of her archenemy, but I will not heed her prayer and bring about what for her would be a favorable result.

Let's look together at some of the Bible passages that speak of My refusing to hear certain prayers to see what they mean.

In the book of Zechariah, the prophet recounted how I refused, with good reason, to listen to the cries of the Israelites. I had repeatedly commanded them to exercise justice, mercy, and compassion; to treat the widows, orphans, aliens, and the poor with dignity; and to deal openly and fairly with others. But they would not listen; they blatantly ignored My repeated commands and warnings. In return, I did not listen—I did not heed their cries when they finally turned to Me for help.[1] As Zechariah reminded the descendants of that rebellious generation of Israelites, their rebellion cost them their land—a land that was left barren and desolate after many of them were taken captive by the Babylonians and many others were scattered throughout the area.[2]

When My people repeatedly disobey Me, I may not heed their prayers unless they are prayers of genuine repentance and not simply sorrow over what they've done or fear over what's about to happen. A genuine repentance is based on a resolve to turn away from evil.[3] That's just as true for entire groups, like the Israelites, as it is for individuals.[4]

Understand that I am speaking here not of an occasional sin; I am speaking of repeated, willful disobedience. Those of you who are parents or have had young children in your care understand that distinction. You consider a pattern of rebellion to be a far more serious issue than you do an occasional act of disobedience.

This is the principle you can apply to those times when it seems as if I have closed My ears to the cries of those who say they love Me: I hear their cries, but because of their willful rebellion, I may not heed them. Many Bible verses that describe Me as refusing to hear the prayers of the unrighteous refer specifically to pleas of the disobedient Israelites who knew Me and knew better than to defy My law.

A similar principle applies to those who do not know Me but continue to commit evil acts against other people. Their *wickedness*—and that's a highly appropriate word for their sinfulness—forces Me to distance Myself from them and refuse to heed their prayers.[5] Remember, though, that when I speak of that kind of evil and wickedness, in contrast to Israel's rebellion and disobedience, I am speaking of individuals and not entire nations or groups. I do not show partiality; I freely welcome anyone from any nation or group who turns to Me and chooses to follow Me.[6]

You can see how I've dealt with My people who are rebellious and evil people who don't yet know Me. Have I ever made exceptions? Yes, I have. When King Ahab humbled himself before Me, I spared him from the devastation that Elijah prophesied would come upon him. Ahab, as many of you know, was a truly wicked man who at first sneered at Elijah. But when he heard what Elijah prophesied about him, he believed his words and began to fast and mourn over what was to come.[7] I alone know the heart of a person,[8] and I alone determine how I will deal with each individual.

JESUS

One of the things that many people today don't understand is that not all Gentiles worshipped Roman gods in first-century Palestine. Some Gentiles were converts to Judaism, while others were attracted to the Father and worshipped with the Jews.[9] One of the Gentiles who believed in God was a Roman centurion named Cornelius, who lived in Caesarea in Samaria, on the Mediterranean Sea. Cornelius had not yet heard about Me, but he and his family were devout Gentiles who prayed regularly and generously gave of what they had to the poor.[10]

One day as Cornelius was in prayer, an angel appeared to him and told him to send for a man named Peter who was in Joppa, just down the coast from Caesarea. This, of course, was My disciple Peter, but Cornelius knew nothing about him. He just did as the angel told him to. Just as Cornelius's servants arrived at the house where Peter was staying, My Spirit told Peter that he was to go with the servants without question.[11]

When Peter and several other of My followers arrived at Cornelius's house several days later, Cornelius told Peter about the angel's appearance and what the angel said to him: "God has heard your prayer and remembered your gifts to the poor."[12] Not only had an angel of God appeared to this Gentile, but the angel also affirmed that God had heard his prayer. An astonished Peter realized for the first time that God heard the prayers of Gentiles and that Gentiles could become My followers.

Peter proceeded to explain to Cornelius and his family—who, like just about everyone else in the area, had heard about Me and My ministry— exactly what My coming to earth meant. I was the Messiah, and I was crucified, I rose from the dead to bring salvation to everyone. As Peter was speaking, the Holy Spirit came upon everyone within hearing range, and, in a language that was new to them, they all began speaking in tongues and praising the Father. Immediately Peter baptized Cornelius and his entire family.[13]

Cornelius is an example of someone whose prayers the Father heard and heeded even though he was neither a Jew nor one of My followers. He understood the Father as well as a Gentile could, and he sought Him in prayer. The Father saw his heart, sent an angel to him, and allowed him to receive the gift of the Holy Spirit. Through that experience, Peter, and later all My Jewish followers, finally and fully understood that everything I had given to them was also available to the Gentiles. This caused no small amount of dissension back in Jerusalem,[14] but once Peter explained what had happened, My Jewish followers also understood that the Gentiles could now be welcomed into the fold, and they began to praise the Father.[15] The conversion of Cornelius and all that it meant marked a turning point for the early church.

34
Why aren't some prayers answered?

Why some prayers aren't answered is a nearly universal question among true believers and skeptics alike. Two God-loving, faith-filled people earnestly pray for a specific concern in their lives, fully believing that God not only can but will answer their prayers. And yet one person's prayer will go unanswered, sometimes during her entire lifetime, while the other person's prayer is answered immediately. It just seems so unfair.

The issue of fairness aside, women want to know why—why God seems to stingily withhold the answer from one person while lavishly bestowing the answer on another. If they could only understand why, then accepting the fact that their prayers aren't answered would be much easier, or so they hope.

Q **God, sometimes we pray for something for decades, and there's not a shred of evidence You're doing anything to answer that prayer. Meanwhile, other women pray for something once and it's as good as done. Why aren't some prayers answered?**

GOD

Your question indicates that you believe your prayers aren't being answered. One of the reasons for that belief is that often when you pray about or for something, you have already determined what the outcome of your prayer should be. My beloved daughters, you think that anything other than that outcome, received by a particular deadline that you have also determined, is an indication that I have not answered your prayer. Consider this possibility: You didn't recognize My answer because it wasn't what you expected—you and millions who came before you. You can't see the full picture of your life that I can, and so I don't expect you always to recognize My answers.

Look at what happened in first-century Palestine. The Jewish people had been praying for centuries for the coming of the Messiah. The vast majority of those people had died before Jesus, the Messiah, made His appearance on earth. But what about those who were alive at the time? Most of them did not recognize the answer to their prayers even though He walked among them because He was not what they were expecting. Even many of those who saw something special in Him failed to recognize Him as the Messiah because they wanted a political leader who would overthrow Roman rule. But I gave the world a far greater answer than a political leader in a small country on the eastern shore of the Mediterranean. I gave them My Son, their Savior.

At times you don't recognize My answer, but it is true that often I withhold My answer for other reasons. As you will recall from our previous discussion, I often denied the Israelites the answers they wanted because of their ongoing rebellion. Sin creates a barrier between My people and Me,[1] one that you have the ability to break down by admitting to your wrongdoing and seeking My forgiveness.[2] Be on guard against pride[3] and arrogance,[4] which can block your prayers and prevent My grace from working in your life.

Women often overlook several other barriers to prayer. One is a failure to care for the poor,[5] and another is having right relationships with the people in your life with whom you're closest. Do you realize that you wives may be married to men whose prayers are blocked because they don't treat you well? It's true. A husband is to treat his wife with consideration, love, respect, and honor, and if he fails to do that, his behavior toward his wife could prove to be a hindrance to his prayers.[6]

But often your prayers go unanswered because you simply don't believe that I will do what I have said I will do, and so you don't even ask Me for what you need.[7] If you are in a true relationship with Me and you pray according to My will, you can have the confidence that I will answer your prayer.[8] I've proven My love for you by giving you My Son; you can have everything else as well.[9]

I know what a hard time you have believing that. I've seen you struggle to have more faith. You strive hard to take Me at My Word and trust Me in every circumstance of your life. You know that if you ask for something but don't really believe that I'll provide, you're not likely to get it.[10] You need to understand how simple the act of believing is. I want My daughters to start relaxing and simply believe that I am trustworthy. That's what walking by faith is all about; instead of trusting in what you see, trust in what you can't see[11]—Me, working behind the scenes of your life, making sure everything works together for your benefit.[12]

You cannot imagine what I have in store for your life.[13] I already know the prayers that you haven't even prayed yet.[14] Believe that I am a faithful God who loves you with an eternal love,[15] who delights in you[16] and longs to show you mercy, compassion, and justice.[17] As long as you live your life with integrity, I will not deny you any good thing.[18]

JESUS

Throughout My ministry, I emphasized to My followers how important it was for them to do the two things the Father just mentioned: make their requests known to Him and believe that He had not only the power to answer their prayers but also the desire. Ask, I told the people; seek what it is you want; knock, and God will open the door to your answers.[19] All they needed to do was believe that they would receive what they asked of the Father.[20]

One of the great joys of My ministry was encountering people who believed without question. One woman in particular exhibited an unusual measure of faith, so much faith, in fact, that she believed all she had to do was touch the bottom of My robe as I walked in front of her and she would be healed. This poor woman had suffered with constant hemorrhaging for twelve years, and she was healed in that moment. All it took was simple faith.[21]

Many men who came to Me for help also trusted Me completely. On one occasion a Roman soldier came to Me and told Me that his servant was paralyzed and suffering terribly. When I offered to go to his home and heal his servant, the soldier said he was not worthy to have Me in his home. Before I could respond, he expressed his confidence that all I had to do was say the word and his servant would be healed. As a man under authority, he understood that My authority came from the Father. I had never witnessed such a pure display of faith in all Israel. I told him to go home, and he would find his servant healed.[22]

Even if you have faith that your prayers will be answered, however, you need to remember that there are other obstacles to having your prayers answered, and I pointed those out during My time on earth. One is lack of forgiveness. Forgiveness is so important that if you refuse to forgive those who have hurt you, betrayed you, or in any other way offended you, you can actually block your own prayers to the Father seeking His forgiveness.[23]

Another hindrance to prayer that I spoke of when I was on earth is hypocrisy. The Pharisees were notorious for this; one of the indications of their hypocrisy was their habit of flaunting their religiosity in public. They would pray on street corners just to be seen as pious by any onlookers. I pointed out that their prayers were worthless; they had already received everything they would ever get from the Father.[24]

Then there's the problem of praying for something that is outside the Father's will, which is something I had to resist as I prayed in the Garden of Gethsemane on the night before My crucifixion. I had gone there with My disciples following our last meal together, and I asked them to wait for Me while I went off by Myself to pray. I knew what I was facing; I was overwhelmed with sorrow at what was to take place the following day. I fell on the ground and pleaded with the Father to spare Me the suffering I knew I would have to endure, but only if it was His will to spare Me. My will was not important; only His will mattered.[25]

The Father's will—what He desires for your life—will always be what is best for you, even if it looks nothing like the outcome you envisioned.

35

Can prayer really make a difference?

The prayers people utter are as varied as the people praying them. Prayers for an end to suffering, disease, poverty, war, and a host of other ills that plague the world are directed toward God every day and every night. And yet all those problems continue to afflict people and societies around the globe. That leads many people to conclude that prayer doesn't make one bit of difference.

Understandably, women, who are especially sensitive to the heartache resulting from tragedies that can often be prevented, want suffering to end. They plead with God to stop disease from spreading, to make a way for the poor to prosper, to change humanity's propensity to wage war. But nothing ever seems to change.

Q **God, regardless of our age, we don't understand why things are not much better today than they were when we were growing up. Some things have improved, but people still suffer unimaginable hardship. Can prayer really make a difference, and if so, how?**

GOD

Prayer changes far more in your life and in the world than you realize. But some of you need more evidence than My Word alone; you're still not sure about Me, and you want proof that what I say is true.

One of My qualities that you need to grasp is My sovereignty, My absolute power and authority over all of life. You have only to read the Bible to discover for yourself the miracles I performed and the marvelous events that occurred because of My activity in the world you live in. Through My prophets, and through other means, I have foretold events that eventually happened. All My plans will be fulfilled, because I have the power to accomplish what I choose to do.[1]

That includes changing events as I please in response to prayer.

As you recall from a previous discussion, King Ahab was a truly evil person who was especially cruel to My prophets. He had been searching throughout his kingdom of Samaria for Elijah, a particularly troublesome servant of Mine; Ahab wanted him dead. Samaria was experiencing an extended drought, and Ahab blamed it on Elijah.

Elijah accused Ahab of causing the drought by turning away from Me. He told Ahab to assemble the so-called prophets of false gods for a contest on Mount Carmel. There, Elijah built an altar for Me, and the false prophets built a wooden altar for their false god, Baal.[2]

A bull was placed on each altar. The false prophets were to pray to Baal to miraculously set the wood on fire, but though they prayed and shouted and even cut themselves with their weapons, nothing happened.[3]

Elijah then added a twist to the competition—after he prepared the altar for Me with the wood and the bull, three times he had the people pour water from four huge jugs all over the wood and the meat, so much that the runoff filled up a ditch he had dug around the altar. The moment he prayed to Me and asked Me to ignite the soaking-wet wood, I sent a powerful fire that consumed the meat, the wood, the ground beneath the altar, and the water in the ditch.[4]

The onlookers who had come to watch this spectacle began bowing before Me and shouting that I was the one true God.[5] As a further sign of My sovereignty and power, I sent a mighty rainstorm that drenched Samaria and ended the drought, in response to Elijah's confident assertions that I would do just that.[6]

Can you see what I accomplished in response to Elijah's challenge and prayer? I ended the drought in Samaria, which was important to the people living there. But I accomplished much more than that. I proved that I was the one true God, and as a result, the people who witnessed My miracle rejected Baal, turned to Me, and acknowledged Me as God. And I provided evidence that prayer can change circumstances. The people saw that Elijah prayed and that I responded. They saw that prayer can bring about change.

Now look at a situation in which I chose not to change one person's circumstances. This situation involved Paul, whom you would assume I would want to bless. And I did bless him in many ways. But I denied him one particular request that he made of Me three times.

Paul told this story in his second letter to the church at Corinth. He began by telling of an incident that occurred fourteen years earlier, which he wasn't sure how to describe except to say that he heard such astounding things that he couldn't repeat them. He stopped just short of boasting about all this.[7] But then he began boasting about his weakness, which you've heard called a thorn in his flesh. He believed that the problem that plagued him and weakened him had served to keep him humble,[8] and he came to that conclusion after begging Me on three occasions to take it away from him.

Each time, I told him the same thing: My grace is all you need to keep you strong; My power is enough to overcome your weakness.[9] Paul knew that had he been any stronger and more capable than he already was, he ran the risk of becoming boastful about his own achievements.[10] In his weakness, I was the one who was glorified, not Paul. I gave him the grace to accomplish what he otherwise would not have been able to do.

In both cases—with Elijah and with Paul—prayer made a difference, but in strikingly different ways. In one case, a huge crowd witnessed My power and My response to prayer. In another case, one person came to understand that his weakness was much more beneficial to Me and My purposes than his healing would have been. Although nothing seemed to change on the outside, a great deal changed on the inside for Paul; the difference that prayer makes is not always visible.

JESUS

There were many times in Paul's life in which prayer made a difference in other ways. He actively sought the prayers of My followers throughout the Mediterranean region. While he was under house arrest in Rome, he wrote to the Colossian church, asking the people to pray that the Father would give him an opportunity to continue to preach about Me in his confinement.[11] Following a severe trial in Ephesus, during which Paul believed he would die for the sake of spreading the good news about Me, he thanked the church at Corinth—in the same letter the Father just mentioned—for the many prayers that were offered up for him, asking that God would deliver him from the trial he'd had to endure.[12] Paul's deliverance was significant, but just as significant were the prayers of the people offered on his behalf.

In another letter written while Paul was under house arrest, he encouraged the church at Ephesus to pray that he would be able to boldly proclaim the good news even though he was in chains. He didn't pray for freedom from prison but for freedom to preach.[13] To the church at Philippi, he expressed confidence that through their prayers and the activity of the Holy Spirit, he would finally be released from prison.[14]

Some people think that because the Father is all knowing, there's no point in praying. If God knows the past, present, and future, why pray? Why ask Him to meet your needs or bless someone else or put an end to world hunger? What difference does it make? Following that line of reasoning, Paul needn't have asked people to pray for him. But Paul knew that the prayers of the people who supported his ministry mattered. They made a difference, not only in the outcome but also in his level of endurance.

HANNAH

Does prayer make a difference? It most certainly does! I lived at the time when Israel was governed by judges, and I was childless, which made me an object of scorn and derision in Israelite society. Even though my husband, Elkanah, loved me, I had to suffer mocking from his other wife, Peninnah, who had borne him several children. One day, I couldn't take it anymore. I ran to the tabernacle and started pouring out my heart to God. I begged Him to remember me and give me a son. In return, I promised to give my son to God, to serve Him in the tabernacle.[15]

Eli, the priest, saw my lips moving but couldn't hear what I was saying. He thought I was drunk But when I told him what my prayer was, he gave me his blessing and affirmed my request for a son.[16]

Soon enough, I became pregnant and gave birth to a son, whom we called Samuel. I honored my promise to God; when Samuel was three, I took him to the tabernacle, where Eli became his guardian and his teacher. Elkanah saw Samuel as the answer to our prayers, and he prayed that God would give us more children. And He did. Despite my earlier barrenness, God gave us three more sons in addition to Samuel and two more daughters.[17] Does prayer make a difference? Yes! For me, it certainly did!

36
Is there one right way to pray?

Among the countless things some women worry about is whether they're praying the right way. They may have heard a sermon, a teaching, or even just a casual conversation about prayer that implied there are wrong ways and right ways to pray, and now they're concerned because they've forgotten what they heard. They want to be sure they're praying correctly, from the words they use to the position of their bodies when they settle down to pray.

Their confusion over how to pray is nothing new. Even though Jesus gave His followers a model for prayer in what is known as the Lord's Prayer, people have pondered the correct method of praying over the intervening two thousand years.

Q
God, some of us were taught to close our eyes and bow our heads when we pray. Others were taught to use high-sounding King James vocabulary. Still others were taught that we should always kneel as a sign of submission. So tell us—is there one right way to pray?

GOD

For millennia, people have been searching for the perfect formula for prayer, as if there were a special key that would unlock the secret of the right way to pray. Some people are so distracted by that search they never take the time to actually pray.

There is no single "right" way to pray, but there are some principles to keep in mind when you pray:

Keep in mind that I am everywhere;[1] not even heaven can contain Me.[2] There is nowhere on earth that you can go and not find Me there.[3] You don't need to go to a special building, like a church, to pray to Me. You can start talking to Me right now, wherever you are.

You can also have a conversation with Me regardless of whether you're sitting, standing, kneeling, or lying down. You don't need to fold your hands in a prayerful position, and you don't need to close your eyes. You can pray when you're driving, jogging, or doing aerobics. The position of your body, your hands, and your eyelids makes no difference whatsoever. What matters is your attitude in prayer, that you approach Me with a willingness to submit to My will. That's much more important to Me than whether you are kneeling as a sign of submission.

You don't need to use formal language when you talk to Me either. You don't use stiff, proper language when you have a normal conversation with someone. I want you to think of prayer as a normal conversation with Me. Don't make the mistake of thinking, as was typical of the pagans when Jesus was on earth, that you need to pray lengthy prayers to make yourself heard; I am aware of your needs already.[4]

In fact, you don't even need to use words at all. Sometimes people's needs are so profound and so intense that they don't even know how to express what they want to say to Me; when that happens, the Holy Spirit takes over and prays for them, translating their thoughts and feelings into "groanings too deep for words."[5]

Some of you wonder if there's a specific time of day when you should pray, particularly those of you who are familiar with the prayer habits of two of My most faithful servants, Daniel and David. Both men made it a habit to pray to Me three times a day.[6] But there's no "should" involved; praying three times a day was their preference, and there was no law dictating that schedule—though theirs is a good model to follow.

When you become more comfortable praying to Me, you may discover that you are carrying on a continual, unspoken conversation with Me[7] throughout the day and on into the night. That ongoing, thought-based conversation is an indication that your heart is always turned in My direction, that your life has taken on an attitude of prayer.

Here's another thing you should never forget: No matter what you've done, no matter how ashamed you are of your behavior, your thought life, or your actions, you can always come to Me, in humility but also in complete confidence that I will extend My mercy and grace to you.[8] I will always accept you when you come to Me in prayer,[9] and I will look upon your request favorably when you ask according to My will, according to what I want to accomplish in your life.[10] Let go of any anxiety you may feel, and come to Me with all your requests, in a spirit of gratitude and thanksgiving.[11]

JESUS

When I was on earth, I found that I needed to spend extended periods of time alone in prayer with the Father. Even after a long day of ministering to huge crowds of people, I would retreat to a solitary place to pray instead of finding a place where I could sleep.[12] When it came time for me to choose twelve apostles—those men whom I would send out on their own to tell people about Me—I retreated to a quiet place on a mountain where I spent the entire night in prayer.[13]

I encouraged My followers to do the same—to go away by themselves to a place where they could have some privacy and spend time in prayer with the Father, who would reward them for not praying just so they could be seen by others, as the Pharisees did.[14] That was in no way meant to discourage them from praying in public, as long as their motivation was pure—again, not like the Pharisees, who wanted to be praised for being religious. Nor was I discouraging them from praying with others, which can be a powerful and effective way of praying, one that also offers assurance of My presence.[15]

If you still have concerns about how to pray and feel you need additional guidance, let's look at the model prayer I gave My disciples to help you understand why it's a good pattern to use for your own prayers.

I taught My disciples to begin their prayers by addressing the Father directly, to focus their attention on Him, and then to indicate their reverence toward Him, using these or similar words: "Our Father in heaven, may your name always be kept holy."[16] I told them to then express their desire that the Father's will be fulfilled, on earth and throughout the spiritual realm.[17] Next they could begin to make their requests: for those things they needed on a daily basis, such as food; for the forgiveness they also needed and the forgiveness others needed from them; and for power over temptation and the devices of the evil one.[18] Finally, I taught them to end their prayer by praising the Father.[19]

Many of you have memorized that prayer, which has come to be known as the Lord's Prayer. If you have, you know that it isn't a long prayer. As the Father said, you should never feel that you have to pray long prayers to be heard. You are free to spend as much time in prayer as you'd like, of course; just remember that the Father doesn't keep a stopwatch ticking to make sure you spend adequate time in prayer or to award you extra points for praying all night. This isn't a game or a contest; points aren't involved at all.

Here's something else that you should always keep in mind, and I told My disciples this on the night before I was crucified: When you ask for anything in My name—according to My purposes and to the glory of God—I will do it for you, so the Father may be glorified through Me.[20] Ask anything of the Father in My name, and you will receive it; the Father wants you to know joy in its fullest measure.[21]

37
Should we pray about only major problems?

People who stand in awe of God as the all-powerful Creator of the universe often have a hard time picturing Him being concerned with the petty problems in their everyday lives. Surely the God who keeps the planets in motion and the stars illuminated and life on earth from disappearing has more important things to think about than their squabbles with colleagues or family members.

Those same people feel it's more appropriate to pray for an Israeli-Palestinian peace accord than for a truce with their neighbors across the backyard fence. Because their personal skirmishes pale in comparison to the magnitude of international conflicts, they believe their minuscule problems are equally diminished from God's perspective.

Q

God, it often feels ridiculous to bother You with things like a minor argument with a coworker or the racket the neighbor's kids make. And yet, these things keep us up at night. Should we pray only about major problems—or can we pray about little things as well?

GOD

Your question assumes that the things you mentioned are minor problems. Those things you think are insignificant to Me will become major problems in your life if you don't deal with them. And the best way to deal with them is to talk them over with Me. A seemingly minor argument with a coworker can create an unnecessary undercurrent of tension at your workplace that could affect everyone you work with, even those who are in no way involved in the dispute. The noise your neighbor's children make—and your sensitivity to it—can be a sign of a much deeper problem that is likely to grow and cause resentment that will become much more difficult to overcome as time goes on. Because their potential for causing strife is immense, these are not minor problems.

My creation is filled with evidence of the damage that can be done by something very small that has been left unattended. Throughout the Scriptures, writers used examples from nature to describe the potentially significant impact of a seemingly insignificant problem. Take, for example, James's comparison of the words you speak to a small fire; if your words are not filled with grace, that small tongue of yours has the potential to create huge problems, just as a small fire can set an entire forest ablaze.[1]

Think, too, of the impact water can have. Over time, dripping water can wear a hole in a hard stone,[2] and if that drip becomes a constant rush of water, it can cause serious erosion. Small things—a small pebble in your shoe, a mosquito that's just landed on your arm, a slight breeze that blows sand in your eyes—can have a big impact. Yes, you can pray to Me about small things, and big things, and everything in between.

When women ask Me questions like this, it signifies that they have forgotten a vitally important aspect of their relationship with Me. You are My children. I affirmed this throughout the Bible, from the writings of Moses[3] through the New Testament.[4] When you truly grasp this truth, you begin to comprehend the many things you can talk to Me about.

Think of the things your own children ask for, or the things you used to ask for when you were a child, for those of you who don't have children of your own. Did you always go to your parents with concerns or requests that seemed big to you at the time, like that shiny bike you saw at the store and wanted with all your heart? Or did you also go to your parents when you saw a spider and wanted them to dispose of it? When Jesus was on earth, He used the example of a child's request for an egg—not a major request, by any means—to symbolize how faithful I am in hearing My children's requests and responding to them, no matter how small or seemingly insignificant those requests may be.[5]

Every time you come to Me with what you think are minor concerns, you give Me an opportunity to help you build up your faith and trust in Me. As you gain greater confidence in Me, your requests become bolder—and I welcome those requests as well.

Abraham boldly challenged Me when I threatened to destroy Sodom and Gomorrah because of the wickedness of the people who lived there. Surely, he said to Me, You would not destroy the righteous who live there as well. You're the judge of all the earth—wouldn't You do what is right?[6] I assured him I would. It was no small thing he asked Me to do, to change My mind if I found any godly people living in those two cities. As an ancient proverb puts it, those who are righteous are as bold as lions,[7] and Abraham certainly proved that true.

JESUS

When I lived on earth, I told several stories about tiny things that can grow into enormous things. Many of you are familiar with the idea of having faith the size of a mustard seed. That originates from the example I gave about the mustard plant, one of the largest plants that grew in Palestine at that time, and yet its seed is very small. I compared the kingdom of God to that seed. From a small seed, the little measure of faith that the disciples had, the kingdom could grow into something much larger than they could imagine.[8]

Though I was speaking specifically about the kingdom of God, the underlying principle of that illustration applies to your prayers for minor things as well. A small concern, placed in the hands of God, can bring about a solution so immense that it will affect far more people and for far longer than you ever thought it could.

Look at a second example I gave to show how this works. I compared the kingdom of God to leaven, or yeast. Now those of you women who have baked bread know what yeast does to a batch of dough. You take the yeast, work it into the dough until it is evenly distributed, and set the dough in a warm place for several hours. What happens? The dough doubles or even triples in size. A small measure of yeast, just a few teaspoons, will produce enough bread to feed a large family. Your prayer for small things increases the yield to yourself and others.[9]

Don't forget the role the Father's angels play in your life either. They're watching over you and guarding you in everything you do. They'll protect you not only from the threat of lions and cobras and serpents but also from the little things—like stubbing your toe.[10]

There's one more point I want to make about the concerns you have in your life. I know how draining your troubles can be. Minor conflicts can rob you of your peace. The pace of your life can leave you feeling worn out and ready to give up. Coming up with the money for a week's groceries can seem as overwhelming as trying to buy a house without a mortgage.

As I looked around at the people of first-century Palestine and saw how life had taken a toll on them, I had great compassion on them. They were oppressed by the Romans, they were oppressed by their own religious leaders, and many of them were oppressed by economic difficulty and other personal problems. I beckoned them to come to Me, where they would find rest for their tired bodies and their weary souls. My gentleness and humility would provide welcome relief from the harsh arrogance they had known, and My teachings would offer them a way to lighten their burdens.[11]

That offer still stands. Let Me become a place of rest for you, a place where you can lay down your burdens and find the relief and refreshment you so desperately need. No burden is too large or too small for Me to handle. I am willing to take on whatever you are willing to turn over to Me. I delight to see you free and joyful once again.

38
Is it okay to pray repetitious prayers?

Conflicts over prayer have abounded for decades. An entire segment of Christendom uses a liturgy that includes written prayers that are prayed over and over again throughout the year, while another segment considers liturgical prayers unbiblical. One preacher may tell the congregation to pray about something one time only and have faith that God will answer that prayer, while another tells a different congregation to pray repeatedly for the same thing until God answers.

It's no wonder some women are puzzled. If this segment of the church is right, then that segment must be wrong. If this preacher says to pray one time only, then that preacher is wrong in telling people to persist in prayer.

Q God, some of us have been told to pray spontaneously and not to pray repetitiously. But sometimes written prayers really help us focus our thoughts, and praying for something repeatedly helps increase our faith. Is it okay to pray written or repetitious prayers?

GOD

I'll respond to your question about written prayers and allow Jesus to respond to the question about persistent or repetitious prayers, which is something He taught about when He was on earth. Much of the misunderstanding and resulting controversy over written prayers stems from Jesus' reference to the "vain repetitions" of the pagans, who thought their gods would hear and respond to the many words they used.[1]

Throughout their history, the Jews have used various prayer books, and the book of Psalms formed a significant portion of the written prayers they recited as part of their liturgy, the standardized rite of worship they used in communal worship services. Christians continued this tradition, also incorporating the book of Psalms into the liturgies they created.

It was only in recent times that some churches abandoned formal liturgies, choosing instead to allow for a more flexible or spontaneous way of worshipping. Some people, however, began interpreting Jesus' words as referring to written liturgy and started teaching that praying written prayers and following a formal liturgy was the same as reciting the vain, or empty and meaningless, repetitions of the pagans.

However, when My people recite a liturgy, it isn't the words themselves that may be empty and meaningless; rather, the people may be saying those words in vain. But no one on earth can determine who is participating in an empty ritual and who genuinely means the words, because no one on earth can see their hearts. Only I can determine which people are using empty and meaningless forms of expression, and those people may be found in churches where spontaneous expression is encouraged just as they can be found in liturgical churches. The hearts of the people are what matters, not how the people express themselves in prayer.

The Psalms appear in the prayer books of both Jews and Christians for good reason. They offer worshippers an opportunity to become immersed in My Word even as they are crying out to Me or expressing their reverence for Me. Jesus Himself prayed passages from the Psalms as He cried out to Me from the cross. When darkness descended on the land during His crucifixion, He called out, "My God, My God, why have You forsaken Me?"[2]—a direct quote from Psalm 22.[3] His last words from the cross, "Father, into Your hands I commit My spirit,"[4] were taken from Psalm 31.[5] In the midst of His greatest suffering and deepest agony, Jesus uttered the written words of Scripture.

The early followers of Jesus also quoted the psalms when they prayed to Me after Peter and John were released following a hearing before the Jewish leaders: "Lord, You are God, who made heaven and earth and the sea, and all that is in them, who by the mouth of Your servant David have said: 'Why did the nations rage, and the people plot vain things? The kings of the earth took their stand, and the rulers were gathered together against the Lord and against His Christ.'"[6] Some of those phrases were taken directly from Psalm 146[7] and Psalm 2.[8]

Over the millennia, My people have discovered that the cry of David's heart often echoed the cry of their own. When they've needed to confess their sins to Me but the words wouldn't come, many have turned to Psalm 51 and repeated what David wrote: "Have mercy on me, O God, because of your unfailing love. Because of your great compassion, blot out the stain of my sins. Wash me clean from my guilt. Purify me from my sin. For I recognize my rebellion; it haunts me day and night. Against you, and you alone, have I sinned; I have done what is evil in your sight. You will be proved right in what you say, and your judgment against me is just."[9]

As you read through the psalms, you will find many that serve as prayers for specific circumstances in your life: Psalm 23 for comfort, for example; or portions of Psalm 36 when you want to praise Me. Those and other psalms can become your prayers whenever their words genuinely express what you want to say to Me.

JESUS

As the Father pointed out, My comment about vain repetitions referred to empty phrases uttered by pagans seeking a response from their false gods. But some of you are concerned even about meaningful repetition, afraid that your repeated prayers over the same problems show a lack of faith or that you're somehow bothering Me and becoming a nuisance.

Let Me tell you a story about someone who was bothered by a woman's persistent pestering. There once was a corrupt judge who had no concern for the Father or for the people whose rights he was supposed to protect. One widow, whose rights had been violated, was determined to get justice even if he was determined not to administer it. She became a constant presence in his life, pestering him to see to it that she got the justice she was entitled to. He ignored her as long as he could, until one day he simply gave up. He still didn't care what God had to say about the matter, and he certainly didn't care about the widow, but her endless carping had finally worn him down. Only then did he see to it that her rights were protected.[10]

That woman's persistence in pursuing what she needed changed the mind of a man who had no compassion on her whatsoever. Imagine what that kind of persistence can accomplish when you bring your requests before your loving heavenly Father. He will act justly on your behalf, and He welcomes the prayers of people of faith who are as persistent as that woman was.[11]

Right after I taught My disciples how to pray, I told them another story about persistent prayer. In that story I asked them to imagine going to a friend's house in the middle of the night and explaining that someone had dropped by unexpectedly but they had nothing to feed him. All they want is three loaves of bread so they can accommodate their guest. But the friend doesn't take kindly to this late-night call and responds from behind the bolted door that his family is asleep, he can't give them anything, and they should just go away.

But they're not about to give up so easily, and they keep knocking and asking the friend to help them out. Eventually he does, but not out of sheer friendship. He gets them food simply because they would not give up. They persisted in asking for help.[12]

Many of you are familiar with what I said next; in fact, some of you have memorized it: "Ask, and you will receive, search and you will find, knock and the door will be opened for you."[13] What your language fails to convey is the persistence embedded in those words. My followers understood that what I was telling them to do was to keep on asking, keep on seeking, and keep on knocking; persistent people are the ones who will receive what they're seeking from their Father.[14]

Do not grieve the Holy Spirit of God, by whom you were sealed for the day of redemption. Let all bitterness, wrath, anger, clamor, and evil speaking be put away from you, with all malice. And be kind to one another, tender-hearted, forgiving one another, even as God in Christ forgave you.

Ephesians 4:30–32 NKJV

RELATIONSHIPS

> *Relationships are often the best part of life, but they can also be the hardest. It isn't always easy to love others, especially when they don't play by the rules or when they treat people badly.*

39. How can we love unlovable people?.................................... 189

40. How can we trust anyone following betrayal? 192

41. How can You expect us to forgive? 196

42. How can we have deeper friendships? 200

43. What's so bad about gossip? 204

44. Why are there restrictions on sex? 208

45. What's wrong with relationships with unbelieving men?.......... 212

46. God, why did You create families? 216

47. What's up with the teaching on submission? 220

48. How can we respect an ungodly boss?................................. 224

39
How can we love unlovable people?

Even if they don't know that the Bible tells them to love every-one, most women seem to understand innately that they should love other people—the good, the bad, and the ugly. But their lives are often peppered with truly unlovable people, like a backstab-bing coworker, an underhanded sister, or an unfaithful husband. Turning the knowledge that they should love other people into actu-ally loving them becomes a monumental challenge.

That challenge is made all the more difficult if their understanding of love is itself skewed. That inaccurate and often superficial under-standing of love results in bitterness—or it leads them to despair of ever imitating Jesus' love and compassion for the unlovely.

Q **God, we know You said we should love other people to the same degree that we love ourselves. But that's an incredibly tall order when we all have people in our lives who are impossible to love. How can we love unlovable people?**

GOD

I'd like you to take the first step toward learning to love that unlovable person in your life by imagining how I feel about her. Do you think that I consider her unlovable? I don't. Can you imagine her doing anything that would cause Me to stop loving her? There isn't a single thing she could do that would cause Me to withdraw My love from her. She is My child, My daughter. I know everything that has happened in her life to make her the person she is today. I know her every fear, insecurity, heartache, and painful memory. And I sent My Son to die on the cross for her.

You can't possibly see that unlovable person in your life the way I see her, but you can understand that I don't see her the way you do. You can't know the multitude of factors that shaped her life, but you can understand that certain factors contributed to the way she behaves today. And you can't yet know why I placed her in your life, but you can understand that I did so for a reason.

As My child whom I also dearly love, you have a wonderful opportunity to show My love to the unlovable. As long as you keep thinking that you have to love her on your own, it's likely that you'll end up tolerating her through gritted teeth and have resentful feelings toward Me for commanding you to love her. But I never give a command without also giving you the power to fulfill it, and I've done that by giving you the Holy Spirit.

To love someone with My love, you need to erase the idea of emotion-based love from your thinking. The love that you give to others in My name is an act of your will and not your emotions. It requires a decision on your part: Will you love this seemingly unlovable person in obedience to Me to show your love for Me? The extent to which you love others, especially the difficult people in your life, is a reflection of your love for Me and your willingness to obey Me.

If you truly want to please Me, then you'll place the highest priority on loving the people I love. It doesn't matter whether you speak in the language of angels or have the ability to prophesy, whether you understand the deep things of the Spirit or have the faith to move mountains—if you don't have love, it's all for nothing. You can give away everything you own and offer yourself as a sacrifice to Me, but without love, none of that matters. You show your love by being patient and kind, by not being jealous or thinking you're better than others or treating others rudely, by not being selfish or easily provoked or thinking wrong thoughts. You show your love by avoiding sin and embracing the truth; by being accepting, trusting, and hopeful; and by enduring all things. That kind of love never fails; it's more important to cultivate that kind of love than it is to cultivate faith and hope. And it's the kind of love I want you to have for others—all others.[1]

Jesus

In one of My final conversations with My disciples, I gave them a new commandment to love one another in the same way I loved them.[2] They didn't fully understand that at the time, but later they realized that kind of love meant sacrificing everything for one another, as I was about to do. A love characterized by that depth and that level of commitment to each other would show the world that they were My followers[3] because no one could love to that extent unless the Spirit of God lived within them.

That commandment applies specifically to My followers' loving one another. If that troublesome person in your life is a Christian, then you both have the responsibility of following the commandment, but there isn't a thing you can do to force her to obey it. What you can do is obey it yourself, treat her with kindness and dignity, pray for her, and ask the Father to show you how to love her—the practical things you can do to help her grow and mature in her relationship with Me.

If she does not already have a relationship with Me, you still have a responsibility to show her the Father's love by loving her the way you love yourself, which you alluded to in your question. I pointed that out in an answer I gave to one of the Jewish leaders who asked Me which of the commandments was the greatest. I responded by quoting from the Jewish scriptures: "The first of all the commandments is: 'Hear, O Israel, the Lord our God, the Lord is one. And you shall love the Lord your God with all your heart, with all your soul, with all your mind, and with all your strength.' This is the first commandment. And the second, like it, is this: 'You shall love your neighbor as yourself.' There is no other commandment greater than these."[4]

Once, a lawyer tried to trip Me up on that by asking Me just who his neighbor was.[5] That's when I told the story that you know as the parable of the good Samaritan.[6] In that story, a man was robbed, beaten, and left for dead on the side of a road. Two Jewish leaders passed him by at different times, and neither one did anything to help him. But then along came a Samaritan—one of a group of people whom the "righteous" Jews looked down on—who tended to his wounds, took him to an inn, stayed with him overnight, and paid for his care until he was healed enough to travel. The lawyer got My point: The Samaritan was a neighbor to the victim because he showed him love and mercy. I told the lawyer, as I am telling you, to "go and do likewise."[7] Show your love for those you consider unlovable by caring for them in practical ways and showing them the Father's love and mercy, as you are guided by the Holy Spirit.

The facts about how you take care of yourself signify the fact of your love for yourself—and the way you love yourself should determine the way you love your neighbor.

40

How can we trust anyone following betrayal?

Some women who have been betrayed—by a friend, a family member, or a "significant other"—have such a trusting nature that they eventually open themselves up to another close relationship. But when the big betrayal comes, when a friend reveals a shameful confidence or a husband moves in with his mistress, the victim of that betrayal may begin to look at everyone as untrustworthy and shut herself off from the close, personal relationships she so desperately needs.

What's especially dangerous is the possibility that she will project human untrustworthiness onto God, believing Him to be just as unfaithful as the people in her life. Even though deep down she wants to trust again, she can't see that happening.

Q **God, some of us have been deeply hurt by people who betrayed our trust, ruining the relationships we once had and hindering our ability to make ourselves vulnerable to others in the future. How can we trust anyone following a betrayal?**

GOD

Betrayal has created huge difficulties among people ever since Cain betrayed Abel;[1] Cain turned a normal activity in their lives—walking out to the field—into an opportunity for murder. Many of the betrayals you have suffered in your lives—infidelity, deception, fraud, violation of privacy or a confidence, dishonesty—have also occurred in the course of your everyday lives, catching you by surprise and causing you to suddenly question so much that you believed to be true.

It's especially painful when the person who betrayed you is someone who claimed to love Me, a person with whom you worshipped and shared faith experiences, a person you trusted. My servant David knew that pain all too well; his pain was so intense that he cried out for the ability to fly so he could escape to the desert, to a shelter, anywhere away from the one who betrayed him [2] But as he said, he could have taken it if an enemy had betrayed him. But it wasn't an enemy. It was a close friend, a man with whom he had enjoyed what he thought was genuine fellowship as they walked together to My house to worship Me.[3] His friend, his betrayer, had deceived him with his smooth speech while his heart was filled with hostility.[4]

In order to endure the anguish he was suffering, David did the one thing that always worked for him, without fail He turned to Me morning, noon, and night, confident that I heard his cries, that I would sustain him, and that I would protect him. His trust in Me remained unshaken.[5]

When you have been betrayed and wonder if you can ever trust again, turn to Me and let Me prove to you how trustworthy I am. I'll heal the hurt in your life[6] and begin to restore you to wholeness. Part of that restoration process, however, involves forgiving the person who hurt you,[7] something you may feel you will never be able to do. But when you place the situation in My hands, you can be confident that I will help you throughout the process and empower you to do much more than you ever hoped for or even dared ask Me to do for you.[8]

Learning to trust other people again will take some time, but that will give you more of an opportunity to spend time with Me and allow Me to give you a critical element when it comes to trust—wisdom. You need only ask, and I will generously share My wisdom with you.[9] My wisdom, which the Holy Spirit will communicate to you as you pray and read My Word, will help you identify the true character of a person before you open your life and your heart to him.

But even as others begin to earn your trust once again, never forget that flawed people will continue to disappoint you at times. Each person is made in My image, and I am at work in each person's life in ways you can never see, but that doesn't make him or her perfect any more than it makes you perfect. For that reason, you need to place your trust in Me, the God who is at work in the lives of those you are beginning to trust.

What all this involves is relinquishment—letting go of the pain, the unforgiveness, the distrust, the barriers you've put around yourself in an effort to keep the potential for future hurt at bay. With relinquishment comes the possibility of transformation. When you let go of painful situations and place them in My hands, I take them and mold them into an entirely new opportunity for you to mature in your faith and trust Me in a deeper way, based on what you experienced with Me and learned from Me in this process. And then you can take that—for example, the comfort I gave you during the healing process—and use it to minister to others in pain.[10] Don't let this experience go to waste; use it to show others where to find the healing they need.

Jesus

I understand fully how it feels to be betrayed. When I was on earth, one of my twelve most trusted disciples turned Me in to the authorities. I had trusted Judas so much that he served as treasurer for My ministry. The one who handled the money betrayed Me for money.

His betrayal took place during the Passover, the Feast of Unleavened Bread, which was one of the main feasts in the Jewish religion. In the early part of Passover week, the Jewish leaders met to determine when and how they would seize Me and kill Me. One thing they didn't want was for this to happen during Passover, because that's when Jerusalem would be filled with visitors, and they were afraid of inciting the crowds to riot.[11]

Judas, however, became upset with Me when I chastised him for criticizing a woman for honoring Me by pouring expensive perfume on Me. He went straight to the council that was meeting and offered to turn Me over to them in return for thirty pieces of silver, the value of a slave.[12]

Later, as we sat down to share the Passover meal together, I told My disciples that one of them would betray Me. They were stunned, and one by one they began trying to determine who the traitor would be. Judas tried to act as if he wasn't the one, but I let him know that I was fully aware of what he had already done and what he was about to do.[13]

Within hours, Judas came after Me in the Garden of Gethsemane, where I had spent the night praying after the Passover meal with My disciples. With him were the Jewish leaders, armed with swords and clubs. Judas greeted Me as if everything were normal; My response indicated I knew that wasn't the case.[14]

From that point until the moment of My death, I was in the custody of either the Jewish leaders or the Roman authorities. Judas's betrayal led directly to My crucifixion. Yes, I understand how it feels to be betrayed and abandoned. My disciples scattered and left Me to face My accusers alone.[15]

What I am about to tell you regarding your ability to trust again is wisdom from God and from experience. You need to pray, not only for the person who betrayed you and about your need to forgive him or her,[16] but also to strengthen yourself for future problems with others.[17] Ask God to bless your betrayer and strive to restore a harmonious relationship with the person.[18]

Never provoke the person,[19] speak ill of him or her,[20] or retaliate in any way.[21] Instead, do what I told My followers to do: turn the other cheek.[22] This is another evidence of the relinquishment the Father mentioned. By turning the left side of your face to someone who has just slapped the right side, you show that you refuse to retaliate and that you have relinquished your right to seek revenge.

Choose to rest in the One who loves you over retaliating against the one who hurt you. Abide in My love.[23] Draw on the grace that God has given you.[24]

41
How can You expect us to forgive?

Like loving our enemies, forgiveness is a most unnatural action. It's not the kind of thing humanity would have ever thought up on its own. Forgiveness is a supernatural action that often requires supernatural power. Only God could have come up with such a radical concept and then expect His people to turn that concept into a reality in their lives.

That's exactly what He expects—but first, He wants His people to understand the nature of true forgiveness and forget much of what the culture around them defines as forgiveness. His kind of forgiveness bears little resemblance to the shallow and insincere form that is all too often extended through gritted teeth.

Q **God, forgiving other people can be so incredibly hard. Sometimes they just don't deserve it. Plus, we're afraid that if we forgive them, they'll just run roughshod over us all over again. How can You possibly expect us to forgive people who have done us wrong?**

GOD

Tucked away in the section of the Old Testament known as the Minor Prophets is a book some of My followers like to refer people to when the subject of forgiveness of others comes up. Don't be surprised if you find this book to be a bit of a surprise when you first read it. I've watched many a person reread passages multiple times, because on their first reading they couldn't believe what I asked Hosea to do.

Let Me give you some background first. The prophet Hosea lived during the eighth century before Jesus came to earth, during the time the prophet Isaiah was also alive. Although Israel's recent history had been marked by a time of relative peacefulness and prosperity, the nation was morally bankrupt, having strayed far from obedience to Me. Israel needed an object lesson that would illustrate My love for them despite their unfaithfulness.

To provide that lesson, I told My prophet Hosea, who had not done anything to upset Me, to marry a harlot[1]—a prostitute whose chosen life-style symbolized what the nation of Israel had become. Hosea loved Gomer relentlessly, even though she was repeatedly unfaithful to him, just as I loved the Israelites relentlessly, despite their unfaithfulness to Me.

Through the example of Hosea and Gomer, I promised Israel that I would forgive them and restore the nation's relationship with Me by attracting them with kind words, an abundance of land, and an offer of hope.[2] I pledged to make a covenant with them to protect them, become united with them in righteousness, justice, lovingkindness, compassion, and faithfulness, and make them My people once again.[3] All this I would do for them despite their own unfaithfulness.

The words the prophet Hosea spoke were meant specifically for the nation of Israel, but the message of My steadfast love and forgiveness is meant for everyone, and it serves as an example of the nature of genuine love and forgiveness. That nature is godly and supernatural. You cannot love and forgive the way I do without relying on My power. It is My nature, not yours, to lavish love upon those who stirred up My anger and abandoned Me as they pursued other lovers.[4]

Make note of this crucial distinction, however. Hosea took Gomer back despite her many betrayals. Does that mean you have to let your betrayer back into your life? Nowhere in My Word do I insist that you welcome an unrepentant person back into your life. Your responsibility is to forgive, regardless of the other person's response or failure to respond. I orchestrated the entire drama involving Hosea and Gomer as an example to the Israelites; your situation involves your free will and that of the person you've forgiven. You need to rely on the guidance of the Holy Spirit to determine how you should proceed in your efforts to reconcile with the person you've forgiven.

My Word is replete with stories of forgiveness. Look at the story of David and Bathsheba. King David, a man after My own heart, lusted after Bathsheba and made sure he got what he wanted. Then when Bathsheba became pregnant with David's child, he gave her soldier husband military leave so he could come home and have sex with his wife so he would think the baby was his. When that backfired, David sent him off to the front lines to be killed.

How forgiving would you be if a scenario like that involved a leader of your country? But I'm not like you, and I not only forgave David when he cried out to Me for mercy but also allowed him to stay in power because he was the right person to rule Israel at the time despite his sin.

Manasseh was someone else I forgave in spite of the evil he had done—which included sacrificing his own children to idols. He was so cruel, so evil, and so good at steering people away from Me that they began to ignore the sound of My voice.[5]

That's when I allowed the Assyrians to attack the land, put a hook in Manasseh's nose and shackles on his feet, and take him off to captivity in Babylon. That brought Manasseh to his senses, and he turned to Me in genuine repentance. I forgave him immediately, even as he prayed, and restored him as king of Judah.[6] When repentance from sin is authentic, My forgiveness is immediate. For you, when you grasp how important it is to forgive others, your forgiveness needs to be just as swift.[7]

Jesus

Look again at the Sermon on the Mount. Right after I taught the people to pray according to the example I gave—the Lord's Prayer—I made a significant point about the connection between prayer and forgiveness. If you pray to the Father for forgiveness but harbor unforgiveness in your heart toward someone else, you block the free flow of forgiveness from the Father to you.[8] Your refusal to extend mercy to others is a poor reflection on how extravagant God is with His forgiveness. If you have received the forgiveness God so freely gives, you should extend your forgiveness to others.[9]

When My friend Peter asked Me how many times he should forgive someone who repeatedly hurt him, I gave him an arbitrary number—490 times, or seventy times seven—to point out the need to keep on forgiving no matter how many times someone hurts you.[10]

I followed that statement by telling a parable about a king who called in one of his servants who had run up a huge debt that he couldn't pay. When the king ordered the servant to be sold as a slave, along with his family, the servant pleaded with him to spare him and give him a chance to pay back the debt. The king was deeply moved and erased the servant's debt. However, as soon as he left the king's presence, he ran into a man who owed him a small amount of money. He seized the man and demanded that he repay the debt immediately.

When the king heard about the servant's despicable behavior, he called the servant before him and berated him for refusing to extend mercy to his debtor after the king had extended mercy to him by erasing his debt entirely. Because the servant refused to forgive the man's small debt, the king forced him to pay back the entire amount that the servant had previously owed.[11]

That's how seriously the Father takes the issue of forgiveness. He expects you to forgive anyone who needs your forgiveness every time you pray so He can be free with His own forgiveness of your sins.[12] There's even more that falls under the issue of extending forgiveness and mercy, things that are hard but not impossible with God's help: Love your enemies and treat them well. Pray for those who mistreat you. Lend to others with no expectation of return. Show others the kind of mercy God has shown.[13] And when it comes to those who are also My followers, be especially careful to treat them with kindness and forgive them as the Father has forgiven you.[14]

42
How can we have deeper friendships?

Women know all about friendship, right? They virtually wrote the basic instructions on making and keeping friends. But in recent decades, deep friendship has been harder to come by, in part because of the mobile nature of the culture and in part because of the ever-increasing busyness of life. Singles and families alike find themselves uprooted and in search of opportunities in other geographical areas, and once they get there, the constant activity that defines twenty-first-century life precludes the opportunity to develop close relationships.

But women continue to yearn for deep friendships. And while modern technology has made it easy to stay in touch with faraway friends, most women still need hugs from a nearby flesh-and-blood friend who truly understands.

Q   **God, our lives are filled with people, and yet some of our relationships feel so superficial. We're tired of friendships that exist only on the surface, but that's what we seem to end up with when our lives are so full of activity. How can we have deeper friendships?**

GOD

Women have an exceptional capacity for intimate friendships and deep relationships with both friends and relatives. But that ability can come with some problems if you are too open and too trusting. You need My wisdom to discern between those friendships that are genuine and healthy—the ones that have the potential to become deep friendships—and those that could bring you to ruin.[1]

Solomon recorded much of the wisdom I gave to him concerning friendships. Here are some things you need to keep in mind when you want to develop close relationships with other women:

* Fewer words lead to fewer opportunities to say the wrong thing. Many friendships have been ruined by a careless tongue. Use the wisdom and the common sense I've given you to protect your friendships by controlling your words.[2]

* Be a trustworthy friend even as you seek out friends who are trustworthy.[3] When you have found a trustworthy friend, heed her advice, especially when others are trying to lead you astray. Choose your friends wisely.[4]

* Don't let arguments and conflicts destroy your friendships. Deal with problems immediately; cultivate an attitude of humility; control your temper.[5]

* Watch out for other women who only want to use you for whatever gain they think their friendship with you will bring.[6] A true friend will continue to love you whether you are prospering or failing and will remain loyal to you no matter what is going on in your life. You can go to her for help just as you would go to a relative.[7]

* Above all, choose to have deep friendships with women who have a solid relationship with Me and will encourage you to do the same. Follow their good example, and give them permission to keep you honest. It's much better to have a friend who will tell you the truth in love than to have one who flatters you and then deceives you behind your back. You know the saying "Iron sharpens iron"—let that characterize your friendships; choose friends who challenge you and keep your faith and your mind sharp.[8]

Genuine friends help one another succeed and lift one another up when they fall; any time you've been alone and in trouble you know the value of a true friend. Friends can offer warmth when the world around you is cold; friends "have your back," as some say—they protect you when others attack you. And it's even better when three people are united in friendship; a rope made of three strands is significantly stronger than one made of two strands. When you and your friend are united with Me, you have an especially strong cord.[9]

Jesus

When I was on earth, I offered My disciples an example of true friendship. Even though they were My followers, I called them My friends because I had revealed to them everything the Father had said to Me. That made our relationship distinctly different from that of, say, master and servant, because servants are never privy to what their master is thinking and planning. Furthermore, My disciples shared in My love and My joy. And, although they didn't fully understand at the time, I made it clear that friends put their lives on the line for one another. Soon after I said those words, I gave My life for them and for everyone.[10]

Friends are there to share in your life, to experience joy with you in the good times and sadness with you during bad times.[11] Your friends are those who will celebrate with you whether you find a lost sheep or a lost coin[12]—or in your society, perhaps a lost iPod or a lost debit card.

But above all, true friends love one another, are devoted to one another, honor one another above themselves, and forgive one another freely, keeping each other from wrongdoing and encouraging each other in doing what is right. As My followers, you know what I expect of you: Be patient with each other, treating each other kindly, gently, and with true humility. My love is what ties all of this together,[13] creating true friendship.

Will you lose friends because of your relationship with Me? Without a doubt. When you begin to live for Me, you know it's time to get rid of any bad habits you used to have when you were trying to fit into a certain group of people. Your entire way of thinking is beginning to change as you start to understand what the Father wants for you—and that what He wants for you is good for you and pleases Him and is in fact the ideal way to live.[14] Those of your friends who don't accompany you into this new life with Me aren't going to like the change in you when you stop living for yourself and doing the things you used to do.[15] But hold on to what you know is true: that you are to love others, and that even when it appears everyone has abandoned you, the Father never will.[16]

Naomi

When people read my story, they see how faithful Ruth was to me, her mother-in-law. When our husbands died,[17] Ruth left her land in Moab to accompany me back to Judah, where my people became her people and my God became her God.[18]

Both Ruth and my other daughter-in-law, Orpah, had always treated me exceedingly well, and their grief at my initial decision to return to Judah alone was touching. But Ruth's decision to go with me was astonishing. The people of Moab and Judah did not take kindly to each other, and in a sense, Ruth was entering hostile territory, even though she was traveling with a native of Judah. She showed an extraordinary level of trust in me, and her pledge to remain with me even to the point of death far exceeded what I ever could have expected from a woman who was neither a blood relative nor an Israelite. She proved herself a true friend, and God blessed her and me by giving her in marriage to Boaz,[19] one of my husband's relatives. Not only did we prosper financially, but she also became the great-grandmother of King David.[20]

The other women in town certainly noticed how Ruth's friendship and loyalty had changed my life. They considered the son born to Boaz and Ruth to be a special blessing in light of all that I had lost in Moab. Even so, the women in my life recognized Ruth's love and devotion and said she was better to me than seven sons.[21] Ruth far exceeded the blessings that a house full of children could ever have brought me.

ELIZABETH

My friendship with Mary, the mother of Jesus, is similar to that of Ruth and Naomi in this way: Naomi and I were both considerably older than Ruth and Mary, even though Mary and I were cousins. But Mary and I were pregnant at the same time, and that created a special bond between us. In addition, we were blood relatives and understood our family.

When Mary came to tell me she was pregnant, the baby in my womb—who would become known as John the Baptist—jumped for joy inside me.[22] We didn't know then the joys and heartaches we both would suffer over the next thirty-three years, but the three months we spent together before John was born helped prepare us for what was to come.

43
What's so bad about gossip?

Gossip—the retelling of either facts or rumors that are of a personal nature—is so pervasive in contemporary society that some people who engage in it don't even realize that what they're doing is gossiping. TV shows routinely pass along gossipy tidbits, and not just the "entertainment news" shows. Many Web sites are notorious for spreading personal information with little regard for the facts or the harm that could result from making the information public.

The cultural disregard for a person's privacy spills over into the lives of people far outside the sphere of celebrity tell-alls. Rumor mills and chatty grapevines keep the flow of personal information spreading from one person to the next—sometimes with tragic consequences.

Q **I don't understand why gossip is such a big deal. All I did was say that I thought a coworker had been fired, and this Christian held up her hand in front of my face and told me she didn't listen to gossip, as if it was a horrible sin. What's so bad about gossip?**

GOD

Let Me start by pointing out what distinguishes gossip from legitimate news or information. In the example you cited, you weren't sure your coworker had been fired, but you were passing along the information anyway. All too often, gossip is based on rumor or hearsay, and if the information turns out not to be true, many problems can result. In your example, your coworker may acquire an undeserved reputation for being a poor employee among those who believe there must have been some truth to the rumor.

Your friend was right to stop you from passing along a rumor because the consequences of gossiping can be significant. The closest of friendships can be destroyed when one of the friends repeats something that was better left unsaid;[1] once you've seriously offended a good friend, winning her back can be more difficult than trying to conquer an entire city.[2]

Ask yourself this: Do you like it when people say things about you that aren't true—or when a supposed friend betrays a confidence? People who have a reputation for being gossips simply can't keep a secret, so it's best that you don't expect them to.[3]

You said your friend treated gossip as if it was a "horrible" sin. You may be interested to know that Paul, writing at the prompting of the Holy Spirit, once offered this description of indecent people whose minds are far from God: They're evil, wicked, greedy, mean people who kill, cheat, start conflicts—and who gossip, saying unimaginably cruel things about other people.[4] Paul didn't think much of people who gossip.

There's no question that gossip causes contention. If you refuse to participate in gossip, you can help defuse a volatile situation; if everyone would agree not to engage in gossip, the whole conflict would die down.[5]

However, if you continue to talk about others in a malicious way, share confidences that you know were meant to be kept secret, and start or perpetuate rumors that you know are not true, you have only yourself to blame when you begin to get a reputation as someone who simply cannot be trusted.[6] It's better not to talk at all—to keep quiet and mind your own business—than to engage in gossip, whether knowingly or unknowingly.[7]

At one time in Israel's history, a war nearly resulted from a rumor that was spread among some of the tribes. This was during the time when Joshua was the leader of the Israelites. Moses had promised the tribes of Reuben and Gad and half the tribe of Manasseh that they would have the right to settle in the land of Gilead, and Joshua had given them his blessing to do so. Once they reached the Jordan River, they built a huge, impressive altar.[8]

But when the remaining Israelites—the members of the other nine tribes and the other half of the tribe of Manasseh—"heard" about the altar, the implication was that the altar was dedicated to another god and not to Me. They gathered at a central location, intent on waging war against the tribes that had presumably turned away from Me and built an altar to a false god.[9]

The Israelites did give Reuben, Gad, and half the tribe of Manasseh a chance to explain before they attacked. As it turned out, the altar had been built as a witness between the two and a half tribes on one side and the nine and a half on the other—a witness to their dedication to Me. Had they not been given a chance to explain, a war among the tribes would have taken place, all because of a rumor.[10]

The ultimate answer to questions like yours lies in your response to another important question that you need to ask: Does this activity reflect the love of God? Think of all the uncomfortable situations you've been in where that question would have helped you determine the right thing to do, and not just with regard to gossip but in every area of your life. If you uphold the principle behind that question—that every activity you engage in should reflect My love—then you will always have an answer when you wonder whether or not something is right, or why something is wrong.

JESUS

As you know, I had many run-ins with the Pharisees. On one occasion, the conflict was over words, the words the Pharisees had used against Me and consequently against God. I used the example of a fruit tree to point out that healthy trees produce good fruit and unhealthy trees produce bad fruit, and you can always tell the health of a tree by the fruit it produces. In the same way, good-hearted people say good things, and evil-hearted people say bad things. And on the Day of Judgment, people will be called to give account of the words they have spoken, and that includes the gossip they've passed along to others.[11]

Paul was careful to address the problem of gossip and other sins of the tongue in the early church, as was My brother James. To the Ephesian church, Paul warned My followers not even to allow unwholesome talk to come out of their mouths and to make sure that whatever they said would help build up other people and prove to be beneficial to them, admonishing them to get rid of a number of ungodly qualities and habits, including slander.[12]

Paul was especially concerned about the potential problem of gossip among the younger widows who would be qualified to receive financial support from the church but would end up spending their time in idle pursuits, which would lead them to engage in gossip and other sins of the tongue.[13]

James reserved his strongest admonitions for those who were considered leaders in the church, which is not surprising since he heard Me do the same when it came to the Jewish leaders. He told those who aspired to be teachers to consider the consequences of an uncontrolled tongue; if they could only control their tongues, he wrote, they could control every aspect of their behavior. To him, the tongue was like a small bit in a horse's mouth or a small rudder on a huge ship; both were capable of steering the direction of something many times their size.[14]

What was especially disturbing to James was how easily a person could bless Me and curse someone else with the same mouth. He compared that with a spring of water, which could not possibly produce both fresh and bitter water; the bitterness would contaminate the entire spring and spoil the fresh water.[15]

The Father mentioned the wisdom He had given to Solomon and the many things Solomon wrote about the evils of gossip. Solomon also gave wise advice on the appropriate use of words, which is something to think about whenever you are tempted to gossip. Some of the images he used are memorable, like kind words being like sweet and healthful honey that does good to both the soul and the body, or like timely words being as beautiful as golden apples in a silver basket.[16]

The next time you hear a choice piece of "news," think before you open your mouth.[17] God will reward you for keeping hurtful information to yourself,[18] and you will spare yourself a great deal of trouble by guarding your mouth.[19]

44
Why are there restrictions on sex?

Sex, at one time a taboo subject in churches, has become so commonplace a topic that an entire sermon series may be devoted to the subject. But while there's a greater openness in talking about sex from the pulpit, there's been no change in the teaching that the act of sex is a gift to be shared only between a wife and her husband—at least, among churches that acknowledge the overriding authority of the Bible.

That leaves some people with the impression that followers of Christ, and God Himself for that matter, are the ultimate killjoys. They see Christians as uptight, puritanical wet blankets who don't enjoy sex and want to make sure no one else enjoys it either.

Q **God, this is a real problem for many of us who are single. Plus, lots of women have strained relationships with daughters who live with their boyfriends, all because of the whole "no sex before marriage" thing. Why did You place restrictions on the act of sex?**

GOD

From the very beginning, I made it clear that sex was My gift to a husband and a wife. In leaving their parents' homes and establishing a new life together, a married couple was given the privilege and joy of becoming "one flesh" through sexual union.[1] And contrary to the thinking of some in your day, gender distinction was no accident or result of evolutionary changes; it was an intentional act on My part.[2] My plan all along was to create a distinct male gender and a distinct female gender, and the two would be joined together in a physical way to reproduce and create the children who would themselves marry and reproduce as well, filling the earth and having a measure of control over it.[3]

In the dawn of sexual union—the physical relationship between Adam and Eve—both the man and the woman were naked and not ashamed;[4] every element in creation was good, including that one.[5] My intention was for male and female to enjoy each other in an unrestricted but pure way. The restrictions that came later resulted from the blatant abuse of this perfect gift that I had given to humanity.

Many of those restrictions are identified in Leviticus 18. By the time of Moses and the establishment of a formal priesthood among the Israelites, many of the surrounding pagan cultures that did not know Me were engaging in sexual perversions that made a mockery of the gift of sex. At the time I gave these laws, the Israelites had been freed from oppression in Egypt. Many of those perversions were customary there and were about to enter the land of Canaan,[6] where sexual perversion also abounded. I wanted to keep My people protected from those practices and remind them of the purpose of sex, which is the expression of love between a husband and wife and the act of procreation.

Through Moses, I gave the Israelites specific instructions: Don't have sex with any of your relatives, including those who are not blood relatives, such as an in-law or a "step" family member. This was a polygamous society at the time, so I had to tell the men not to have sex with their father's other wives.[7] And I had to tell them not to commit adultery,[8] which I had earlier included in the Ten Commandments.[9]

Remember, too, that sex was intended for pleasure, not just for procreation. Through the writings of Solomon, I pointed out that there is a specific time for sexual love to be awakened, to be experienced,[10] and through him I encouraged couples to find sexual pleasure in each other.[11] Paul also encouraged couples to enjoy each other sexually, abstaining only by mutual agreement for periods of prayer and fasting,[12] echoing another of Solomon's sayings.[13]

JESUS

I also encouraged couples to marry and unite in sex.[14] The Father designed sex as a means for a husband to show his love for his wife just as I showed My love for the church and just as I sacrificed My life for the church. In addition, a husband's responsibility is to love his wife as much as he loves his own body—in other words, to treat her as well as he treats himself.[15]

You need to understand how important this is. Marriage is to mirror the relationship between My church and Me.[16] When you marry, you become physically united with your husband; when you become My follower, you become spiritually united with Me.[17] Do you recall the relationship between the Father and Israel—how Israel often abandoned the Father and worshipped other gods? That's a form of spiritual adultery. Being physically united with someone other than your husband mirrors the spiritual adultery that Israel committed against the Father and also that My followers commit when they worship other gods, like consumerism, physical beauty, wealth, and yes, sexual pleasure outside marriage.

Although the instances of adultery are more numerous today, physical and spiritual adultery are clearly nothing new. The city of Corinth was so plagued by sexual immorality that Paul had to tell the early Christians there to flee sexual sin, pointing out that immorality was unlike other sins in that it was a sin against your own body,[18] and that sexual sin had infiltrated the church, with one of the members having sex with his father's wife.[19] Paul reminded the church there that their bodies now belonged to Me and were no longer to be used for immoral purposes.[20] And he pointed out that many members of the church at Corinth had, in fact, regularly engaged in sex outside of marriage but were now living in obedience to Me, so there was hope for everyone.[21]

The early church needed many reminders of the fact that sex was meant to be confined to marriage,[22] that sex before marriage was a sin, and that those who scorned the sanctity of sex within marriage—the fornicators and adulterers—would be judged.[23] Paul mentioned the need to be sexually pure in nearly every one of his letters. He reminded the Colossians of the redemption that comes when people are delivered from the darkness of perversion and told them to put to death fornication.[24]

To the Thessalonians, Paul wrote that part of God's will for them was to be holy, so they were to avoid all sexual sin,[25] and he told the Ephesians that because they were God's people, they needed to make sure no one could say that any of them were immoral or indecent.[26]

Those are just a few of the references Paul made to sexual immorality in his letters to the churches throughout the Mediterranean. But even after chastising the church at Corinth for allowing sexual sin to flourish in their midst, he wrote in a second letter how grieved he was to hear about those who had not repented.[27] There will always be people in churches who have heard that the Father wants them to reject their immoral lifestyle, many of whom have been confronted with the evidence of their sin, but who refuse to begin living the way the Father wants them to. And there will always be people who justify their sin by pointing to My followers who refuse to listen. But they are not examples to be followed. The only example you should follow is Mine.

The good news, of course, is that those who have committed sexual sins can find immediate freedom when they repent and receive the gift of the Holy Spirit.[28] God will forgive them and purify them,[29] and they can then experience a new start, serving God with a clear conscience that has been washed clean by My sacrifice.[30]

There's more good news: The temptation to commit sexual sin is so common to humanity that it isn't as if you're going through something unusual. But the Father is so faithful that He will always give you a way out; He'll always see to it that you are not tempted beyond what you are able to withstand.[31] And that applies to any temptation, not just sexual immorality.

45

What's wrong with relationships with unbelieving men?

In many churches, it doesn't take more than a quick glance around the room to see that women outnumber men, sometimes by a significant margin—and the men who are there are often married family men. Young women and older women alike realize right away that the worst place to find an unattached man who shares their faith and values may be the one place they'd hoped to do so—at church.

It's no wonder, then, that some women become involved with men whose beliefs don't exactly line up with their own. They may be decent, kind, loyal men who treat women with the utmost respect, but they don't have a strong faith in God.

Q God, it hasn't been easy for me to find someone I'm compatible with. But when I started dating a guy at work that I like hanging out with, a friend warned me to break it off since I'm a Christian and he's not. What's wrong with relationships with unbelieving men?

GOD

My daughters, you are so precious to Me that My heart aches when I see you settling for anything other than My best. So often, I have seen My daughters innocently develop friendships with men who have many good qualities but who don't understand what it means to be completely committed to Me. When those friendships blossom into romance, the potential for heartache increases significantly, and when romance leads to marriage, My daughters are setting themselves up for a lifetime of disappointment. As your relationship with Me deepens, you will want to share that joy with your husband, but you will not be able to.

But the most serious ramification of being in a relationship with an unbelieving man is the distinct possibility that your love for him will compromise your relationship with Me. Once more, look at My relationship with the Israelites and their relationships with surrounding cultures that did not know Me and did not worship Me.

Early on in the Israelites' history—actually, starting with Abraham, before I gave the law of Moses to the Israelites—they were warned not to intermarry with neighboring pagan tribes. When Abraham sought a wife for his son Isaac, he sent his servant to Abraham's ancestral land in Mesopotamia to find an appropriate mate for Isaac, even though at the time Abraham was living among the pagan-worshipping Canaanites. Abraham took this matter so seriously that he made his servant swear a particular oath that he would not return with a Canaanite from nearby but would travel the much greater distance to find the right woman for his son.[1]

Even without the law, Abraham understood the potential danger of marrying off his son to a woman who worshipped other Gods. Isaac himself witnessed the problems that can result when My followers marry outside the faith; his elder son, Esau, married two women from the pagan-worshipping Hittite culture, and his two wives caused Isaac and Rebekah a great deal of grief.[2] Rebekah was so disturbed by Esau's decision that when it came time for their younger son, Jacob, to marry, she despaired of what her life would be like if he, too, married a pagan. Isaac ordered Jacob to seek a wife from among Rebekah's family.[3]

When I gave the law to Moses, I specifically prohibited the Israelites from intermarrying with the Canaanites for the reason that My people would turn away from Me and begin to serve the Canaanite gods instead. And that is exactly what happened. After I led the Israelites out of the wilderness and had performed one miracle after another on their behalf, they disobeyed Me and began to intermarry with the pagans in the cultures that surrounded the land I had promised to them.[4]

In no time, the Israelites forgot all about Me and began to serve the Baals and the Asherahs, the pagan gods of the Canaanites. My people had begun to do so much evil that I could not withhold My punishment any longer. I gave them over to a despotic king, whom they were forced to serve for eight years.[5] Finally, the Israelites cried out to Me for deliverance, and I sent them Othniel, a judge who served as their leader for the next forty peaceful years.[6]

That wasn't the last time My people caused havoc by intermarrying. One man whose decision to marry pagan women caused Me to grieve in a profound way was King Solomon. Though his father, David, made his share of mistakes, his love for Me was unquestioned. Solomon, however, tried to love Me halfway by sharing his love for Me with the many pagan women who were numbered among his seven hundred wives and princesses, and three hundred concubines, mistresses who didn't have the same status as wives.[7]

I had given Solomon the gift of wisdom,[8] but he squandered it when in his old age he unwisely allowed his wives to turn his heart away from Me, to the point of building altars to his wives' gods.[9] In his younger years, I had appeared to him twice and gave him far more than he asked of Me; I had blessed him beyond measure throughout his lifetime. His idolatry so angered Me that I pledged to dismantle his kingdom.[10]

Solomon could not plead ignorance. He knew what he was doing. He knew I had warned the Israelites that I would not tolerate their worship of other gods, just as he knew his children would also bear the consequences of his rejection of Me. After Solomon died, the nation of Israel split in two and his kingdom was dismantled as I had warned would happen. His own son rejected the wise counsel of the elders and helped bring about the division among My people.[11]

That was a tragedy that had serious consequences for generations, all caused by one man whose love for pagan women caused him to forget his love for Me—and My love for him.

JESUS

Solomon didn't set out to disobey the Father. Many women are like Solomon in that respect; their relationships with unbelieving men start out innocently enough. But when you realize you're beginning to rationalize that relationship, it's time to step back and take a clear-eyed look at what you're doing.

I've heard your many prayers as you cried out to the Father for a mate who loves Him as you do. I've also heard the cries of discouragement from those of you who look around at the people you worship with and see only happily married couples. *All the good men are taken*, I've heard you say so many times. And so you settle. You settle for men with whom you share other interests. Your relationship seems right. But I want you to understand that it isn't; it will only end in heartache for you.[12]

Paul understood that and made it clear to My followers in Corinth that they were not to become entangled in relationships with people who were not My followers. The term he used was "yoked,"[13] a crystal-clear image for the people of that day. When two oxen are yoked together, they have to walk together; the yoke keeps them from going in separate directions. When you are yoked with one of My followers, you walk in step with each other. My yoke provides an added measure of insurance that if one of you starts to stray off My path, the other will pull you back.

But when you are yoked with someone who doesn't follow Me, the two of you don't even start out on an equal footing. Your steps start out wobbly, and as you try to walk together, your attempts become increasingly uncomfortable, especially as you each begin to pursue your own interests. The yoke that seemed so romantic when you first made a commitment to each other becomes a heavy burden that keeps you from fully following Me and your unbelieving husband from fully participating in his own interests—or worse, from following someone else. You're likely to find yourselves throwing off the yoke altogether as you go your separate ways following divorce court.

My brother James warned My early followers that knowing what God wants you to do and not doing it is an example of sin.[14] Does the Father want you to be in a close, yoked relationship with unbelievers? No. Does He want you to follow your unbelieving husband into a life that pulls you away from Him? No. Neither does He want you to divorce your husband.

By becoming involved in a relationship with an unbelieving man, you set yourself up for the possibility of a lifetime with him and a difficult life with few truly satisfying choices. Your only hope will be to turn back to the Father, trust your unbelieving husband into His care, and believe that He will redeem an unhappy marriage that your obedience could have prevented.

46
God, why did You create families?

Families can be the greatest joy in life and the greatest challenge. While most women find comfort and security in the people they're related to by birth or marriage, women who have suffered abuse or other trauma in their families feel tethered to the very people who caused them so much pain, all in the name of family.

To such a woman, family can be a dirty word, because of the father who took advantage of her while her mother looked the other way, or, later in life, because of the husband who betrayed her but remains a part of her life due to the children they share. Family? That word doesn't evoke warm and loving memories for her.

Q **God, sometimes I want to run away and have a good cry when I hear my friends talk about their families, even if they're complaining. My experience with family was so painful that I can't talk about it, let alone complain. Why did You create families anyway?**

GOD

From the very beginning, I conceived the idea of loving, caring families that would fill the earth and be responsible for all of creation.[1] Men and women were to marry, become one flesh through sexual union, and have children,[2] forming this unit known as a family.

They were to take care of one another, providing a model for society as a whole. But then disobedience entered the world. The potential dissolution of the family that many people in your society fear has its roots all the way back to the garden of Eden. Adam and Eve passed their sinful natures along to their children, and most of you know the tragedy that resulted: Cain killed his brother, Abel. When I asked Cain where his brother was, I knew that he had murdered him in a jealous rage. Cain's response—"Am I my brother's keeper?"—was purely rhetorical.[3] Cain knew the answer to his own question; yes, he was his brother's keeper. He was responsible for his brother's welfare, just as every family member is responsible for every other family member's welfare. That was my intention in creating the family, and Cain knew it. He had killed someone who was his responsibility to protect—and someone who was responsible to protect him. Cain killed one of the few people he could count on.

Throughout the history of My people, I repeatedly emphasized the importance of the family. When I drew individuals into a special relationship with Me, I drew their families as well. Noah is a good example of this. When I established My covenant with him and gave him instructions for surviving the Flood, I included his entire family in the covenant, or contract, that I made with him.[4] The same held true for Abraham. When I called him to leave his father's house and travel from Haran to a land I would reveal to him when he arrived there, I told him to bring his family, including Lot, his nephew, with him.[5] Through Abraham, I would bless all the families on earth.[6] Also through Abraham, I established My covenant with everyone in his household and not just his relatives by blood or marriage, which meant that I included his servants in that contract.[7]

Later, when I created a contract with the entire nation of Israel, I included stipulations designed to underscore the importance of the family to Me. That contract, known as the Ten Commandments, included My order that all the people of Israel should treat their mothers and fathers with respect so I could bless them with a long life.[8] That was the fifth commandment. The seventh commandment stated that the Israelites must not commit adultery.[9] Joining yourself sexually with someone who is not your husband degrades the sacredness of the marriage covenant and undermines the family structure. Breaking either of those family-oriented commandments is a sin.

Because you live in a flawed world, your family life will never be perfect. That was true throughout the history of My people just as it is true for people today. Still, you can find examples of a healthy family life in My Word. One example is the story of Esther, who rose from obscurity to become a queen. When the Jews were living in captivity in Babylon, Mordecai took full responsibility for Esther, his younger cousin, after her parents died.[10] Once she was taken into the king's palace to prepare to become queen, Mordecai checked on her welfare every day.[11] When the lives of all the Jews in Babylon were at stake, Mordecai advised Esther to take action,[12] and her action saved the Jews from certain annihilation.[13] As an orphan, Esther could have had a miserable existence, but Mordecai's excellent care of her caused her to be blessed and to be a blessing to an entire group of people.

Learn to see your family for the blessing that it is, even though some days that may seem difficult. And be a blessing to your family as well. I established the family to be source of love, support, and protection, and as a family member, you can be both recipient and provider of all that and more.

JESUS

One of the concepts about family that I introduced is one that is a struggle for some of you. This happened when I was speaking to a large crowd. I had just rebuked the Pharisees and the scribes once again and had turned my attention back to the people who had been following Me that day. Someone came to tell Me that Mary, My mother, and My brothers wanted to talk to Me and were waiting for Me outside of where the crowd had assembled.[14]

I turned and asked a question that puzzled many in the crowd that day and has continued to puzzle people ever since: "Who is My mother and who are My brothers?"[15] I asked. And then I pointed to My disciples, announcing that they were My mother and My brothers; those who obeyed My Father in heaven were My true family.[16]

In saying that, I was not abandoning My physical family; even in the midst of the intense agony I suffered on the cross, I made sure My mother would be taken care of after I died.[17] Instead, I was pointing out that the Father was creating a new family, one that would be characterized by obedience to Him.

From the beginning, the Father's plan for the physical family was a model for the spiritual family that He would create through My sacrifice on the cross. My resurrection brought about the resurrection of individuals to a new life in God. And those individuals would be called the children of God; they would possess an eternal spirit.[18] People who repent of their sins, experience baptism, and receive God's Spirit are God's family.[19] That truth is confirmed by the Holy Spirit.[20]

The Father explained how He extended the covenant He made with Abraham to Abraham's entire household, and He did the same with several families in the early church. One such example followed the conversion of Lydia—you've already heard from her; Lydia's entire household was baptized after she responded to Paul's discussion about Me.[21]

Not long after, an earthquake destroyed part of the jail where Paul and Silas were imprisoned. The frightened jailer was certain that the prisoners had escaped, which would have meant humiliation and execution for him. Instead of facing the Roman soldiers, the jailer was ready to kill himself with his own sword. He would have, too, if Paul hadn't shouted and told him that all the prisoners were accounted for.[22]

The jailer knew something miraculous had just happened, and he humbled himself before Paul and Silas, asking how he could be saved. They told him about Me and assured him that his entire household would also be saved if they placed their trust in Me. Even though it was the middle of the night, he took the two men to his house, washed their wounds, and prepared a meal for them—but only after he and everyone in his home were baptized.[23]

God cared deeply for Lydia's family and the Philippian jailer's family—so deeply that He revealed the truth about Me to everyone in their families, and their entire households were baptized at the same time. God cares just as deeply for your family.

47
What's up with the teaching on submission?

In his letter to the Ephesian church, Paul taught that wives must submit to their husbands. While this was seldom a popular teaching among women, widespread opposition to it began during the movement for women's equality in the 1960s. Since then, Bible teachers have interpreted what Paul meant as everything from the absolute control of men over women, to cultural distinctions that limit the teaching to Paul's place and time.

Those wide-ranging interpretations are of little help to wives who want to obey God and have a place in His kingdom that is not a place of subjection to their husbands. Neither is it of help to single women who want to be married—but not if that means servitude.

Q **We've had it up to here with men saying women must submit to their husbands. Sometimes they're teasing us and trying to be funny, but the idea that we have to obey them isn't a joke. What's up with the teaching on submission—do we have to follow it?**

GOD

My daughters, before I clarify what you call the teaching on submission, I want to make several truths so clear to you that you will never again doubt them. All these truths are found in My Word, and yet they are often overshadowed by one or two verses that people have misinterpreted for two thousand years. Here are the truths I want you to grab hold of and never let out of your grasp:

You are made in My image. Women are not inferior to men. I created women in My image, not in the image of some lesser form of man.[1] When I looked out over all that I created, I determined all of it to be good.[2]

I created women and men to be co-laborers. I commanded Adam and Eve together to fill the earth with their descendants and to take responsibility for all that I created.[3] Woman does not have any lesser responsibility over creation than man.

I created woman to be a suitable mate for man, not an assistant who is subordinate to him. One reason I created you was to help your mate in the same way that I help humanity, which is in no way a subordinate form of help. The word in Genesis that refers to woman as a helper of man[4] is the same word that refers to Me as David's "help" in Psalm 23, the psalm that offers you so much comfort.[5]

In marriage, the wife and husband become one. I fashioned Eve out of Adam's rib, and Eve took her place at his side just as he was at her side. Through the act of sex, they became one again; they became whole.[6] You cannot be united as one body or united in wholeness if one partner is considered superior or inferior to the other.

Women are not solely responsible for introducing sin to the world. I have heard the cries of women who have been told that because Eve ate of the apple first, women are to blame for the sin that is in the world. I want you to understand that Adam is equally responsible. He ate of the tree just as Eve did.[7]

You are to be controlled by the Holy Spirit, not by any person. Some of you have asked Me how much control your husband is allowed to have over you. The marital relationship is a loving one in which the kind of control you've prayed to Me about has no place. Christians are never to "lord it over" those who have been entrusted to their care.[8] All the biblical references that describe your relationship with the Holy Spirit—be filled with the Spirit,[9] walk in the Spirit, live by the Spirit,[10] be led by the Spirit[11]—add up to being controlled by the Spirit. You have one Master—Me. You cannot serve two masters,[12] and you must obey Me over any human being.[13]

There is only one mediator between you and Me, and that mediator is Christ. The term "priest of the household" does not appear in Scripture, and that concept is not one I established. Yes, husbands are to come to Me on behalf of their wives and children, just as wives are to come to Me on behalf of their husbands and children. But that is simply through the act of prayer. Neither can stand in as a mediator for the other, and neither is accountable for the other. Each person approaches Me and stands before Me as an individual, through the work that Jesus accomplished on the cross.[14]

Now to the issue of submission. In marriage, the wife and husband are to submit to each other.¹⁵ Theirs is to be a relationship built on a foundation of mutual love, respect, and cooperation, but even more basic than that, it is to be built on a foundation of faith in Jesus Christ. Earlier you looked at a Bible verse that describes a three-strand rope as one that cannot be easily broken. When Jesus forms the third strand of the cord that binds you together, not only will your relationship be stronger, but also your commitment to love, respect, and cooperation will be stronger.

I know the objections some of you are raising in your minds right now. Your husbands are God-fearing men, and it's because of their faith in Me that they feel they must assume their rightful place of authority over their wives and children. Depending on how they were taught about their role, they may call themselves head of the household, priest of the family, or the final authority in the family. They believe they are fulfilling the responsibility I have placed in the hands of husbands. However, they've misunderstood what the women and men in the early church understood clearly, that through the teaching on submission—or to use a better word, *yielding*—men were to model submission for their wives through the way they submitted to the lordship of Christ.¹⁶

Your submission is a voluntary yielding of your will out of respect for your husband, just as you voluntarily yield your will to Me. That yielding cannot be coerced; it results from a heart that is softened by love. If your husband loves you in the way that he genuinely loves Me, then it's likely that your heart has already been softened by his love.¹⁷

JESUS

Among the things I accomplished in coming to earth was breaking down the barriers between groups of people—between the Jews and the non-Jews (or Gentiles); between slaves and those who were free; and between male and female. In Me, people from different groups that were often at enmity with each other became united. Paul compared this to putting on new clothes. When people put on new clothes, their entire demeanor often changes; when people clothe themselves with the new life I offer, their demeanor changes to one of love for people who once were not like them at all.¹⁸

In Paul's letter to the Ephesians, which is where you'll find the teaching on submission that the Father just referred to, he spoke of submission outside the context of authority. Paul mentioned the husband as the "head" of the wife[19] in the same way he mentioned that concept in his first letter to the Corinthian church. There, he stated that Christ is the head of the man, the man is the head of the women, and God is the head of Christ.[20] In both passages, Paul was referring to the "head" as the origin or source of life: The life of Christ originated in God, and the life of woman originated in man. In the letter to Corinth, he elaborated on this by emphasizing that in Me, woman and man are not independent of each other. Woman originally came from man—Eve originally came from Adam—but since then, man has come from woman through birth.[21] There is no suggestion in his illustrations that one is subservient or inferior to the other. And of course, all life originates with the Father.

If your husband has been "lording it over" you, take heart from the writings of Peter, who encouraged women to cultivate a quiet and gentle spirit so that they could influence their husbands without having to say a word. The way you live your life, the respect you have for God, the inner beauty that is so precious to God, the evidence that God has blessed you just as He has blessed your husband—all those things can have a profound effect on your husband.[22]

48
How can we respect an ungodly boss?

It happens all too frequently in the workplace: Employees are asked—or told—to do something unethical or even illegal. Those who are committed to their relationship with God find themselves in a situation in which the choice is between doing what is right at the risk of disciplinary action or outright dismissal, and doing what is wrong with the certainty that it will displease God.

For women, having an ungodly male boss can have more-personal implications. Despite laws against sexual harassment in the workplace, ungodly men in authority can make the work environment exceedingly uncomfortable for female employees without technically crossing any legal lines. Women often feel they have no recourse but to tolerate their boss's disrespectful behavior.

Q **The Bible says we're supposed to obey those in authority over us and do our work as if we're working directly for You. That's asking a lot when our boss bears no resemblance to You and asks us to do things You hate. How can we respect an ungodly boss?**

GOD

There's a difference between treating a person with respect and having respect for what she does, and that's an important distinction to keep in mind when you're being asked to obey someone in authority and work as if you're working for Me. You can treat a person with respect because of her position, even though you have no respect for the fact that she's behaving in an underhanded way in order to get ahead at work.

Still, there's a line that you must draw when a person in authority over you asks or demands that you do something that is contrary to My will. My laws are higher than the laws or policies of any government, company, or institution you work for, and they're certainly higher than those of any individual in authority over you. The followers of Christ learned that early on when the ruling Jewish religious council demanded that the apostles stop preaching.[1] Had they obeyed, they would have violated the direct command from Jesus to make disciples from every ethnic group, teaching them and baptizing them.[2]

Look at several examples of times when women were commanded to do things that would have violated one or more of My laws; their disobedience to human authority showed their high regard for My authority.

When the Hebrews were living as slaves under the rule of the Egyptians, the pharaoh, or king, became alarmed at the population increase among the Hebrews and summoned two of the Hebrew midwives to a meeting, ordering them to kill all the male babies they delivered. But the midwives believed in Me and My commands and refused to obey Pharaoh's orders. Despite the danger their disobedience to Pharaoh put them in, they chose to obey Me, and I blessed them and the Israelites with even more children.[3]

Later in the Israelites' history, a prostitute named Rahab saved the lives of two men who had been sent by Joshua to spy on the city of Jericho and the surrounding area. When the king of Jericho heard that the spies were staying with Rahab, he demanded that she send them outside. Instead, she hid the men and told the king's messenger that they had already left the city, but she didn't know where they had gone.[4] Later that night, she told the spies that she had heard how I had delivered the Israelites from Egypt and about other miracles I had done on their behalf. She believed in Me, and that was why she was helping them.[5] They soon left Jericho in safety, promising to reward Rahab by sparing her family when they returned to attack.

In both those cases, the women knew they would be violating My law if they obeyed the authorities. Jesus will now tell you how to handle a boss who hasn't asked you to disobey Me but is still a difficult person to respect.

JESUS

Paul directly addressed the work relationship, although he was writing to slaves and their masters, hardly the relationship you have with your boss. But the same principles apply; there's a great deal of wisdom in what Paul wrote about obedience to authority.

First, he advised slaves, or in your case employees, to obey their earthly authorities and treat them with the same measure of genuine respect they show Me. Knowing human nature, he made sure to point out that their obedient behavior needed to stem from an obedient heart; it wasn't good enough to be on best behavior only when those in authority were watching. The object was not to please earthly masters but to please the Father.[6]

He told workers to go a step further and do their jobs with enthusiasm, as if I were right there on the job with them and they were serving Me through their work rather than serving a human authority such as a boss. Their obedience, he wrote, would earn them a reward, not necessarily from their boss but from Me.[7]

Paul continued with an admonition to Christians who owned slaves that they should treat their slaves well, just as God treats all His children equally well.[8] But nowhere in this section does Paul imply that slaves, or employees, should obey only if those in authority over them are good, kind, decent supervisors.

In fact, in one of his letters, Peter made a point of telling Christians that they were to obey dishonest authorities just as they were to obey those who were good and kind; this is what My followers are called to do. That may seem unfair, but doing good in the face of evil pleases God. He used the unfair treatment of Me as an example for you to follow. When people insulted Me or caused Me to suffer, I didn't retaliate. I left it up to the Father to judge those who mistreated Me.[9]

Remember, too, that you have a great many tools at your disposal for dealing with people who seem to be difficult, bearing in mind that although your struggle may appear to be with an ungodly boss, the real culprit is the evil spirit behind your boss's behavior. That's when you need to find your strength and power in Me by putting on a full suit of armor, just as if you were experiencing hand-to-hand combat in a full-fledged spiritual war.[10]

Many of you already know the pieces that this suit of armor includes. First, there's the belt of truth. The integrity of the belt—the truth of who God is and who you are in God—holds the armor in place and keeps you standing strong, because you believe the truth and are certain that you are fighting on the side of truth. Second, there's your chest protection, which is like a bulletproof vest. If someone wants to do serious damage to you, where do they aim? They aim for your heart. If the forces of evil want to hurt you spiritually, that's also where they'll aim. But if you protect your heart with the righteousness of God—the power to live the way He wants you to—neither your boss nor anyone else can harm you.[11]

The third and fourth pieces are the shoes you wear and the shield you carry. The right shoes enable you to move about swiftly when you need to and to stand firm when that's what is needed. Your shoes represent peace, which is what you always need to aim for. Paul told My followers that their spiritual shields—their faith in Me—would deflect fiery arrows and render them harmless. Early Christians understood that image perfectly, having seen the Roman shields. Arrows were covered with pitch, and the shields, which were covered with leather, were soaked in water to extinguish the flames.[12]

Finally, you need to wear the helmet of salvation, which protects your head—your mind—from the ungodly thoughts that an attack might provoke, and you need to carry the sword of the Spirit, which is God's Word. The sword, the words from the Bible that God will cause you to remember, will not only strengthen you but will also enable you to discern between right and wrong. It will help you discern between those things your boss asks you to do that may be unpleasant but with which you must comply, and those things that are contrary to God's commands and with which you must not comply.[13]

This suit of armor will serve to protect you from a difficult situation at work, as well as any other difficulties in your life. If you use it, all of it, you will still be standing strong even after the difficulties have passed.[14]

With my whole heart I agree with the Law of God. But in every part of me I discover something fighting against my mind, and it makes me a prisoner of sin that controls everything I do. What a miserable person I am. Who will rescue me from this body that is doomed to die? Thank God! Jesus Christ will rescue me.

Romans 7:22–25 CEV

GOOD AND EVIL

Evil abounds in the world, and it seems to be getting more pervasive. It sometimes seems as if good is being squeezed out. People question whether good is powerful enough to keep evil at bay.

49. How can evil coexist with Your love? 231

50. Why do Your followers have to suffer? 235

51. Are all sins the same to You? 239

52. How can some unbelievers be so good? 243

53. How can You forgive truly evil criminals? 246

54. What about people who continue to sin? 250

55. How can anybody find good in tragedy? 254

49

How can evil coexist with Your love?

The pervasiveness of evil in the world is so evident that it often seems as if evil is winning. Especially in a world in which news of violence and hateful acts is available twenty-four hours a day in a bewildering array of formats, it takes genuine effort to seek out news of anything good happening around the globe.

And yet, every day, in every dot on the map, there's abundant evidence of God's love. It's hard to imagine at times how so much goodness can live on the same planet where there's so much evil. It's equally hard to imagine how so much goodness can live in some people and so much evil in others.

Q **God, we can't get away from the news unless we live in complete isolation. But when we hear about the horrible things people do to each other, we can't reconcile that with Your love. How can so much evil coexist with the love You have for humanity?**

GOD

Your question, of course, comes as no surprise to Me. Many people are uncomfortable with life's mysteries, and this is one of them. Let Me clear up at least some of the mystery for you, although in the end you will likely realize that this is one of many things you simply have to trust to Me.

It's vitally important that you look at the world from this perspective: The fact that evil has not overwhelmed the world is evidence of just how powerful My love is. When sin entered the world, its potential for devastation was immense. All you need do is look at your own nature to understand what I mean. If you did not have a relationship with Me, or if you did not have a moral code that you lived by, can you imagine what you might do? Most people, especially My people, don't like to think about that or admit to it, but I know that the human heart is desperately wicked.[1]

Look around you. Look at your neighborhood, your community, the people you know, and the people you love. Most of you will be able to say that goodness and not evil dominates your lives. Even those of you who live in neighborhoods where evil is rampant are able to find pockets of love and goodness somewhere in your area, even if it's only in your own home. Despite the fact that everyone has the potential to do evil to others, most choose not to. That's because of the power of My love.

My love keeps the forces of evil from wreaking havoc on the earth. Where you see people doing horrible things to each other, I see the myriad places where My love prevented people from doing much worse. You see a piece of the puzzle; I see the entire picture that the puzzle creates.

Consider what you know about the times I've used evil to serve My purposes for individuals and for humanity as a whole. I take everything that happens and make it work out according to what I've planned and what I want.[2] I'll give you an example that many of you are familiar with: the story of Joseph in the Old Testament.

Joseph's brothers had become jealous of him after he told them about a dream he had in which they all bowed down to him. They didn't realize that the dream was prophetic, and they tired quickly of what they saw as Joseph's boastfulness. They sold him into slavery and told their father, Jacob, that a wild beast had killed him.

They didn't know it then, but I was at work turning their evil act into a future blessing for them and their entire family. Joseph became a prominent official in the Egyptian government, and when a famine threatened Jacob's household, he sent most of his sons to Egypt to buy some grain, since the famine had not affected that area.

Now the fate of Jacob and his family was in Joseph's hands, because he was the one in charge of selling Egypt's surplus to outsiders. Joseph immediately recognized his brothers, but they failed to recognize him, and he chose not to reveal who he was right away. But when he did, his brothers were understandably terrified. Here was the brother they had sold to slave traders, and their fate was in his hands. He could have snapped his fingers and had them all tortured or killed or both. But he didn't. He wept and embraced them and blessed them with more than they ever asked for or expected.[3]

Why would Joseph do such a thing? Was he blind to what his brothers had done to him? Was he so young when he was sold into slavery that he forgot how he got there? Joseph was able to forgive his brothers and bless them for one reason: He knew Me. All the time Joseph was in Egypt, he remained in relationship with Me, trusting Me to provide wisdom when he needed it, again through the dreams he had, and allowing Me to create a heart of love and forgiveness within him. When his brothers showed their astonishment at his gracious behavior toward them, Joseph pointed out a truth that has kept evil from overtaking the world to this day: People may mean to do evil to others, but I can turn their evil intentions around and provide a blessing instead.[4]

JESUS

There's no greater evidence of the evil people can do to another person than the evil that was done to Me on earth. Even before I reached the cross, one of My closest friends betrayed Me, and all My disciples abandoned Me, fleeing from Me out of fear that they would face the same kind of death I was facing. The people who had hailed Me as their king just a few days earlier turned against Me and rejected Me.

The Roman government, knowing they would kill Me, staged what amounted to a mock trial and turned Me over to the Jewish leaders. Cruelly beaten and tortured, I was forced to carry through the streets of the city the heavy cross on which I would die. I was barely able to bear up under the weight of it, and I was wearing a crown made out of thorns that pierced My skin and drew blood that streamed down My face and hair.

All that happened before the first nail was hammered into My body.

It's at the cross that you find the intersection of ultimate evil and ultimate love: monumental injustice and unthinkable cruelty inflicted on an innocent man, the only sinless man who ever lived, and yet, the greatest act of love that the world would ever know and would ever need. The Father's powerful love ripped evil to shreds that day as He sacrificed His Son on the cross. The intense pain and agony I experienced was meant for evil, but the Father turned it around for good as He placed the world's sins on Me so you wouldn't have to carry them anymore.

Evil and love coexisted at the foot of the cross, but love won. And love continues to win. My death on the cross and all that it accomplished was a one-time act whose effects will last throughout eternity. There is no greater evidence of God's love than the cross.[5]

Here's the part that remains a mystery to most of the world: The Father not only allowed Me to suffer as I did, but He actually planned it all.[6] That may not sound like love to you, but every step I took on the way to Calvary was part of God's plan to take unconscionable evil, nail it to the cross with Me, and transform it into good, the ultimate good.

Wherever you see evil in the world, you can be certain that the Father's love is there in the midst of it, keeping greater evil at bay, transforming lives, and being poured out on all who suffer in the presence of evil. Evil and love can coexist because God allows it to happen. He allows His love to occupy the same space where misery has taken root, to show His mercy to a world that would otherwise be overwhelmed by sin.

50
Why do Your followers have to suffer?

People come into relationship with God for different reasons—they may turn to Him because of a tragedy, a friend's encouragement, an emptiness in their lives, or the simple realization that what the Bible says is true. But those who turn to God because they expect an easy life discover soon enough that the rain falls on those who follow God just as hard as it does on those who reject Him.

That's disconcerting to some people. They wonder what point there is in living God's way when they suffer pain and illness just as much as the next guy, the one who wants nothing to do with God. In fact, that guy often suffers less!

Q **God, we all know Christians who suffer with terminal illness or from overwhelming loss and tragic events in their lives. That seems so unfair; they often lived lives of total dedication to You, and they ended up in horrible situations. Why do Your followers have to suffer?**

GOD

As you already know, when Adam and Eve sinned in the garden of Eden, all creation was tarnished by their disobedience. Their sin had consequences not only for themselves but also for all humanity and even for the earth itself.[1] Some of the suffering that people undergo is a result of the curse that affected the earth; people suffer due to extreme heat or extreme cold, famine, drought, crop failure brought on by extreme weather, and natural disasters like earthquakes, tornadoes, hurricanes, and floods. These are natural consequences of the sin that has ravaged the earth, and they affect My followers as well as those who don't know Me. I intervene at times and spare My followers, but in any natural disaster, you are likely to find My people among its casualties.

What your question implies, however, is that you wonder why My followers have to suffer the effects of man-made or seemingly random tragedies. You wonder why, for example, a woman who has dedicated her entire life to Me, has diligently and lovingly served other people in My name, and has shared My love with just about everyone she ever met should die as a result of cervical cancer. Why didn't I spare her? How could I watch her suffer the pain caused by the disease and the distressing effects of the treatment she received?

Let Me direct you to the story of Job. Most of you are familiar with it. The story tells of a righteous man named Job who had everything: wealth, friends, family, everything a person in his culture would have wanted. He loved Me and obeyed Me. That made the evil one very unhappy and very sarcastic, and he snidely pointed out that of course Job worshipped Me; why wouldn't he? He had it all, and so he had no cause to challenge Me or defy Me, but what would happen if I took it all away?

I took on the challenge from the evil one and left Job with nothing but some shards of pottery that he used to scrape the wounds that were festering on his body.[2] Yes, that's how bad things were for Job. His own wife told him he should just curse Me and die.[3]

But Job didn't curse Me and die, not even when some of his friends stopped by and made him feel even worse, three of them insisting there had to be some sin in his life for Me to deal so severely with him. A fourth friend, however, couldn't take it any longer. Three men were telling Job he had sinned and Job was telling them that he hadn't; all the while the Spirit of God was bottled up inside Elihu, who held his tongue out of respect for the older men.[4]

When Elihu released the Spirit inside him, it burst forth with an abundance of wisdom about the nature and purpose of suffering[5] as well as some harsh words for Job, in some respects as harsh as those of the other three men. But Elihu spoke wisdom, such as when he castigated Job for complaining that I did not answer his cries for understanding. Elihu rightly disputed that and enumerated the ways I speak to people.[6] He continued by reminding Job of My sense of justice, My goodness, and My majesty,[7] all while Job was still suffering.

Then I spoke, challenging Job to admit that his attitude implied he knew more than I did. I did so by asking him questions about creation that I knew he could not answer. My questions silenced him; he realized that he had no greater understanding of suffering than he had about how I laid the foundations of the earth or how I determined where the ocean waves would stop as they neared the shoreline.[8]

By the time I finished speaking, Job saw himself more clearly than he ever had before; he realized that he had little understanding of My ways,[9] and he repented of his sin, the sin of self-righteousness. His suffering was necessary to bring him to that point, to bring him to the end of himself so he could finally see Me.[10]

JESUS

Let's follow that up with a look at the benefits of suffering, the good fruit that suffering produces. As we continue this discussion, I want you to keep in mind the good fruit that My suffering produced: the salvation of the entire world. That was worth every lashing, every hammer blow, every piercing I experienced before and during My crucifixion.

That brings us to a significant point we haven't talked about yet, the fact that earth is not your real home and that everything you experience on earth is a prelude to your life with God after you die a natural death. Peter described My followers as "aliens and strangers" on earth,[11] who the writer of Hebrews said were longing to leave their earthly home for their home in the heavenly city.[12] Paul was so convinced of the glories of heaven that he called his suffering on earth—of which he experienced an abundance—a "light and momentary" affliction.[13] His sufferings, he wrote, weren't even worth comparing to the glory that would eventually be revealed to the Father's people.[14]

Until you reach that heavenly city, however, you can be assured that at times you will suffer on earth. How will you respond? Peter told My followers that they should never be surprised at the suffering that tested their faith. Rather, they should rejoice that they were able to share in My suffering.[15] Furthermore, he wrote that they should greatly rejoice because the testing would prove the authenticity of their faith, which was worth more than gold.[16] And at the end of their suffering, they could be assured that I would restore and strengthen them.[17]

The early Christians could rejoice in their suffering because they understood that suffering developed their character[18] and contributed to their ongoing process of maturity.[19] It also kept them in prayer; they knew they could give their troubles to the Father, who would sustain them no matter what they had to endure.[20] Those of My followers who were Jews, as well as those Gentiles who attended Jewish religious services, were familiar with the words of Psalm 46: "God is our refuge and strength, a very present help in trouble. Therefore we will not fear, even though the earth be removed, and though the mountains be carried into the midst of the sea; though its waters roar and be troubled, though the mountains shake with its swelling."[21] They would have clung to that type of sentiment as they endured hardship.

Paul saw an even greater purpose to suffering. He knew that those who had experienced suffering, especially persecution for their faith, were in a better position to "rejoice with those who rejoice, and weep with those who weep."[22] But he also knew they would not be left alone in their sufferings; by giving their anxiety to the Father in prayer, His peace would protect their hearts and minds in ways they couldn't even comprehend.[23] He encouraged My followers by reminding them of his conviction that nothing, not even the suffering or the persecution or the danger they experienced, could ever separate them from My love:[24] "I am convinced that neither death, nor life, nor angels, nor principalities, nor things present, nor things to come, nor powers, nor height, nor depth, nor any other created thing, will be able to separate us from the love of God, which is in Christ Jesus our Lord."[25]

51
Are all sins the same to You?

One woman really, really wants a spacious kitchen like her sister has. Another woman wants, and gets, the hunk of a husband that her best friend has—or used to have. By New Testament standards, both women have sinned. But clearly, the second woman's sin is much greater. Or maybe not; maybe in the eyes of God, sin is sin, and one sin is no worse than another.

It's nearly impossible for most people to wrap their heads around that possibility. In fact, to them it's ludicrous even to suggest such a thing. Like lies, "little white sins" exist. And God certainly makes a distinction between those and the really bad sins people commit. Or maybe not?

Q God, we've heard people say that to You, one sin is as bad as another. That doesn't make sense. How can the sins of someone who pilfers a box of pens from work be as bad as those of a serial killer? Are all sins really the same to You?

GOD

I understand your confusion. I, too, have heard people say that "sin is sin" and that every sin is equal in My eyes. Although the people who convey that thought are well intentioned, their words trivialize the sin of mass murder and magnify the sin of petty theft. Their intention is to discourage people from dismissing the sin in their lives as insignificant, but that thought is better expressed by simply explaining that sin creates a barrier between My people and Me, and that turning away from sin offers the possibility of reconciliation with Me.

Under the Old Testament law, sins were assigned different penalties, a clear indication that I don't view all sins as equal. And I considered certain sins to be an abomination, an atrocity. Among those were such things as statues of other gods,[1] bringing money earned through prostitution into My house,[2] arrogance, dishonesty, murder, evil scheming, passion for evil, false

239

witness, and creating division among brothers.[3] Under the law, the death penalty was required for eleven sins in all, while such sins as theft simply required restitution.

That said, it's important never to make light of sin, even though you no longer live under the law. The leaders of the early church understood this concept well. They were the first followers of Christ to be liberated from the law through their faith in Jesus, and yet they realized the harmful effects of sin. Even though grace (My favor, which cannot be earned by keeping the law) and mercy (My lovingkindness, which I extend to you instead of punishment) replaced the law, My followers knew that the consequences of sin were serious, and not only because it interfered with our relationship but also because of the damage to them personally.

Sexual sin is a good example of that concept. Is sexual sin the worst sin you can possibly commit? No. But we saw in our earlier discussion on sex that sexual sin is the one sin that a person commits against her own body. Paul warned the Corinthians to flee from sexual sin not because sin is "dirty," as so many in your culture assume, but because it violates the unity you have with Me. When you are in a relationship with Me, we are united in spirit. Your body becomes a temple, a sacred space where the Holy Spirit dwells. The Holy Spirit is My gift to you, just as sex is My gift to you. When you treat your body with respect, you honor Me and you honor the fact that our relationship came at a high price, the death of My Son. You no longer belong to yourself. You now belong to Me.[4]

Here's another point to remember about sin. Under the Old Testament law, if you broke one law, you broke the entire law. Once the Pharisees started adding their own laws to the laws I gave Moses, it became impossible for anyone to have a shred of hope that they would never break a single law. The Pharisees couldn't even keep the laws they imposed.

But under the law of love—the new approach to sin that Jesus established on the cross—sin became better defined as a violation of love.[5] That means your understanding of what sin is and the difference in the seriousness of individual sins is guided by the overarching principle of love. Does a particular action reflect your love for Me, your spouse, your neighbor, or yourself? If the action is murder or adultery, the answer is a clear no. In the situation I mentioned earlier—being dishonest to avoid hurting a friend—your love for your friend may outweigh the consequences of lying, but that isn't always the case. Sometimes a well-intended lie can have adverse effects, and you are likely better off not saying anything at all.

JESUS

The belief you refer to in your question stems from another misinterpretation of one of My teachings. In the Sermon on the Mount, I had just set the stage for a discussion on the seriousness of all sin by telling the people that if they continued to try to keep the law, they would need to be more righteous than the scribes and Pharisees to enter heaven.[6] The people would soon realize that no one was fit to enter the kingdom of heaven if the example of the Jewish leaders was the one they followed.

Then I made several points about the nature and seriousness of sin. First, I said that being angry with another person would incur judgment from God in the same way that murdering another person would. In fact, calling someone a fool was worthy of spending eternity in hell.[7] Furthermore, I said that looking at someone else's spouse in a lustful way or simply thinking about being unfaithful was just like actually committing adultery.[8]

Now, do you believe that I consider thinking about adultery to be equal in seriousness to committing adultery? Do you believe that the Father would consign someone to hell for being angry enough to kill someone but not actually committing murder? If you answered yes to either of those questions, you have gravely misunderstood My teaching. My audience that day recognized the principle behind My words, and that principle is this: Thinking about a particular sin and acting on that thought are both violations of the same law, and both are harmful to your relationship with the Father.

Consider the potential consequences if My followers had believed that My meaning was literal. If they became angry with someone, they might as well kill the person if they had already incurred a strict judgment by merely thinking about it. The same would be true for committing adultery; if thinking about it and doing it were the same thing, then they might as well go through with it once the thought crossed their minds.

Violating the law of love is an offense, but the extent to which you violate it determines the seriousness of the offense. Although My teaching that day applied to everyone, My comments were directed to the Pharisees in particular. They needed to stop placing so much emphasis on outward behavior and begin to recognize the evil that was in their own hearts and minds.[9] Throughout My ministry, I made a point of also emphasizing that the sins of the Pharisees were much greater than those of other people because they strutted around with an air of importance and took advantage of others,[10] and because they focused on trivial matters while ignoring the more important aspects of the law.[11]

Don't forget how seriously I take the sin of unforgiveness. We've already discussed the story I told about the servant whose debt was forgiven but who refused to forgive the debt of another servant who owed him money. I compared the punishment that the unforgiving servant received from his master to that which the unforgiving people in My audience would receive from the Father.[12]

In one very limited sense, then, all sin is the same to the Father, because all sin separates people from the Father. But all sin isn't the same when you consider the seriousness of the offense and the severity of the corresponding punishment. However, all sin is alike in one important sense: All sin can be forgiven when people turn to God in genuine repentance.

52
How can some unbelievers be so good?

It may sometimes be hard for God's people to admit this, but it's true: Among the kindest, most thoughtful and generous people they know are those who have no place in their lives for a relationship with God. Neither do they have any knowledge of the Bible or its moral code, except what they may have picked up somewhere along the way.

What's especially maddening is when those people prove to be more compassionate and understanding than their Christian counterparts. It just doesn't compute. Some followers of Christ have to make an intentional—and in some cases, exceedingly difficult—effort to develop Christlike qualities, while some unbelievers seem to have acquired those qualities by osmosis.

Q **God, those of us who are new to this whole Christian thing have noticed something very unsettling—some people who want nothing to do with You are so much more Christlike than the Christians in our lives. How can that be? How can some unbelievers be so good?**

GOD

Your question reflects the nature of the fallen world you live in, a world of division. Fallen humanity seeks to justify its sinful nature by creating an imaginary world in which everyone who is like them is good and everyone who is not like them is bad. Not everyone believes or behaves this way, of course, but the fact that many people do is evident. Whether it's their country, their race, their economic system, their faith, their gender, or so on, some people allow no possibility that those who are different from them can be right, good, or just.

Let's go back to the garden once again, the garden of Eden. Do you recall the pattern I used when I created woman and man? I used Myself as a pattern. I made woman and man in My own image.[1] But which women and men? Only those who obey Me and follow Christ and strive to live godly lives? No. I made everyone in My image. And what did I call My creation? I called it good—very good.[2]

Then sin entered the world and tarnished the loveliness and purity of the world and the people I had created. But sin is not powerful enough to eradicate My image from the nature of humanity. Every person on earth—every Hindu, atheist, Sikh, Protestant, Buddhist, Catholic, nature worshipper, agnostic—everyone is made in My image. But everyone has also inherited a sinful nature. If you believe that those who are not like you do not have the capacity to be good, then you must believe that they somehow inherited a greater portion of sin, a portion so powerful that it obliterates My image in their lives. That way of thinking dishonors Me.

The first-century Jews also lived in a world of division. Paul was one of the Jews who grasped the concept that everyone is made in My image. He wrote that even the Gentiles—the non-Jews, those who were different from him—lived by a moral code even though most of them were unaware of the law of Moses, which gave the Jews their standards of right and wrong. Gentiles who were obedient to the law of God written on their hearts were in better standing with Me than were those Jews who had the entire law memorized but failed to follow it.[3] That was a radical concept at the time, and it's just as radical today. Many people today call themselves Christians because they said one specific prayer but then went on with their lives, following their old ways rather than following Me, as if nothing monumental had happened. Meanwhile, others who have never fully understood the significance of who Christ is, if they've heard of Him at all, adhere to the moral code I wrote on their hearts. The second group is obedient to My law, even though they may not be aware of it.

That's how unbelievers can be good. But I didn't create people just to be good. I created people to be in a relationship with Me.

There is no question that being good makes the world a better place for everyone to live in. Kindness, compassion, generosity, patience, love, decency, and similar qualities serve to strengthen relationships and create a harmonious environment in families and entire communities. The people who cultivate those qualities because they're following the moral code written on their hearts help keep evil from overwhelming the world, as much as that is in their power.

But their influence and capacity for good is limited to a horizontal plane, the plane on which relationships between human beings exist. I sent My

Son to earth to break wide open the vertical plane, the one where My relationship with My people exists. I didn't create people to live merely on a horizontal level, treating each other well and inching the world back to the goodness of Eden. I created people to be in relationship with Me and thereby becoming not good but holy, as I am holy.[4]

JESUS

One day a young man came to Me and asked Me what "good thing" he had to do to receive eternal life. I responded with a question of My own: why was he asking Me about what was good? I told him that only God is good.[5] In saying that, I wasn't denying My divinity but leading him to understand that by asking Me about goodness, he was acknowledging the Spirit of God in Me.

What I said to him was and is true: Only God is good. My brother James elaborated on that in a letter in which he wrote that everything that is good, every good and perfect gift, finds its source in the Father.[6] If only God is good, if everything good comes from God, if God has written His moral code on the hearts of every person, then no person and no thing can be good apart from God, whether or not people acknowledge God as the source of their goodness and whether or not they even believe in God.

As the Father said, being good is not the important issue; having a relationship with the Father and becoming holy, not good, is what's important. We've talked about holiness before, but let Me remind you that being holy doesn't require living a celibate life in a cloister or a monastery, thinking only about Me, talking only to Me, and reading only My words. Holiness requires one thing: acknowledging that My work on the cross paid the penalty for your sins, enabling and empowering you to live a life that is holy and pleasing to the Father. Then your life—your work, your relationships, your everyday routine—becomes sacred, right here on earth, as you submit your life to Me. By the grace and power of God, you have the very life, the sacred life, that you love.[7]

53
How can You forgive truly evil criminals?

Shortly before He died, Jesus assured a thief who was nailed to a cross next to His that God would welcome him into His presence upon his death. In modern society, criminals such as serial killer Ted Bundy who have committed heinous acts claim that they have experienced God's love and forgiveness as they sat on death row.

While some people rejoice over this, many more believe that forgiving evildoers is a slap in the face of good people, while others refuse to believe that the likes of Ted Bundy were actually forgiven at all. They believe that God can't possibly forgive certain sins, and they find no comfort in the testimonies of those who say He has.

Q **God, my friend's daughter was date-raped at a frat party a week after she started college. The boy was convicted and did jail time, and he now claims that he found You and Your forgiveness in jail. But she has never recovered. How can You forgive truly evil criminals?**

GOD

The anger you feel toward this young man is understandable. What he did was reprehensible; the suffering of the young woman grieves Me as it grieves her friends and family. His behavior was inexcusable. But as difficult as it is for you to understand, it is not unforgivable.

Let Me assure you that you are not alone in questioning how I can extend forgiveness to this young man and countless other people who have committed heinous crimes. People have become furious with Me over My generous and gracious forgiveness, and some have turned their backs on the loving relationship we once had with each other. I grieve when that happens as well, but My offer of forgiveness still stands. It's an offer that I extend to anyone who will seek My forgiveness in genuine repentance for what they have done.

That last bit is where you and so many others get stuck. Every day I hear the comments people make about the authenticity of a person's repentance, especially if that person is a criminal, and even more especially, if that person is a criminal on death row. People who consider themselves to be good cannot believe that a criminal's heart can be so softened that he could come to a place of genuine repentance—a complete turning away from sin and evil and crime, and a complete turning toward Me and all that is good and righteous.

Here's one of the many differences between humans and Me: People judge others by what they can see, but I look straight through to a person's heart.[1] What do you see when you think about the young man you mentioned in your question? You see a rapist. You see a bad person who ruined someone else's life. You see a convicted criminal undeserving of justice or forgiveness.

Now let Me tell you what I see. I see My Son, beaten and bloodied and breathing His last breath on the cross, all to pay for this young man's sins. And I see that young man's heart so broken by the horrible reality of what he had done that he could not face Me as he sat in that cell and wanted to end his life. I see another prisoner as well, a hardened criminal who cried out to Me years ago and now ministers to others in jail. I see him trying to get through to the young man, tears streaming down his face, as he attempts to assure him that I will forgive him. I see every meeting they have, until the one day when My Spirit penetrates his heart and he finally gets it—he finally understands that My Son died on the cross for everyone,[2] even him. I see his utter shame and humiliation in the presence of My grace and mercy. And then I see him rejoice in the freedom from sin that he has found in his confinement. He will still have to serve his sentence because in the eyes of the justice system he is still guilty. But in My eyes his guilt has been erased by My Son's blood.

My Son did not suffer and die just so people could feel free to drive over the speed limit and know they would be forgiven. He didn't endure betrayal and abandonment just so they could feel free to curse their enemies and know they'd be forgiven. And He didn't hang in pain and agony just so they could feel free to judge others and know they'd be forgiven.

Jesus suffered and died to pay the price for every one of your sins, including the worst acts of evil people can imagine and commit. None of the atrocities people have committed against one another are beyond the reach of the cross. Once a person turns to Me and cries out for forgiveness with a truly repentant heart, her sins are all forgiven because of the blood Jesus shed on the cross.[3]

JESUS

What you need to keep your eyes on is not the extent of the crimes a person has committed but rather the enormity of My sacrifice on the cross. That sacrifice was sufficient to cover the sins of billions upon billions of people, some of whose sins are unimaginable. When I uttered My last words from the Cross—"It is finished"—it truly was finished. The penalty for sin had been paid, once and for all.

Even before that work was accomplished, however, I made one final request of the Father, that He would forgive those who were responsible for My suffering. As I hung there, the searing, agonizing pain cutting through every part of My body, I reminded the Father that they truly did not understand that they were crucifying the Messiah, and I asked Him to forgive them.[4] Seeking forgiveness for those who have caused you unimaginable suffering can only come through the grace and power of the living God. That's how I could seek forgiveness for My tormentors, and that's how you can trust that God knows what He is doing when He forgives people who have committed horrible crimes.

The forgiveness the Father extends does not overlook the sin or in any way imply approval of the criminal's actions. For a criminal's repentance to be genuine—for his heart to make even the slightest turn in the Father's direction—he first has to come to terms with the evil he has committed. The Father sees everything that goes on in a person's heart and mind, and He knows whether a person has come face-to-face with the horrific act he has committed. But when a person looks at his sin head-on and acknowledges his utter depravity, that's when his heart begins to soften toward God. And that's when his repentance becomes real.

WOMAN CAUGHT IN ADULTERY

You have to understand just how incredible it is to be forgiven of your sins when those sins came with a death sentence. I found myself in that situation when Jesus was on earth. I had been caught in the act of adultery, and that sin was punishable by death—stoning. It was just after dawn, and

Jesus had already started teaching a group of people outside the temple. The Pharisees and Jewish teachers made a big show of bringing me to Him and forcing me to stand in front of all those people, including Jesus. I was humiliated.

They told Jesus, and everybody else, that I had been caught in the act of adultery. They reminded Him that the punishment was stoning. Then they challenged Him to make some kind of response. It seemed they were trying to trap Him into saying something they considered to be wrong. Jesus got really quiet and seemed to be ignoring them. He even bent down and started writing on the ground, but they kept questioning Him. Eventually He stood up and told them that if any of them were without sin in their lives, that person should be the one to throw the first stone at me.

You should have seen them. One by one they walked away, until only Jesus and I were left. He looked right at me and asked where my accusers were; who was there to condemn me? I told Him no one was, and then He assured me that He didn't condemn me either. He told me simply to go and leave my life of sin behind. I had been spared a painful stoning and certain death. His refusal to condemn me meant I had been forgiven, forgiven of a crime worthy of death.[5] Did I deserve forgiveness? No. But He gave it anyway.

54
What about people who continue to sin?

Not everyone who comes into a relationship with God succeeds in giving up old ways. Some continue to follow the same sinful patterns that characterized their lives before they knew God. Most Christians understand that they need to be patient with people like that, but when weeks stretch into months and months stretch into years with no visible change in their habits, it's difficult to believe that those people care at all about the change God wants to see in their lives.

Others follow God for a while, return to their old way of living, repent, begin living God's way again, but then go back to their former life once more. The cycle seems to have no end.

Q **God, we know some people who turned their lives over to You, but eventually they went back to the way they lived before they met You. They say they still believe in You but can't live according to Your rules. What happens to people like that who continue to sin?**

GOD

When My people continue to practice the sinful habits of their old lifestyles, it's often because they lack a knowledge of the Scriptures[1] and don't understand how they can have victory over sin, such as through the power of the Holy Spirit. Because the Bible is inspired by My Spirit, it teaches people the truth, helps them see what's wrong in their lives, corrects them when they're wrong, and teaches them how to live the right way. Without knowledge of the Bible, people are ill-equipped and ill-prepared to face the temptations that confront them.[2]

Here is a good example of how ignorance of the entire message of the Bible—or picking and choosing certain passages over others—can keep people trapped in sin. Paul, the great theologian of the early church, battled his sinful nature daily. He found this puzzling: Why couldn't he practice the righteous way he wanted to live? Why was he doing the very thing he hated? He concluded that he was no longer the one who wanted to sin; it was his flesh—his body, his sin nature—that insisted on sinning. Despite the fact that Paul found great joy in the good news of Christ and agreed fully with the right way of living that Jesus taught, his flesh wanted to go in another direction. This paradox tormented Paul, and he looked to Jesus to free him from the war that waged within him.[3]

That is contained in one passage of his letter to the church in Rome. But he didn't leave his thoughts there, stuck in a place of torment. Just a little further on in the same letter, he explained how to find that freedom from sin. When you live in agreement with the Spirit, he wrote, your mind is focused on what the Spirit wants and not on what your body wants; your body is dead to sin, but your spirit is alive to God. Put your sin nature to death and be led by the Spirit as a child of God.[4]

There's another passage, this time from the apostle John, that makes it clear that if a person is truly committed to Me, she simply cannot continue living a sinful lifestyle by virtue of the fact that My Spirit lives in her.[5] That doesn't mean she is perfect and lives a sin-free life. As long as she is living an earthly existence, she will sin, sometimes even on purpose. But if My Spirit lives inside her, she cannot continue a sinful lifestyle without having her conscience catch up with her at some point. Take someone who claims to know Me but continually defies godly counsel, which others can see, and the promptings of My Spirit, which only I can see. That person is living a life dominated by sin, the sin of rebellion, and not the leading of My Spirit. That's an example of continuing to live in sin.

Still, there is always hope, always, right up until she takes her last breath, that a person's heart will be turned back to Me and that she will repent and begin living life the right way. If you have a friend in such a situation, encourage her to read and memorize passages in the Bible that will help her stay in relationship with Me. Remind her that her knowledge of the Bible and the way she applies its truth to her life will help keep her on the right path[6] and help her avoid returning to her old sinful habits.[7]

Even so, remember this: Because of Jesus, those who live for Me no longer have to live under the fear of condemnation, even though they are still subject to the lure of sin. Their new life in Christ has set them free from the oppression of fearing punishment for the sin in their lives.[8]

JESUS

Even though I reserved My harshest words for the scribes and the Pharisees, I didn't go soft on sin. Some of the most difficult things I said referred to the consequences of continuing to live in sin, or worse, causing others to sin. Do you recall one of the times when the disciples asked Me who was the greatest person in the kingdom? I called a young child over to Me, spoke a bit about the natural humility children have, and then gave a warning. If anyone ever caused a child who believes in Me to sin, it would be better if that person had someone put "cement shoes" on her—a term you understand better than the millstone image I once used—and throw her into the deepest part of the ocean to drown.[9] That's graphic, I know, but too often people who have returned to a sinful life after following Me will try to lure their newfound Christian friends into a life of sin with them.

I continued this thought with a few more graphic images. Once again, I had some harsh words for those who cause others to sin, along with any thing that causes people to sin. If your hand or your foot causes you to sin, I said, cut it off! Throw it away! If one of your eyes causes you to sin, gouge it out! Throw it away! You're better off not having a hand or a foot or an eye than having to wage a constant battle against sin.[10]

You know, it's not just judgment or condemnation or God's punishment that My followers need to be concerned about when they return to a life of sin. They also need to be concerned about the natural consequences of sin. Those consequences may be legal, judicial, or relational. You have a saying that if you play with fire, you will be burned. Well, that saying is nothing new; Solomon conveyed the same idea in some of the proverbs he wrote. Here's one passage from him: "Can you build a fire in your lap and not burn your pants? Can you walk barefoot on hot coals and not get blisters?" In that context, he was writing about the consequences of committing adultery, but the principle applies to all sin. Every sin has an ugly consequence.[11]

It's important to understand how serious a matter sin is to the Father, just as it's important to understand how profound His grace and mercy are when you have sinned. If you confess your sins to the Father, He will be faithful to fulfill His promise to you, the promise that He will forgive your sins and wash them away, leaving you clean and ready to start a new life with Me.[12]

When My followers sin, they have Me to turn to; I stand before the Father as their advocate.[13] So that they may receive even more grace from God, My followers must never take forgiveness as a license to continue in sin. You must consider yourselves as dead to your former way of life, the sinful habits that once characterized your lifestyle.[14]

55
How can anybody find good in tragedy?

When tragedy strikes anywhere in the world, it isn't unusual to hear someone mention the good that came out of the situation. Though people like that are often in the minority, their words echo around the world because of the striking contrast between their attitude and the aftermath of the tragic event. Many people scratch their heads in bewilderment as they try to make sense of the hopeful words they just heard.

In like manner, some who are victims of horrible crimes emerge stronger after having surviving their ordeal. They, too, have managed to find something positive, some glimmer of hope, that turned a nightmare into a reason to go on living.

Q **God, I don't understand how some people respond to tragedy. Even though I'm sure You help people through crises, I don't think I could ever be like those who get up from the rubble of an earthquake and praise You. How can anybody find good in tragedy?**

GOD

History and experience have shown people that great good can come out of terrible tragedy, which is why even those people who don't know Me will begin to look for the good once the immediate shock of the tragedy passes. They may not recognize My hand in the blessings that come in the wake of tragedy, but they expect good to follow. You only have to watch the news coverage of a major catastrophe to find evidence of that. Earthquake coverage will include a tally of the fatalities and other casualties, the number of buildings destroyed or damaged, and the estimated dollar loss. But it will also include stories of heroic rescues, strangers rallying together to provide food and water to devastated areas, and volunteers leaving the safety and comfort of their homes around the world to travel to the stricken area so they can be of help. A bigger news story would be if that kind of good did not follow a tragedy.

You say you don't think you could be like the kind of people who praise Me in the midst of tragic circumstances. Many of the people who have praised Me under those circumstances believed they could never be like that either because they, like you, had never before lived through such a horrifying situation and therefore had never experienced My presence in the midst of tragedy. Today, however, they know that no matter what kind of disaster they may face in the future, they can say, along with My prophet Habakkuk, "Yet I will exult in the LORD, I will rejoice in the God of my salvation. The Lord GOD is my strength."[1]

Many survivors of tragedy will also attest to the overwhelming comfort My presence has brought them. In his second letter to the Corinthians, Paul called me the "God of all comfort,"[2] the One whose consoling and soothing presence surrounds you in the midst of your afflictions. Bear in mind the experiences of the man who wrote that. Later on in the same letter, Paul recounted some of his "afflictions." On five occasions he was lashed thirty-nine times with whips; on three occasions he was beaten; and on one occasion he was stoned. He was involved in two shipwrecks and once spent an entire night and day in the sea. He stayed on the move, facing real threats from bandits, the Jews, the Gentiles, and even some people who claimed to be Christians. He found himself in dangerous situations in cities and in the countryside, at sea and in raging rivers. He experienced hard labor, sleeplessness, hunger, thirst, cold, and nakedness.[3] Yet he continued to praise Me, because he had experienced My comfort in the midst of every affliction.

Paul made another point about the comfort I bring. One of the purposes of My comfort is that it enables you to pass it along to others when they face tragedies in their lives,[4] and that makes it one of the ways in which you can share your love of Christ with other people. I am the source of all that is good,[5] including the compassion you have for those who are enduring hardship. And don't be surprised if you are on the receiving end of the comfort that My followers will share with you when you face difficulties of your own.

Keep in mind that people respond to tragedy in different ways. Some people become hysterical, some hopeless, some fearful, and so on. You can be the calming influence in the middle of tragic circumstances by building up your faith in Me now, by testing My faithfulness when your life is relatively calm and things are going well for you. Then when disaster strikes, you can be that woman who rises from the rubble, praises Me, and becomes a source of comfort for those who do not yet know Me.

JESUS

I want you to consider a much larger view of tragedy than the individual events you may be thinking about at the moment—the natural disasters, like floods, earthquakes, and tsunamis, as well as man-made tragedies like fatal accidents, terrorist attacks, and mass murder. Think instead of the Father's involvement with the world you live in. Because the Father is the Creator and sustainer of all that is, and because He is a personal God who loves His people and wants to be in close relationship with them, you can be assured that every tragedy on earth is steeped in deep and profound meaning. Yes, some acts of violence seem senseless, but the Father saturates those acts with His loving presence, bringing sense to what seems senseless and meaning to what seems meaningless.

Not everyone, however, can see that sense and that meaning because they don't recognize or acknowledge the Father's hand in the aftermath of tragedy. Those of you who can see it have an opportunity to bring the message of its significance to the survivors of tragedy, even if you count yourself among them. Even if your own house is destroyed by a tornado, your understanding of who the Father is and how He relates to the world, in addition to your personal relationship with Him, places you in a remarkable position to bring peace and hope and comfort to a chaotic situation. You don't need to preach or expound on the evidence of God's hand in the tragedy.

You will be able to minister to people in the worst circumstances of their lives if you begin now to commit your life to getting to know the Father better and using what you know of Him to serve the hurting world around you. All your questions for God have been leading up to the questions you now need to ask yourself: *How can I, as a woman, use my unique, personal perspective on God to serve the people in my life? What is God saying to me in the context of the myriad things going on in my life right now? What does God want to say through me to other people in the context of the myriad things going on in their lives? How can I better serve God by better serving other people?*

Those questions require ongoing reflection, but that's something you can do in the course of your everyday life if you stay connected with the Father throughout your day. Keep your heart turned toward the Father, and lean into your relationship with Him in an intentional way. You will start to find the good in all of life, in the routine moments, in the exciting moments, in the hilarious moments, in the boring moments. When tragedy strikes, you'll be the one who brings the Father's love, compassion, and comfort to those who are waiting desperately for someone to help them make sense of the devastation that surrounds their lives.

Never forget that of all the roles you fill in your life, you are first a daughter of the Most High God. And He will never leave you or abandon you.[6] He is always with you, in your joy and laughter, in your grief and sorrow, in ordinary times and tragic times. And that infuses your life with profound meaning.

NOTES

Chapter 1: God, why don't You just reveal Yourself?

1.   They heard the sound of the LORD God walking in the garden in the cool of the day, and Adam and his wife hid themselves from the presence of the LORD God among the trees of the garden. (Genesis 3:8 NKJV)

2.   The LORD appeared to him by the oaks of Mamre, while he was sitting at the tent door in the heat of the day. (Genesis 18:1 NASB)

3.   He built an altar there, and called the place El-bethel, because there God had revealed Himself to him when he fled from his brother . . . Then God appeared to Jacob again when he came from Paddan-aram, and He blessed him. (Genesis 35:7, 9 NASB)

4.   The LORD spoke to Moses face to face, as a man speaks to his friend. (Exodus 33:11 NKJV)

5.   [Moses said:] "At the mountain the LORD spoke to you face to face from the heart of the fire. I stood as an intermediary between you and the LORD, for you were afraid of the fire and did not want to approach the mountain. He spoke to me, and I passed his words on to you." (Deuteronomy 5:4–5 NLT)

6.   They stayed at a distance and said to Moses, "Speak to us yourself and we will listen. But do not have God speak to us or we will die." . . . Then the LORD said to Moses, "Tell the Israelites this: 'You have seen for yourselves that I have spoken to you from heaven.'" (Exodus 20:18–19, 22 NIV)

7.   The basic reality of God is plain enough. Open your eyes and there it is! By taking a long and thoughtful look at what God has created, people have always been able to see what their eyes as such can't see: eternal power, for instance, and the mystery of his divine being. So nobody has a good excuse. (Romans 1:19–20 MSG)

8.   The heavens declare the glory of God; and the firmament shows his handiwork. (Psalm 19:1 NKJV)

9.   The scribes who came down from Jerusalem said, "He has Beelzebub," and, "By the ruler of the demons He casts out demons." (Mark 3:22 NKJV)

10.   Matthew 22:15–46: Teacher, we know that you are honest. You teach the truth about what God wants people to do. And you treat everyone with the same respect, no matter who they are. Tell us what you think! Should we pay taxes to the Emperor or not? (vv. 16–17 CEV); Teacher, Moses wrote that if a married man dies and has no children, his brother should marry the widow. Their first son would then be thought of as the son of the dead brother. Once there were seven brothers who lived here. The first one married, but died without having any children. So his wife was left to his brother. The same thing happened to the second and third brothers and finally to all seven of them. At last the woman died. When

259

God raises people from death, whose wife will this woman be? She had been married to all seven brothers (vv. 24–28 CEV); Teacher, what is the most important commandment in the Law? (v. 36 CEV)

11. As he was drawing near—already on the way down the Mount of Olives—the whole multitude of his disciples began to rejoice and praise God with a loud voice for all the mighty works that they had seen, saying, "Blessed is the King who comes in the name of the Lord! Peace in heaven and glory in the highest!" And some of the Pharisees in the crowd said to him, "Teacher, rebuke your disciples." (Luke 19:37–39 ESV)

12. "I know, Father Abraham," [the rich man said,] "but they're not listening. If someone came back to them from the dead, they would change their ways." Abraham replied, "If they won't listen to Moses and the Prophets, they're not going to be convinced by someone who rises from the dead." (Luke 16:30–31 MSG)

Chapter 2: Why do we have to face temptation?

1. Let no one say when he is tempted, "I am being tempted by God"; for God cannot be tempted by evil, and He Himself does not tempt anyone. (James 1:13 NASB)

2. No test or temptation that comes your way is beyond the course of what others have had to face. All you need to remember is that God will never let you down; he'll never let you be pushed past your limit; he'll always be there to help you come through it. (1 Corinthians 10:13 MSG)

3. My counsel is this: Live freely, animated and motivated by God's Spirit. Then you won't feed the compulsions of selfishness. For there is a root of sinful self-interest in us that is at odds with a free spirit, just as the free spirit is incompatible with selfishness. These two ways of life are antithetical, so that you cannot live at times one way and at times another way according to how you feel on any given day. Why don't you choose to be led by the Spirit and so escape the erratic compulsions of a law-dominated existence? (Galatians 5:16–18 MSG); If you live according to the flesh you will die; but if by the Spirit you put to death the deeds of the body, you will live. (Romans 8:13 NKJV)

4. Let God work his will in you. Yell a loud *no* to the Devil and watch him scamper. (James 4:7 MSG)

5. God, with undeserved kindness, declares that we are righteous. He did this through Christ Jesus when he freed us from the penalty for our sins. (Romans 3:24 NLT)

6. If we confess our sins, He is faithful and just to forgive us our sins and to cleanse us from all unrighteousness. (1 John 1:9 NKJV)

7. He said to me, "My grace is sufficient for you, for my power is made perfect in weakness." (2 Corinthians 12:9 NIV)

8. It is written, "Man shall not live by bread alone, but by every word that proceeds from the mouth of God" (Matthew 4:4 NKJV). Read the full account in Matthew 4:1–11.

9. Ephesians 6:17 NLT.

10. Lead us not into temptation, but deliver us from evil. (Matthew 6:13 ESV)

11. Stay alert; be in prayer so you don't wander into temptation without even knowing you're in danger. (Matthew 26:41 MSG)

12. Now that we know what we have—Jesus, this great High Priest with ready access to God—let's not let it slip through our fingers. We don't have a priest who is out of touch with our reality. He's been through weakness and testing, experienced it all—all but the sin. So let's walk right up to him and get what he is so ready to give. Take the mercy, accept the help. (Hebrews 4:14–16 MSG)

13. By these He has granted to us His precious and magnificent promises, so that by them you may become partakers of the divine nature, having escaped the corruption that is in the world by lust. (2 Peter 1:4 NASB)

14. In all these things we are more than conquerors through Him who loved us. (Romans 8:37 NKJV)

Chapter 3: Why should we trust You?

1. God is greater than our worried hearts and knows more about us than we do ourselves. (1 John 3:20 MSG)

2. Regarding Israel, God said, "All day long I opened my arms to them, but they were disobedient and rebellious." (Romans 10:21 NLT)

3. I will thank you forever, because you have done it. I will wait for your name, for it is good, in the presence of the godly. (Psalm 52:9 ESV)

4. See 1 Samuel 21:1–9; 22:6–23.

5. Suddenly a voice came from heaven, saying, "This is My beloved Son, in whom I am well pleased." (Matthew 3:17 NKJV)

6. At the ninth hour Jesus cried out with a loud voice, saying, "Eloi, Eloi, lama sabachthani?" which is translated, "My God, My God, why have You forsaken Me?" (Mark 15:34 NKJV)

7. Near the cross of Jesus stood his mother, his mother's sister, Mary the wife of Clopas, and Mary Magdalene. When Jesus saw his mother there, and the disciple whom he loved standing nearby, he said to his mother, "Dear woman, here is your son," and to the disciple, "Here is your mother." From that time on, this disciple took her into his home. (John 19:25–27 NIV)

8. These all continued with one accord in prayer and supplication, with the women and Mary the mother of Jesus, and with His brothers. (Acts 1:14 NKJV)

Chapter 4: How are we made in Your image?

1. Genesis 1:26–27 NLT.

2. God is Spirit, and those who worship Him must worship in spirit and truth. (John 4:24 NKJV)

3. If we are the God-created, it doesn't make a lot of sense to think we could hire a sculptor to chisel a god out of stone for us, does it? (Acts 17:29 MSG)

4.   God is love. (1 John 4:16 NKJV)

5.   Let me give you a new command: Love one another. In the same way I loved you, you love one another. This is how everyone will recognize that you are my disciples—when they see the love you have for each other. (John 13:34–35 MSG)

6.   God saw everything that he had made, and behold, it was very good. And there was evening and there was morning, the sixth day. (Genesis 1:31 ESV); When Adam sinned, sin entered the world. Adam's sin brought death, so death spread to everyone, for everyone sinned. (Romans 5:12 NLT)

7.   In reference to your former manner of life, you lay aside the old self, which is being corrupted in accordance with the lusts of deceit, and that you be renewed in the spirit of your mind, and put on the new self, which in the likeness of God has been created in righteousness and holiness of the truth. (Ephesians 4:22–24 NASB)

8.   God blessed them and said, "Be fruitful and multiply. Fill the earth and govern it. Reign over the fish in the sea, the birds in the sky, and all the animals that scurry along the ground." (Genesis 1:28 NLT)

9.   This Son perfectly mirrors God, and is stamped with God's nature. He holds everything together by what he says—powerful words! (Hebrews 1:3 MSG)

10.   I and the Father are one. (John 10:30 ESV)

11.   Jesus said, "Father, forgive them, for they don't know what they are doing." And the soldiers gambled for his clothes by throwing dice. (Luke 23:34 NLT)

Chapter 5: How can Your spirit live in us?

1.   The Spirit himself testifies with our spirit that we are God's children. (Romans 8:16 NIV)

2.   You Gentiles have also heard the truth, the Good News that God saves you. And when you believed in Christ, he identified you as his own by giving you the Holy Spirit, whom he promised long ago. The Spirit is God's guarantee that he will give us the inheritance he promised and that he has purchased us to be his own people. He did this so we would praise and glorify him. (Ephesians 1:13–14 NLT)

3.   You, however, are controlled not by the sinful nature but by the Spirit, if the Spirit of God lives in you. And if anyone does not have the Spirit of Christ, he does not belong to Christ. (Romans 8:9 NIV)

4.   You realize, don't you, that you are the temple of God, and God himself is present in you? No one will get by with vandalizing God's temple, you can be sure of that. God's temple is sacred—and you, remember, *are* the temple. (1 Corinthians 3:16–17 MSG)

5.   There are different kinds of spiritual gifts, but the same Spirit is the source of them all. There are different kinds of service, but we serve the same Lord. God works in different ways, but it is the same God who does the work in all of us. A spiritual gift is given to each of us so we can help each other. To one person the Spirit gives the ability to give wise advice; to another the same Spirit gives a

message of special knowledge. The same Spirit gives great faith to another, and to someone else the one Spirit gives the gift of healing. He gives one person the power to perform miracles, and another the ability to prophesy. He gives someone else the ability to discern whether a message is from the Spirit of God or from another spirit. Still another person is given the ability to speak in unknown languages, while another is given the ability to interpret what is being said. It is the one and only Spirit who distributes all these gifts. He alone decides which gift each person should have. (1 Corinthians 12:4–11 NLT)

6. The Friend, the Holy Spirit whom the Father will send at my request, will make everything plain to you. He will remind you of all the things I have told you. (John 14:26 MSG)

7. I keep asking that the God of our Lord Jesus Christ, the glorious Father, may give you the Spirit of wisdom and revelation, so that you may know him better. (Ephesians 1:17 NIV)

8. Don't worry about what you'll say or how you'll say it. The right words will be there; the Spirit of your Father will supply the words. (Matthew 10:19–20 MSG)

9. The Spirit helps us in our weakness. For we do not know what to pray for as we ought, but the Spirit himself intercedes for us with groanings too deep for words. And he who searches hearts knows what is the mind of the Spirit, because the Spirit intercedes for the saints according to the will of God. (Romans 8:26–27 ESV)

10. The fruit of the Spirit is love, joy, peace, longsuffering, kindness, goodness, faithfulness, gentleness, self-control. Against such there is no law. And those who are Christ's have crucified the flesh with its passions and desires. If we live in the Spirit, let us also walk in the Spirit. (Galatians 5:22–25 NKJV)

11. Rabbi, we all know you're a teacher straight from God. No one could do all the God-pointing, God-revealing acts you do if God weren't in on it. (John 3:2 MSG)

12. Jesus answered, "Most assuredly, I say to you, unless one is born of water and the Spirit, he cannot enter the kingdom of God. That which is born of the flesh is flesh, and that which is born of the Spirit is spirit." (John 3:5–6 NKJV)

13. The Spirit gives life; the flesh counts for nothing. The words I have spoken to you are spirit and they are life. (John 6:63 NIV)

Chapter 6: Who's controlling our lives—You or us?

1. I, too, give witness to the greatness of GOD, our Lord, high above all other gods. He does just as he pleases—however, wherever, whenever. (Psalm 135:5–6 MSG)

2. By Him all things were created that are in heaven and that are on earth, visible and invisible, whether thrones or dominions or principalities or powers. All things were created through Him and for Him. And He is before all things, and in Him all things consist. (Colossians 1:16–17 NKJV)

3. Jeremiah 10:23–24 MSG.

4.   Whoever listens to me will dwell secure and will be at ease, without dread of disaster. (Proverbs 1:33 ESV); I know the thoughts that I think toward you, says the LORD, thoughts of peace and not of evil, to give you a future and a hope. (Jeremiah 29:11 NKJV)

5.   Trust in the LORD with all your heart, and lean not on your own under-standing; in all your ways acknowledge Him, and He shall direct your paths. (Proverbs 3:5–6 NKJV); Thus says the LORD, your Redeemer, the Holy One of Israel, "I am the LORD your God, who teaches you to profit, who leads you in the way you should go." (Isaiah 48:17 NASB)

6.   I will instruct you and teach you in the way you should go; I will guide you with My eye. (Psalm 32:8 NKJV); The LORD will guide you continually. (Isaiah 58:11 NLT)

7.   I will make with them an everlasting covenant, that I will not turn away from doing good to them. And I will put the fear of me in their hearts, that they may not turn from me. (Jeremiah 32:40 ESV)

8.   Oh, magnify the LORD with me, and let us exalt His name together. (Psalm 34:3 NKJV)

Chapter 7: Why don't You prevent disasters from happening?

1.   Blessed be the God and Father of our Lord Jesus Christ, the Father of mer-cies and God of all comfort. (2 Corinthians 1:3 NKJV)

2.   The creation waits in eager expectation for the sons of God to be revealed. For the creation was subjected to frustration, not by its own choice, but by the will of the one who subjected it, in hope that the creation itself will be liberated from its bondage to decay and brought into the glorious freedom of the children of God. (Romans 8:19–21 NIV)

3.   Who kept the sea inside its boundaries as it burst from the womb, and as I clothed it with clouds and wrapped it in thick darkness? For I locked it behind barred gates, limiting its shores. I said, "This far and no farther will you come. Here your proud waves must stop!" (Job 38:8–11 NLT)

4.   There were present at that season some who told Him about the Galileans whose blood Pilate had mingled with their sacrifices. And Jesus answered and said to them, "Do you suppose that these Galileans were worse sinners than all other Galileans, because they suffered such things? I tell you, no; but unless you repent you will all likewise perish." (Luke 13:1–3 NKJV)

5.   Or those eighteen on whom the tower in Siloam fell and killed them, do you think that they were worse sinners than all other men who dwelt in Jerusalem? I tell you, no; but unless you repent you will all likewise perish." (Luke 13:4–5 NKJV)

6.   There's a way of life that looks harmless enough; look again—it leads straight to hell. Sure, those people appear to be having a good time, but all that laughter will end in heartbreak. (Proverbs 14:12–13 MSG)

7.   Who will separate us from the love of Christ? Will tribulation, or distress,

or persecution, or famine, or nakedness, or peril, or sword? . . . But in all these things we overwhelmingly conquer through Him who loved us. For I am convinced that neither death, nor life, nor angels, nor principalities, nor things present, nor things to come, nor powers, nor height, nor depth, nor any other created thing, will be able to separate us from the love of God, which is in Christ Jesus our Lord. (Romans 8:35, 37–39 NASB)

8. God is our refuge and strength, a very present help in trouble. Therefore we will not fear though the earth gives way, though the mountains be moved into the heart of the sea, though its waters roar and foam, though the mountains tremble at its swelling. (Psalm 46:1–3 ESV)

9. You let the world, which doesn't know the first thing about living, tell you how to live. You filled your lungs with polluted unbelief, and then exhaled disobedience. (Ephesians 2:2 MSG)

10. I heard a loud voice from heaven saying, "Behold, the tabernacle of God is with men, and He will dwell with them, and they shall be His people. God Himself will be with them and be their God. And God will wipe away every tear from their eyes; there shall be no more death, nor sorrow, nor crying. There shall be no more pain, for the former things have passed away." (Revelation 21:3–4 NKJV)

Chapter 8: Jesus, are You really God's Son?

1. When the wicked one appears, Satan will pretend to work all kinds of miracles, wonders, and signs. (2 Thessalonians 2:9 CEV)

2. The story of Lazarus and the meeting of the Sanhedrin is found in John 11:1–53.

3. Matthew 14:33 NIV.

4. Matthew 16:16 MSG.

5. Matthew 26:33–35, 69–75.

6. 2 Peter 1:1 NKJV.

7. I believe that You are the Christ, the Son of God, who is to come into the world. (John 11:27 NKJV)

8. Matthew 27:54 NIV.

9. John 20:28 NIV.

10. Jesus answered, "I tell you the truth, before Abraham was even born, I AM!" At that point they picked up stones to throw at him. But Jesus was hidden from them and left the Temple. (John 8:58–59 NLT)

11. Mark 14:61–64; John 10:30; 14:11 NIV.

12. See John 1:1–18.

13. This is My beloved Son, in whom I am well pleased. (Matthew 3:17 NKJV)

14. These will make war with the Lamb, and the Lamb will overcome them, for He is Lord of lords and King of kings; and those who are with Him are called, chosen, and faithful. (Revelation 17:14 NKJV); "I am the Alpha and the Omega, the

Beginning and the End," says the Lord, "who is and who was and who is to come, the Almighty." (Revelation 1:8 NKJV)

Chapter 9: Why did You come to earth anyway?

1. That which was from the beginning, which we have heard, which we have seen with our eyes, which we have looked upon, and our hands have handled, concerning the Word of life—the life was manifested, and we have seen, and bear witness, and declare to you that eternal life which was with the Father and was manifested to us—that which we have seen and heard we declare to you, that you also may have fellowship with us; and truly our fellowship is with the Father and with His Son Jesus Christ. And these things we write to you that your joy may be full. (1 John 1:1–4 NKJV)

2. I am the resurrection and the life. Anyone who believes in me will live, even after dying. Everyone who lives in me and believes in me will never ever die. (John 11:25–26 NLT)

3. My dear children, don't let anyone divert you from the truth. It's the person who *acts* right who is right, just as we see it lived out in our righteous Messiah. Those who make a practice of sin are straight from the Devil, the pioneer in the practice of sin. The Son of God entered the scene to abolish the Devil's ways. (1 John 3:7–8 MSG)

4. Truly, truly, I say to you, he who hears My word, and believes Him who sent Me, has eternal life, and does not come into judgment, but has passed out of death into life. (John 5:24 NASB)

5. The Spirit of the LORD is upon me, for he has anointed me to bring Good News to the poor. He has sent me to proclaim that captives will be released, that the blind will see, that the oppressed will be set free. (Luke 4:18 NLT)

6. I have come that they may have life, and that they may have it more abundantly. (John 10:10 NKJV)

7. Do not think that I have come to abolish the Law or the Prophets; I have not come to abolish them but to fulfill them. (Matthew 5:17 ESV)

8. You've observed how godless rulers throw their weight around, how quickly a little power goes to their heads. It's not going to be that way with you. Whoever wants to be great must become a servant. Whoever wants to be first among you must be your slave. That is what the Son of Man has done: He came to serve, not be served—and then to give away his life in exchange for the many who are held hostage. (Matthew 20:25–28 MSG)

9. You say rightly that I am a king. For this cause I was born, and for this cause I have come into the world, that I should bear witness to the truth. Everyone who is of the truth hears My voice. (John 18:37 NKJV)

10. God so loved the world that He gave His only begotten Son, that whoever believes in Him should not perish but have everlasting life. (John 3:16 NKJV)

11. God knew what would happen, and his prearranged plan was carried out when Jesus was betrayed. With the help of lawless Gentiles, you nailed him to a

cross and killed him. But God released him from the horrors of death and raised him back to life, for death could not keep him in its grip. (Acts 2:23–24 NLT)

12.   When the Messiah arrived, high priest of the superior things of this new covenant, he bypassed the old tent and its trappings in this created world and went straight into heaven's "tent"—the true Holy Place—once and for all. He also bypassed the sacrifices consisting of goat and calf blood, instead using his own blood as the price to set us free once and for all. If that animal blood and the other rituals of purification were effective in cleaning up certain matters of our religion and behavior, think how much more the blood of Christ cleans up our whole lives, inside and out. Through the Spirit, Christ offered himself as an unblemished sacrifice, freeing us from all those dead-end efforts to make ourselves respectable, so that we can live all out for God. (Hebrews 9:11–15 MSG)

13.   The Lord Himself shall give you a sign: Behold, the virgin shall conceive and bear a Son, and shall call His name Immanuel. (Isaiah 7:14 NKJV)

14.   He will be great and will be called the Son of the Most High. And the Lord God will give to him the throne of his father David, and he will reign over the house of Jacob forever, and of his kingdom there will be no end. (Luke 1:32–33 ESV)

15.   See Luke 2:25–38.

Chapter 10: Why was a virgin birth necessary?

1.   To Adam He said, "Because you have listened to the voice of your wife, and have eaten from the tree about which I commanded you, saying, 'You shall not eat from it'; cursed is the ground because of you; in toil you will eat of it all the days of your life." (Genesis 3:17 NASB)

2.   Just as through one man sin entered into the world, and death through sin, and so death spread to all men, because all sinned. (Romans 5:12 NASB)

3.   Luke 1:34 NIV.

4.   Luke 1:34–38 NIV.

5.   Blessed are you among women, and blessed is the fruit of your womb! But why is this granted to me, that the mother of my Lord should come to me? For indeed, as soon as the voice of your greeting sounded in my ears, the babe leaped in my womb for joy. Blessed is she who believed, for there will be a fulfillment of those things which were told her from the Lord. (Luke 1:42–45 NKJV)

6.   Mary said: "My soul magnifies the Lord, and my spirit has rejoiced in God my Savior. For He has regarded the lowly state of His maidservant; for behold, henceforth all generations will call me blessed. For He who is mighty has done great things for me, and holy is His name. And His mercy is on those who fear Him from generation to generation. He has shown strength with His arm; He has scattered the proud in the imagination of their hearts. He has put down the mighty from their thrones, and exalted the lowly. He has filled the hungry with good things, and the rich He has sent away empty. He has helped His servant Israel, in remembrance of His mercy, as He spoke to our fathers, to Abraham and to his seed forever." (Luke 1:46–55 NKJV)

7. This is how Jesus Christ was born. A young woman named Mary was engaged to Joseph from King David's family. But before they were married, she learned that she was going to have a baby by God's Holy Spirit. Joseph was a good man and did not want to embarrass Mary in front of everyone. So he decided to quietly call off the wedding. While Joseph was thinking about this, an angel from the Lord came to him in a dream. The angel said, "Joseph, the baby that Mary will have is from the Holy Spirit. Go ahead and marry her. Then after her baby is born, name him Jesus, because he will save his people from their sins." So the Lord's promise came true, just as the prophet had said, "A virgin will have a baby boy, and he will be called Immanuel," which means "God is with us." After Joseph woke up, he and Mary were soon married, just as the Lord's angel had told him to do. (Matthew 1:18–24 CEV)

8. The Lord Himself will give you a sign: Behold, the virgin shall conceive and bear a Son, and shall call His name Immanuel. (Isaiah 7:14 NKJV)

Chapter 11: Did You physically rise from the dead?

1. Thomas (called Didymus), one of the Twelve, was not with the disciples when Jesus came. So the other disciples told him, "We have seen the Lord!" But he said to them, "Unless I see the nail marks in his hands and put my finger where the nails were, and put my hand into his side, I will not believe it." (John 20:24–25 NIV)

2. Reach your finger here, and look at My hands; and reach your hand here, and put it into My side. Do not be unbelieving, but believing. (John 20:27 NKJV)

3. This story can be found in Luke 24:13–32.

4. Jesus said to them, "Come and eat breakfast." Yet none of the disciples dared ask Him, "Who are You?"—knowing that it was the Lord. Jesus then came and took the bread and gave it to them, and likewise the fish. (John 21:12–13 NKJV)

5. His brothers said, "Why don't you leave here and go up to the Feast so your disciples can get a good look at the works you do? No one who intends to be publicly known does everything behind the scenes. If you're serious about what you are doing, come out in the open and show the world." His brothers were pushing him like this because they didn't believe in him either. (John 7:3–5 MSG)

6. After that, he was seen by more than 500 of his followers at one time, most of whom are still alive, though some have died. Then he was seen by James and later by all the apostles. (1 Corinthians 15:6–7 NLT)

7. "Look at my hands and my feet and see who I am! Touch me and find out for yourselves. Ghosts don't have flesh and bones as you see I have." After Jesus said this, he showed them his hands and his feet. The disciples were so glad and amazed that they could not believe it. Jesus then asked them, "Do you have something to eat?" They gave him a piece of baked fish. He took it and ate it as they watched. Jesus said to them, "While I was still with you, I told you that everything written about me in the Law of Moses, the Books of the Prophets, and

in the Psalms had to happen." (Luke 24:39–44 CEV); For forty days after Jesus had suffered and died, he proved in many ways that he had been raised from death. He appeared to his apostles and spoke to them about God's kingdom. While he was still with them, he said: Don't leave Jerusalem yet. Wait here for the Father to give you the Holy Spirit, just as I told you he has promised to do. John baptized with water, but in a few days you will be baptized with the Holy Spirit. While the apostles were still with Jesus, they asked him, "Lord, are you now going to give Israel its own king again?" Jesus said to them, "You don't need to know the time of those events that only the Father controls. But the Holy Spirit will come upon you and give you power. Then you will tell everyone about me in Jerusalem, in all Judea, in Samaria, and everywhere in the world." (Acts 1:3–8 CEV)

8. Jesus came and said to them, "All authority in heaven and on earth has been given to me. Go therefore and make disciples of all nations, baptizing them in the name of the Father and of the Son and of the Holy Spirit, teaching them to observe all that I have commanded you. And behold, I am with you always, to the end of the age." (Matthew 28:18–20 ESV)

9. When they heard these things they were cut to the heart, and they gnashed at him with their teeth. But he, being full of the Holy Spirit, gazed into heaven and saw the glory of God, and Jesus standing at the right hand of God, and said, "Look! I see the heavens opened and the Son of Man standing at the right hand of God!" Then they cried out with a loud voice, stopped their ears, and ran at him with one accord; and they cast him out of the city and stoned him. And the witnesses laid down their clothes at the feet of a young man named Saul. And they stoned Stephen as he was calling on God and saying, "Lord Jesus, receive my spirit." Then he knelt down and cried out with a loud voice, "Lord, do not charge them with this sin." And when he had said this, he fell asleep. (Acts 7:54–60 NKJV)

10. Saul/Paul's conversion is covered in Acts 9:1–31.

11. Do not be afraid, for I know that you seek Jesus who was crucified. He is not here; for He is risen, as He said. Come, see the place where the Lord lay. And go quickly and tell His disciples that He is risen from the dead, and indeed He is going before you into Galilee; there you will see Him. Behold, I have told you. (Matthew 28:5–7 NKJV)

12. They left the tomb and broke the news of all this to the Eleven and the rest. Mary Magdalene, Joanna, Mary the mother of James, and the other women with them kept telling these things to the apostles, but the apostles didn't believe a word of it, thought they were making it all up. (Luke 24:9–11 MSG)

13. Suddenly Jesus met them. "Greetings," he said. They came to him, clasped his feet and worshiped him. Then Jesus said to them, "Do not be afraid. Go and tell my brothers to go to Galilee; there they will see me." (Matthew 28:9–10 NIV)

Chapter 12: Did You experience human emotions on earth?

1. The world must learn that I love the Father and that I do exactly what my Father has commanded me. (John 14:31 NIV)

2.   As the Father loved Me, I also have loved you; abide in My love. (John 15:9 NKJV)

3.   John 11:3 NIV.

4.   Jesus wept. So the Jews said, "See how he loved him!" But some of them said, "Could not he who opened the eyes of the blind man also have kept this man from dying?" (John 11:35–37 ESV)

5.   There was reclining on Jesus' bosom one of His disciples, whom Jesus loved. (John 13:23 NASB); She came running to Simon Peter and the other disciple, the one Jesus loved, and said, "They have taken the Lord out of the tomb, and we don't know where they have put him!" (John 20:2 NIV); The disciple Jesus loved said to Peter, "It's the Master!" (John 21:7 MSG)

6.   When Jesus saw his mother and the disciple whom he loved standing nearby, he said to his mother, "Woman, behold, your son!" (John 19:26 ESV)

7.   John 15:13 NLT.

8.   When he looked out over the crowds, his heart broke. (Matthew 9:36 MSG)

9.   Moved with compassion, Jesus reached out and touched him. "I am willing," he said. "Be healed!" (Mark 1:41 NLT); Deeply moved, Jesus touched their eyes. They had their sight back that very instant, and joined the procession. (Matthew 20:34 MSG); When Jesus went out He saw a great multitude; and He was moved with compassion for them, and healed their sick. (Matthew 14:14 NKJV)

10.   Read the story in Matthew 15:32–39.

11.   Jesus saw the huge crowd as he stepped from the boat, and he had compassion on them because they were like sheep without a shepherd. So he began teaching them many things. (Mark 6:34 NLT)

12.   He sighed deeply in His spirit, and said, "Why does this generation seek a sign? Assuredly, I say to you, no sign shall be given to this generation." (Mark 8:12 NKJV)

13.   Mark 8:21 MSG.

14.   When the Passover Feast, celebrated each spring by the Jews, was about to take place, Jesus traveled up to Jerusalem. He found the Temple teeming with people selling cattle and sheep and doves. The loan sharks were also there in full strength. Jesus put together a whip out of strips of leather and chased them out of the Temple, stampeding the sheep and cattle, upending the tables of the loan sharks, spilling coins left and right. He told the dove merchants, "Get your things out of here! Stop turning my Father's house into a shopping mall!" That's when his disciples remembered the Scripture, "Zeal for your house consumes me." (John 2:13–17 MSG)

15.   Read the account in Matthew 26:17–27:50.

16.   These things I have spoken to you, that My joy may remain in you, and that your joy may be full. (John 15:11 NKJV)

17.   Matthew 11:19 NASB.

Chapter 13: Is it true that You never sinned?

1. Just as through one man sin entered into the world, and death through sin, and so death spread to all men, because all sinned. (Romans 5:12 NASB)

2. The Holy Spirit will come upon you, and the power of the Highest will overshadow you; therefore, also, that Holy One who is to be born will be called the Son of God. (Luke 1:35 NKJV)

3. We do not have a high priest who is unable to sympathize with our weaknesses, but we have one who has been tempted in every way, just as we are—yet was without sin. (Hebrews 4:15 NIV)

4. Let no one say when he is tempted, "I am being tempted by God"; for God cannot be tempted by evil, and He Himself does not tempt anyone. (James 1:13 NASB)

5. You remain the same, and your years will never end. (Hebrews 1:12 NIV); Jesus Christ is the same yesterday, today, and forever. (Hebrews 13:8 NKJV)

6. God put the wrong on him who never did anything wrong, so we could be put right with God. (2 Corinthians 5:21 MSG)

7. At just the right time, when we were still powerless, Christ died for the ungodly. Very rarely will anyone die for a righteous man, though for a good man someone might possibly dare to die. But God demonstrates his own love for us in this: While we were still sinners, Christ died for us. (Romans 5:6–8 NIV); As through one man's offense judgment came to all men, resulting in condemnation, even so through one Man's righteous act the free gift came to all men, resulting in justification of life. For as by one man's disobedience many were made sinners, so also by one Man's obedience many will be made righteous. (Romans 5:18–19 NKJV)

8. There is one God and one mediator between God and men, the man Christ Jesus, who gave himself as a ransom for all men—the testimony given in its proper time. (1 Timothy 2:5–6 NIV)

9. You know that it was not with perishable things such as silver or gold that you were redeemed from the empty way of life handed down to you from your forefathers, but with the precious blood of Christ, a lamb without blemish or defect. (1 Peter 1:18–19 NIV); The next day John saw Jesus coming toward him and said, "Look! The Lamb of God who takes away the sin of the world!" (John 1:29 NLT)

10. Jesus Christ is the same yesterday and today and forever. (Hebrews 13:8 NASB)

11. Christ has rescued us from the curse pronounced by the law. When he was hung on the cross, he took upon himself the curse for our wrongdoing. For it is written in the Scriptures, "Cursed is everyone who is hung on a tree." (Galatians 3:13 NLT)

12. We wait for the blessed hope, the glorious appearing of our great God and Savior, Jesus Christ, who gave himself for us to redeem us from all wickedness and to purify for himself a people that are his very own, eager to do what is good. (Titus 2:13–14 NIV)

13. What marvelous love the Father has extended to us! Just look at it—we're called children of God! That's who we really are. But that's also why the world doesn't recognize us or take us seriously, because it has no idea who he is or what he's up to. But friends, that's exactly who we are: children of God. And that's only the beginning. Who knows how we'll end up! What we know is that when Christ is openly revealed, we'll see him—and in seeing him, become like him. All of us who look forward to his Coming stay ready, with the glistening purity of Jesus' life as a model for our own. All who indulge in a sinful life are dangerously lawless, for sin is a major disruption of God's order. Surely you know that Christ showed up in order to get rid of sin. There is no sin in him, and sin is not part of his program. (1 John 3:1–5 MSG)

14. 1 Peter 2:21–25 MSG.

Chapter 14: Did You really die to save everyone?

1. God so loved the world that He gave His only begotten Son, that whoever believes in Him should not perish but have everlasting life. (John 3:16 NKJV)

2. The judgment is based on this fact: God's light came into the world, but people loved the darkness more than the light, for their actions were evil. All who do evil hate the light and refuse to go near it for fear their sins will be exposed. But those who do what is right come to the light so others can see that they are doing what God wants. (John 3:19–21 NLT)

3. Even Death and Destruction hold no secrets from the LORD. How much more does he know the human heart! (Proverbs 15:11 NLT)

4. The thief comes only to steal and kill and destroy; I came that they may have life, and have it abundantly. (John 10:10 NASB)

5. In My Father's house are many mansions; if it were not so, I would have told you. I go to prepare a place for you. (John 14:2 NKJV)

6. Eye has not seen, nor ear heard, nor have entered into the heart of man the things which God has prepared for those who love Him. (1 Corinthians 2:9 NKJV)

7. Look! I stand at the door and knock. If you hear my voice and open the door, I will come in, and we will share a meal together as friends. (Revelation 3:20 NLT)

8. Do I take any pleasure in the death of the wicked? declares the Sovereign LORD. Rather, am I not pleased when they turn from their ways and live? . . . for I take no pleasure in the death of anyone, declares the Sovereign LORD. Repent and live! (Ezekiel 18:23, 32 NIV)

9. He will wipe away every tear from their eyes, and death shall be no more, neither shall there be mourning nor crying nor pain anymore, for the former things have passed away. (Revelation 21:4 ESV)

10. Don't overlook the obvious here, friends. With God, one day is as good as a thousand years, a thousand years as a day. God isn't late with his promise as some measure lateness. He is restraining himself on account of you, holding back the End because he doesn't want anyone lost. He's giving everyone space

and time to change (2 Peter 3:8–9 MSG)

11. Do you think lightly of the riches of His kindness and tolerance and patience, not knowing that the kindness of God leads you to repentance? (Romans 2:4 NASB)

12. I urge you, first of all, to pray for all people. Ask God to help them; intercede on their behalf, and give thanks for them . . . This is good and pleases God our Savior, who wants everyone to be saved and to understand the truth. For there is only one God and one Mediator who can reconcile God and humanity— the man Christ Jesus. He gave his life to purchase freedom for everyone. This is the message God gave to the world at just the right time (1 Timothy 2:1, 3–6 NLT)

13. Whoever confesses that Jesus is the Son of God, God abides in him, and he in God. And we have known and believed the love that God has for us. God is love, and he who abides in love abides in God, and God in him. (1 John 4:15–16 NKJV)

14. Love is made complete among us so that we will have confidence on the day of judgment, because in this world we are like him. There is no fear in love. But perfect love drives out fear, because fear has to do with punishment. The one who fears is not made perfect in love. (1 John 4:17–18 NIV)

15. We know that this is indeed the Savior of the world. (John 4:42 ESV); We have seen and testify that the Father has sent his Son to be the Savior of the world. (1 John 4:14 ESV)

16. The next day John saw Jesus coming toward him, and said, "Behold! The Lamb of God who takes away the sin of the world!" (John 1:29 NKJV)

17. We see Jesus, who was made a little lower than the angels, for the suffering of death crowned with glory and honor, that He, by the grace of God, might taste death for everyone. (Hebrews 2:9 NKJV); He gave his life to purchase freedom for everyone. This is the message God gave to the world at just the right time. (1 Timothy 2:6 NLT)

18. Go therefore and make disciples of all the nations, baptizing them in the name of the Father and the Son and the Holy Spirit. (Matthew 28:19 NASB); You will receive power when the Holy Spirit has come upon you; and you shall be My witnesses both in Jerusalem, and in all Judea and Samaria, and even to the remotest part of the earth. (Acts 1:8 NASB)

19. Romans 10:9–10 NLT.

Chapter 15: Who actually wrote the Bible?

1. Every part of Scripture is God-breathed and useful one way or another— showing us truth, exposing our rebellion, correcting our mistakes, training us to live God's way. (2 Timothy 3:16 MSG); This is what we speak, not in words taught us by human wisdom but in words taught by the Spirit, expressing spiritual truths in spiritual words. (1 Corinthians 2:13 NIV)

2. No prophecy of Scripture comes from someone's own interpretation. For no prophecy was ever produced by the will of man, but men spoke from God as they were carried along by the Holy Spirit. (2 Peter 1:20–21 ESV)

3. [Jesus said:] "For a long time now people have tried to force themselves into God's kingdom. But if you read the books of the Prophets and God's Law closely, you will see them culminate in John, teaming up with him in preparing the way for the Messiah of the kingdom. Looked at in this way, John is the 'Elijah' you've all been expecting to arrive and introduce the Messiah." (Matthew 11:12–14 MSG); see also Matthew 5:17.

4. Beginning at Moses and all the Prophets, He expounded to them in all the Scriptures the things concerning Himself. (Luke 24:27 NKJV)

5. At that moment, open-eyed, wide-eyed, they recognized him. And then he disappeared. Back and forth they talked. "Didn't we feel on fire as he conversed with us on the road, as he opened up the Scriptures for us?" (Luke 24:31–32 MSG)

6. I am convinced that neither death, nor life, nor angels, nor principalities, nor things present, nor things to come, nor powers, nor height, nor depth, nor any other created thing, will be able to separate us from the love of God, which is in Christ Jesus our Lord. (Romans 8:38–39 NASB)

7. A Jew named Apollos, a native of Alexandria, came to Ephesus. He was a learned man, with a thorough knowledge of the Scriptures. He had been instructed in the way of the Lord, and he spoke with great fervor and taught about Jesus accurately, though he knew only the baptism of John. He began to speak boldly in the synagogue. When Priscilla and Aquila heard him, they invited him to their home and explained to him the way of God more adequately. (Acts 18:24–26 NIV)

Chapter 16: Must we obey everything in the Bible?

1. I will establish My covenant with you; and you shall go into the ark—you, your sons, your wife, and your sons' wives with you. (Genesis 6:18 NKJV); I establish My covenant with you: Never again shall all flesh be cut off by the waters of the flood; never again shall there be a flood to destroy the earth. (Genesis 9:11 NKJV)

2. I will establish My covenant between Me and you and your descendants after you throughout their generations for an everlasting covenant, to be God to you and to your descendants after you. (Genesis 17:7 NASB)

3. "If you obey me fully and keep my covenant, then out of all nations you will be my treasured possession. Although the whole earth is mine, you will be for me a kingdom of priests and a holy nation." These are the words you are to speak to the Israelites. (Exodus 19:5–6 NIV)

4. This means that anyone who belongs to Christ has become a new person. The old life is gone; a new life has begun! (2 Corinthians 5:17 NLT)

5. There is therefore now no condemnation for those who are in Christ Jesus. For the law of the Spirit of life has set you free in Christ Jesus from the law of sin and death. (Romans 8:1–2 ESV)

6. If we confess our sins, He is faithful and righteous to forgive us our sins and to cleanse us from all unrighteousness. (1 John 1:9 NASB)

7. Don't suppose that I came to do away with the Law and the Prophets. I did not come to do away with them, but to give them their full meaning. (Matthew 5:17 CEV)

8. I tell you not to resist an evil person. But whoever slaps you on your right cheek, turn the other to him also. (Matthew 5:39 NKJV)

9. Matthew 5:44 NIV.

10. Matthew 22:37–40 NLT.

Chapter 17: Did all those miracles really happen?

1. Remember the things I have done in the past. For I alone am God! I am God, and there is none like me. Only I can tell you the future before it even happens. Everything I plan will come to pass, for I do whatever I wish. (Isaiah 46:9–10 NLT)

2. Nothing will be impossible with God. (Luke 1:37 NASB)

3. The boat was a long way from the shore. It was going against the wind and was being tossed around by the waves. A little while before morning, Jesus came walking on the water toward his disciples. When they saw him, they thought he was a ghost. They were terrified and started screaming. At once, Jesus said to them, "Don't worry! I am Jesus. Don't be afraid." (Matthew 14:24–27 CEV)

4. Jesus said to them, "Fill the waterpots with water." So they filled them up to the brim. And He said to them, "Draw some out now and take it to the head-waiter." So they took it to him. When the headwaiter tasted the water which had become wine, and did not know where it came from (but the servants who had drawn the water knew), the headwaiter called the bridegroom, and said to him, "Every man serves the good wine first, and when the people have drunk freely, then he serves the poorer wine; but you have kept the good wine until now." (John 2:7–10 NASB)

5. That evening the disciples came to him and said, "This is a remote place, and it's already getting late. Send the crowds away so they can go to the villages and buy food for themselves." But Jesus said, "That isn't necessary—you feed them." "But we have only five loaves of bread and two fish!" they answered. "Bring them here," he said. Then he told the people to sit down on the grass. Jesus took the five loaves and two fish, looked up toward heaven, and blessed them. Then, breaking the loaves into pieces, he gave the bread to the disciples, who distributed it to the people. They all ate as much as they wanted, and afterward, the disciples picked up twelve baskets of leftovers. About 5,000 men were fed that day, in addition to all the women and children! (Matthew 14:15–21 NLT)

6. To him who is able to do immeasurably more than all we ask or imagine, according to his power that is at work within us, to him be glory in the church and in Christ Jesus throughout all generations, for ever and ever! Amen. (Ephesians 3:20–21 NIV)

7. Sarah laughed to herself, saying, "After I have become old, shall I have pleasure, my lord being old also?" And the LORD said to Abraham, "Why did Sarah

laugh, saying, 'Shall I indeed bear a child, when I am so old?' Is anything too difficult for the LORD? At the appointed time I will return to you, at this time next year,
and Sarah will have a son." Sarah denied it however, saying, "I did not laugh"; for
she was afraid. And He said, "No, but you did laugh." (Genesis 18:12–15 NASB)

8.   See Exodus 7:20–12:30.

9.   They went to the Jordan and began to cut down trees. As one of them was
cutting down a tree, the iron axhead fell into the water. "Oh, my lord," he cried out,
"it was borrowed!" The man of God asked, "Where did it fall?" When he showed
him the place, Elisha cut a stick and threw it there, and made the iron float. "Lift it
out," he said. Then the man reached out his hand and took it. (2 Kings 6:4–7 NIV)

Chapter 18: Which biblical promises apply to us today?

1.   Are you tired? Worn out? Burned out on religion? Come to me. Get
away with me and you'll recover your life. I'll show you how to take a real rest.
(Matthew 11:28 MSG)

2.   You are tempted in the same way that everyone else is tempted. But God
can be trusted not to let you be tempted too much, and he will show you how to
escape from your temptations. (1 Corinthians 10:13 CEV)

3.   If any of you lacks wisdom, let him ask of God, who gives to all liberally
and without reproach, and it will be given to him. (James 1:5 NKJV)

4.   The Lord is faithful, and he will strengthen and protect you from the evil
one. (2 Thessalonians 3:3 NIV)

5.   James 4:10 NLT.

6.   If you ask Me anything in My name, I will do it. (John 14:14 NASB)

7.   I tell you, love your enemies. Help and give without expecting a return.
You'll never—I promise—regret it. Live out this God-created identity the way our
Father lives toward us, generously and graciously, even when we're at our worst.
Our Father is kind; you be kind. (Luke 6:35–36 MSG)

8.   When Jesus spoke again to the people, he said, "I am the light of the
world. Whoever follows me will never walk in darkness, but will have the light of
life." (John 8:12 NIV)

9.   The Holy Spirit will come and help you, because the Father will send the
Spirit to take my place. The Spirit will teach you everything and will remind you
of what I said while I was with you. (John 14:26 CEV)

10.   Seek first the kingdom of God and His righteousness, and all these things
shall be added to you. (Matthew 6:33 NKJV)

11.   Revelation 3:20 NIV.

12.   John 4:14 CEV.

Chapter 19: How can the Bible still be relevant?

1.   The grass withers, the flower fades, but the word of our God stands forever. (Isaiah 40:8 NKJV)

2. It was to us that God revealed these things by his Spirit. For his Spirit searches out everything and shows us God's deep secrets. No one can know a person's thoughts except that person's own spirit, and no one can know God's thoughts except God's own Spirit. And we have received God's Spirit (not the world's spirit), so we can know the wonderful things God has freely given us. (1 Corinthians 2:10–12 NLT)

3. God lives fully in Christ. (Colossians 2:9 CEV)

4. It was by faith that Abraham obeyed when God called him to leave home and go to another land that God would give him as his inheritance. He went without knowing where he was going . . . And so a whole nation came from this one man who was as good as dead—a nation with so many people that, like the stars in the sky and the sand on the seashore, there is no way to count them. (Hebrews 11:8, 12 NLT)

5. To the woman He said, "I will greatly multiply your pain in childbirth, in pain you will bring forth children; yet your desire will be for your husband, and he will rule over you." Then to Adam He said, "Because you have listened to the voice of your wife, and have eaten from the tree about which I commanded you, saying, 'You shall not eat from it'; cursed is the ground because of you; in toil you will eat of it all the days of your life. Both thorns and thistles it shall grow for you; and you will eat the plants of the field; by the sweat of your face you will eat bread, till you return to the ground, because from it you were taken; for you are dust, and to dust you shall return." (Genesis 3:16–19 NASB)

6. Adam slept with Eve his wife. She conceived and had Cain. She said, "I've gotten a man, with GOD's help!" Then she had another baby, Abel. Abel was a herdsman and Cain a farmer. (Genesis 4:1–2 MSG)

7. Jesus said to her, "Your brother will rise again." (John 11:23 NIV)

Chapter 20: What can Bible women teach us?

1. If the king agrees, let him pronounce a royal ruling . . . that Vashti is permanently banned from King Xerxes' presence. (Esther 1:19 MSG)

2. Mordecai had a cousin named Hadassah, whom he had brought up because she had neither father nor mother. This girl, who was also known as Esther, was lovely in form and features, and Mordecai had taken her as his own daughter when her father and mother died. (Esther 2:7 NIV)

3. Esther had not revealed her people or family, for Mordecai had charged her not to reveal it. (Esther 2:10 NKJV)

4. If you remain silent at this time, relief and deliverance for the Jews will arise from another place, but you and your father's family will perish. And who knows but that you have come to royal position for such a time as this? (Esther 4:14 NIV.)

5. Judges 4:6–16. In verse 8, Barak, the Israelite army commander, told Deborah, "If you go with me, I will go; but if you don't go with me, I won't go" (NIV).

6. Deborah said to Barak, "Go! This is the day the LORD has given Sisera into your hands. Has not the LORD gone ahead of you?" (Judges 4:14 NIV)

7. If we claim to know him and don't obey him, we are lying and the truth isn't in our hearts. (1 John 2:4 CEV)

8. See Judges 4:14 in note 6, Deborah's second command and reminder to Barak.

9. In Your presence is fullness of joy; at Your right hand are pleasures forevermore. (Psalm 16:11 NKJV)

Chapter 21: Is there a purpose to life?

1. You are worthy, O Lord our God, to receive glory and honor and power. For you created all things, and they exist because you created what you pleased. (Revelation 4:11 NLT); All things were created by him and for him. (Colossians 1:16 NIV)

2. Psalm 73:25 NLT.

3. God knew what he was doing from the very beginning. He decided from the outset to shape the lives of those who love him along the same lines as the life of his Son. The Son stands first in the line of humanity he restored. We see the original and intended shape of our lives there in him. (Romans 8:29 MSG)

4. Don't be like the people of this world, but let God change the way you think. Then you will know how to do everything that is good and pleasing to him. (Romans 12:2 CEV)

5. We all, with unveiled face, beholding as in a mirror the glory of the Lord, are being transformed into the same image from glory to glory, just as by the Spirit of the Lord. (2 Corinthians 3:18 NKJV)

6. All of us who have had that veil removed can see and reflect the glory of the Lord. And the Lord—who is the Spirit—makes us more and more like him as we are changed into his glorious image. (2 Corinthians 3:18 NLT); My children, I am in terrible pain until Christ may be seen living in you. (Galatians 4:19 CEV); He handed out gifts of apostle, prophet, evangelist, and pastor-teacher to train Christ's followers in skilled servant work, working within Christ's body, the church, until we're all moving rhythmically and easily with each other, efficient and graceful in response to God's Son, fully mature adults, fully developed within and without, fully alive like Christ. (Ephesians 4:11–13 MSG)

7. Christ encourages you, and his love comforts you. God's Spirit unites you, and you are concerned for others. Now make me completely happy! Live in harmony by showing love for each other. Be united in what you think, as if you were only one person. Don't be jealous or proud, but be humble and consider others more important than yourselves. Care about them as much as you care about yourselves and think the same way that Christ Jesus thought: Christ was truly God. But he did not try to remain equal with God. He gave up everything and became a slave, when he became like one of us. Christ was humble. He obeyed God and even died on a cross. Then God gave Christ the highest place and

honored his name above all others. So at the name of Jesus everyone will bow down, those in heaven, on earth, and under the earth. And to the glory of God the Father everyone will openly agree, "Jesus Christ is Lord!" My dear friends, you always obeyed when I was with you. Now that I am away, you should obey even more. So work with fear and trembling to discover what it really means to be saved. God is working in you to make you willing and able to obey him. (Philippians 2:1–13 CEV)

8. Philippians 2:12–13 NLT.

9. See Matthew 9:10–17; 26:20–30; Luke 7:36–50; 11:37–54; 14:1–24; John 12:1–8.

10. The Friend, the Holy Spirit whom the Father will send at my request, will make everything plain to you. He will remind you of all the things I have told you. (John 14:26 MSG); It is not you who speak, but it is the Spirit of your Father who speaks in you. (Matthew 10:20 NASB); The One that God sent speaks God's words. And don't think he rations out the Spirit in bits and pieces. (John 3:34 MSG)

Chapter 22: How do we know what You want?

1. Here's what I want you to do, God helping you: Take your everyday, ordinary life—your sleeping, eating, going-to-work, and walking-around life—and place it before God as an offering. Embracing what God does for you is the best thing you can do for him. Don't become so well-adjusted to your culture that you fit into it without even thinking. Instead, fix your attention on God. You'll be changed from the inside out. Readily recognize what he wants from you, and quickly respond to it. Unlike the culture around you, always dragging you down to its level of immaturity, God brings the best out of you, develops well-formed maturity in you. (Romans 12:1–2 MSG)

2. New Testament scholar Richard Bauckham and others maintain that Paul's repeated emphasis on the consistent oral tradition handed down from the disciples and eyewitnesses gave him such credibility that believers considered what he wrote to be a continuation of that tradition and therefore worth remembering.

3. Do not be conformed to this world, but be transformed by the renewing of your mind, so that you may prove what the will of God is, that which is good and acceptable and perfect. (Romans 12:2 NASB)

4. He found a Jew named Aquila, a native of Pontus, having recently come from Italy with his wife Priscilla, because Claudius had commanded all the Jews to leave Rome. He came to them, and because he was of the same trade, he stayed with them and they were working, for by trade they were tent-makers. (Acts 18:2–3 NASB)

5. Your old life is dead. Your new life, which is your *real* life—even though invisible to spectators—is with Christ in God. *He* is your life. (Colossians 3:3 MSG)

6. They know the truth about God because he has made it obvious to them. For ever since the world was created, people have seen the earth and sky.

Through everything God made, they can clearly see his invisible qualities—his eternal power and divine nature. So they have no excuse for not knowing God. (Romans 1:19–20 NLT)

7.   They don't worship the glorious and eternal God. Instead, they worship idols that are made to look like humans who cannot live forever, and like birds, animals, and reptiles. (Romans 1:23 CEV)

8.   Long ago when the judges ruled Israel, there was a shortage of food in the land. So a man named Elimelech left the town of Bethlehem in Judah to live in the country of Moab with his wife and his two sons. (Ruth 1:1–2 NCV)

9.   Where you go, I will go. Where you live, I will live. Your people will be my people, and your God will be my God. (Ruth 1:16 NCV)

10.   The Old Testament book of Judges.

Chapter 23: Can we ever be free of guilt?

1.   Where is the god who can compare with you—wiping the slate clean of guilt, turning a blind eye, a deaf ear, to the past sins of your purged and precious people? You don't nurse your anger and don't stay angry long, for mercy is your specialty. That's what you love most. And compassion is on its way to us. You'll stamp out our wrongdoing. You'll sink our sins to the bottom of the ocean. (Micah 7:18–19 MSG)

2.   If we admit our sins—make a clean breast of them—he won't let us down; he'll be true to himself. He'll forgive our sins and purge us of all wrongdoing. (1 John 1:9 MSG)

3.   Even if we don't feel at ease, God is greater than our feelings, and he knows everything. (1 John 3:20 CEV)

4.   Let us draw near with a true heart in full assurance of faith, having our hearts sprinkled from an evil conscience and our bodies washed with pure water. (Hebrews 10:22 NKJV)

5.   Romans 6:14 NLT.

6.   Peter came to him and asked, "Lord, how often should I forgive someone who sins against me? Seven times?" "No, not seven times," Jesus replied, "but seventy times seven!" (Matthew 18:21–22 NLT)

Chapter 24: Jesus, what does following You involve?

1.   "Who do you say I am?" Peter replied, "You are the Messiah." (Mark 8:29 NLT); The first thing Andrew did was to find his brother Simon and tell him, "We have found the Messiah" (that is, the Christ). (John 1:41 NIV)

2.   Anyone who intends to come with me has to let me lead. You're not in the driver's seat; I am. Don't run from suffering; embrace it. Follow me and I'll show you how. Self-help is no help at all. Self-sacrifice is the way, my way, to saving yourself, your true self. What good would it do to get everything you

want and lose you, the real you? What could you ever trade your soul for? (Mark 8:34–37 MSG)

3. I consider that the sufferings of this present time are not worthy to be compared with the glory that is to be revealed to us. (Romans 8:18 NASB)

4. God's kingdom isn't about eating and drinking. It is about pleasing God, about living in peace, and about true happiness. All this comes from the Holy Spirit. (Romans 14:17 CEV)

5. Just think—you don't need a thing, you've got it all! All God's gifts are right in front of you as you wait expectantly for our Master Jesus to arrive on the scene for the Finale. And not only that, but God himself is right alongside to keep you steady and on track until things are all wrapped up by Jesus. God, who got you started in this spiritual adventure, shares with us the life of his Son and our Master Jesus. He will never give up on you. Never forget that. (1 Corinthians 1:7–9 MSG)

6. Again I say to you, it is easier for a camel to go through the eye of a needle, than for a rich man to enter the kingdom of God. (Matthew 19:24 NASB)

7. How can you say, "My friend, let me take the speck out of your eye," when you don't see the log in your own eye? You showoffs! First, get the log out of your own eye. Then you can see how to take the speck out of your friend's eye. (Luke 6:42 CEV)

8. Luke 14:26–27 NKJV.

Chapter 25—God, do You really forgive and forget?

1. You have burdened Me with your sins, you have wearied Me with your iniquities. I, even I, am He who blots out your transgressions for My own sake; and I will not remember your sins. (Isaiah 43:24–25 NKJV)

2. Micah 6:3 NIV.

3. Who is a God like You, who pardons iniquity and passes over the rebellious act of the remnant of His possession? He does not retain His anger forever, because He delights in unchanging love. He will again have compassion on us; He will tread our iniquities under foot. Yes, You will cast all their sins into the depths of the sea. (Micah 7:18–19 NASB)

4. Psalm 103:11–12 NASB.

5. Because Your lovingkindness is better than life, my lips shall praise You. (Psalm 63:3 NKJV)

6. Jeremiah 31:34 NLT.

7. There is not a just man on earth who does good and does not sin. (Ecclesiastes 7:20 NKJV); If we claim to be without sin, we deceive ourselves and the truth is not in us. (1 John 1:8 NIV); All of us have sinned and fallen short of God's glory. (Romans 3:23 CEV)

8. The Lord is not slack concerning His promise, as some count slackness, but is longsuffering toward us, not willing that any should perish but that all should come to repentance. (2 Peter 3:9 NKJV)

9. Luke 7:44–47 MSG.

10. Luke 7:48 MSG.

11. The story of the town harlot is found in Luke 7:36–50. Direct quotations are taken from The Message (MSG).

Chapter 26: Do we have to go to church?

1. Encourage each other and give each other strength, just as you are doing now. (1 Thessalonians 5:11 NCV)

2. Care for the flock that God has entrusted to you. Watch over it willingly, not grudgingly—not for what you will get out of it, but because you are eager to serve God. (1 Peter 5:2 NLT)

3. Be responsive to your pastoral leaders. Listen to their counsel. They are alert to the condition of your lives and work under the strict supervision of God. Contribute to the joy of their leadership, not its drudgery. Why would you want to make things harder for them? (Hebrews 13:17 MSG)

4. With a loud command and with the shout of the chief angel and a blast of God's trumpet, the Lord will return from heaven. Then those who had faith in Christ before they died will be raised to life. Next, all of us who are still alive will be taken up into the clouds together with them to meet the Lord in the sky. From that time on we will all be with the Lord forever. Encourage each other with these words. Encourage each other with these words. (1 Thessalonians 4:16–18 CEV)

5. If you have sinned, you should tell each other what you have done. Then you can pray for one another and be healed. The prayer of an innocent person is powerful, and it can help a lot. (James 5:16 CEV)

6. We loved you so much that we shared with you not only God's Good News but our own lives, too. Don't you remember, dear brothers and sisters, how hard we worked among you? Night and day we toiled to earn a living so that we would not be a burden to any of you as we preached God's Good News to you. (1 Thessalonians 2:8–9 NLT)

Chapter 27: What about women in ministry?

1. It happened, when the king heard the words of the Book of the Law, that he tore his clothes. Then the king commanded Hilkiah the priest, Ahikam the son of Shaphan, Achbor the son of Michaiah, Shaphan the scribe, and Asaiah a servant of the king, saying, "Go, inquire of the LORD for me, for the people and for all Judah, concerning the words of this book that has been found; for great is the wrath of the LORD that is aroused against us, because our fathers have not obeyed the words of this book, to do according to all that is written concerning us." (2 Kings 22:11–13 NKJV)

2. Hilkiah the priest, Ahikam, Achbor, Shaphan, and Asaiah went to Huldah the prophetess, the wife of Shallum the son of Tikvah, the son of Harhas, keeper of the wardrobe. (She dwelt in Jerusalem in the Second Quarter.) And they spoke with her. (2 Kings 22:14 NKJV)

3. She said to them, "Thus says the LORD God of Israel, 'Tell the man who sent you to Me, "Thus says the LORD: 'Behold, I will bring calamity on this place and on its inhabitants—all the words of the book which the king of Judah has read—because they have forsaken Me and burned incense to other gods, that they might provoke Me to anger with all the works of their hands. Therefore My wrath shall be aroused against this place and shall not be quenched.'"' But as for the king of Judah, who sent you to inquire of the LORD, in this manner you shall speak to him, 'Thus says the LORD God of Israel: "Concerning the words which you have heard—because your heart was tender, and you humbled your-self before the LORD when you heard what I spoke against this place and against its inhabitants, that they would become a desolation and a curse, and you tore your clothes and wept before Me, I also have heard you," says the LORD. "Surely, therefore, I will gather you to your fathers, and you shall be gathered to your grave in peace; and your eyes shall not see all the calamity which I will bring on this place."'" So they brought back word to the king." (2 Kings 22:15–20 NKJV)

4. There was a prophetess, Anna the daughter of Phanuel, of the tribe of Asher. She was advanced in years and had lived with her husband seven years after her marriage. (Luke 2:36 NASB); On the next day we left and came to Caesarea, and entering the house of Philip the evangelist, who was one of the seven, we stayed with him. Now this man had four virgin daughters who were prophetesses. (Acts 21:8–9 NASB)

5. Joel the prophet wrote about what is happening here today: "God says: In the last days I will pour out my Spirit on all kinds of people. Your sons and daughters will prophesy. Your young men will see visions, and your old men will dream dreams. At that time I will pour out my Spirit also on my male slaves and female slaves, and they will prophesy." (Acts 2:16–18 NCV)

6. You are all sons of God through faith in Christ Jesus. For as many of you as were baptized into Christ have put on Christ. There is neither Jew nor Greek, there is neither slave nor free, there is neither male nor female, for you are all one in Christ Jesus. (Galatians 3:26–28 NKJV)

7. 1 Timothy 2:12 NLT.

8. 1 Timothy 5:23 NIV.

9. I have not shunned to declare to you the whole counsel of God. (Acts 20:27 NKJV)

10. God has revealed it to us by his Spirit. (1 Corinthians 2:10 NIV)

11. A vision appeared to Paul in the night: a man of Macedonia was standing and appealing to him, and saying, "Come over to Macedonia and help us." (Acts 16:9 NASB)

12. On the Sabbath we went outside the city gate to the river, where we expected to find a place of prayer. We sat down and began to speak to the women who had gathered there. (Acts 16:13 NIV)

13. A certain woman named Lydia heard us. She was a seller of purple from the city of Thyatira, who worshiped God. The Lord opened her heart to heed the things spoken by Paul. (Acts 16:14 NKJV)

14. When they came out of the jail, they went to Lydia's house where they saw some of the believers and encouraged them. Then they left. (Acts 16:40 NCV)

15. At that hour of the night the jailer took Paul and Silas and washed their wounds. Then he and all his people were baptized immediately. (Acts 16:33 NCV)

Chapter 28: How can we do it all?

1. She had a sister, Mary, who sat before the Master, hanging on every word he said. (Luke 10:39 MSG)

2. Martha was pulled away by all she had to do in the kitchen. Later, she stepped in, interrupting them. "Master, don't you care that my sister has abandoned the kitchen to me? Tell her to lend me a hand." (Luke 10:40 MSG)

3. Luke 10:41 MSG.

4. Only one thing is needed. Mary has chosen what is better, and it will not be taken away from her. (Luke 10:42 NIV)

5. The faith which you have, have as your own conviction before God. Happy is he who does not condemn himself in what he approves. (Romans 14:22 NASB)

6. My yoke is easy, and My burden is light. (Matthew 11:30 NIV)

7. The thief comes only to steal and kill and destroy; I came that they may have life, and have it abundantly. (John 10:10 NASB)

8. A thief comes only to rob, kill, and destroy. I came so that everyone would have life, and have it in its fullest. (John 10:10 CEV)

Chapter 29: How can we stop worrying so much?

1. I sought the LORD, and He answered me, and delivered me from all my fears." (Psalm 34:4 NASB)

2. Worry weighs a person down; an encouraging word cheers a person up. (Proverbs 12:25 NLT)

3. Do not be wise in your own eyes; fear the LORD and depart from evil, It will be health to your flesh, and strength to your bones. (Proverbs 3:7–8 NKJV)

4. It is useless for you to work so hard from early morning until late at night, anxiously working for food to eat; for God gives rest to his loved ones. (Psalm 127:2 NLT)

5. Trust in the LORD with all your heart and lean not on your own understanding; in all your ways acknowledge him, and he will make your paths straight. (Proverbs 3:5–6 NIV)

6. All your children shall be taught by the LORD, and great shall be the peace of your children. (Isaiah 54:13 ESV)

7. Train up a child in the way he should go; even when he is old he will not depart from it. (Proverbs 22:6 ESV)

8. My God will supply every need of yours according to his riches in glory in Christ Jesus. (Philippians 4:19 ESV)

9. There is great gain in godliness with contentment, for we brought nothing

into the world, and we cannot take anything out of the world. But if we have food and clothing, with these we will be content. (1 Timothy 6:6–8 ESV); Keep your life free from love of money, and be content with what you have, for he has said, "I will never leave you nor forsake you." (Hebrews 13:5 ESV)

10. Is anyone thirsty? Come and drink—even if you have no money! Come, take your choice of wine or milk—it's all free! Why spend your money on food that does not give you strength? Why pay for food that does you no good? Listen to me, and you will eat what is good. You will enjoy the finest food. (Isaiah 55:1–2 NLT)

11. The LORD is on my side; I will not fear. What can man do to me? The LORD is on my side as my helper; I shall look in triumph on those who hate me. It is better to take refuge in the LORD than to trust in man. It is better to take refuge in the LORD than to trust in princes. (Psalm 118:6–9 ESV)

12. Why are you downcast, O my soul? Why so disturbed within me? Put your hope in God, for I will yet praise him, my Savior and my God. (Psalm 42:5 NIV)

13. This is the confidence that we have toward him, that if we ask anything according to his will he hears us. And if we know that he hears us in whatever we ask, we know that we have the requests that we have asked of him. (1 John 5:14–15 ESV)

14. I tell you not to worry about your life. Don't worry about having something to eat, drink, or wear. Isn't life more than food or clothing? Look at the birds in the sky! They don't plant or harvest. They don't even store grain in barns. Yet your Father in heaven takes care of them. Aren't you worth more than birds? (Matthew 6:25–26 CEV)

15. Why are you anxious about clothing? Consider the lilies of the field, how they grow: they neither toil nor spin, yet I tell you, even Solomon in all his glory was not arrayed like one of these. But if God so clothes the grass of the field, which today is alive and tomorrow is thrown into the oven, will he not much more clothe you, O you of little faith? (Matthew 6:28–30 ESV)

16. Can worry make you live longer? (Matthew 6:27 CEV)

17. Seek first the kingdom of God and his righteousness, and all these things will be added to you (Matthew 6:33 ESV)

18. Do not be anxious about tomorrow, for tomorrow will be anxious for itself. Sufficient for the day is its own trouble. (Matthew 6:34 ESV)

19. Go and announce to them that the Kingdom of Heaven is near. Heal the sick, raise the dead, cure those with leprosy, and cast out demons. Give as freely as you have received! (Matthew 10:7–8 NLT)

20. When you are arrested, don't worry about how to respond or what to say. God will give you the right words at the right time. For it is not you who will be speaking—it will be the Spirit of your Father speaking through you. (Matthew 10:19–20 NLT)

21. Don't spend all of your time thinking about eating or drinking or worrying about life. If you do, the final day will suddenly catch you. (Luke 21:34 CEV)

22. Don't fret or worry. Instead of worrying, pray. Let petitions and praises

shape your worries into prayers, letting God know your concerns. Before you know it, a sense of God's wholeness, everything coming together for good, will come and settle you down. It's wonderful what happens when Christ displaces worry at the center of your life. (Philippians 4:6–7 MSG)

23. Hope does not disappoint, because the love of God has been poured out within our hearts through the Holy Spirit who was given to us. (Romans 5:5 NASB)

24. God cares for you, so turn all your worries over to him. (1 Peter 5:7 CEV)

Chapter 30: Is it possible to find genuine peace?

1. I ask Euodia and Syntyche to agree in the Lord. And I ask you, my faithful friend, to help these women. They served with me in telling the Good News, together with Clement and others who worked with me, whose names are written in the book of life. (Philippians 4:2–3 NCV)

2. Christ encourages you, and his love comforts you. God's Spirit unites you, and you are concerned for others. Now make me completely happy! Live in harmony by showing love for each other. Be united in what you think, as if you were only one person. Don't be jealous or proud, but be humble and consider others more important than yourselves. Care about them as much as you care about yourselves. (Philippians 2:1–4 CEV)

3. If one part suffers, every part suffers with it; if one part is honored, every part rejoices with it. (1 Corinthians 12:26 NIV)

4. Let everyone see that you are gentle and kind. The Lord is coming soon. (Philippians 4:5 NCV)

5. Do not worry about anything, but pray and ask God for everything you need, always giving thanks. (Philippians 4:6 NCV)

6. God's peace, which is so great we cannot understand it, will keep your hearts and minds in Christ Jesus. (Philippians 4:7 NCV)

7. Brothers and sisters, think about the things that are good and worthy of praise. Think about the things that are true and honorable and right and pure and beautiful and respected. (Philippians 4:8 NCV)

8. Do what you learned and received from me, what I told you, and what you saw me do. And the God who gives peace will be with you. (Philippians 4:9 NCV)

9. When Jesus heard about it he said, "Lazarus's sickness will not end in death. No, it happened for the glory of God so that the Son of God will receive glory from this." (John 11:4 NLT)

10. John 11:16 NKJV.

11. This story is found in John 11:17–44.

12. The next day the large crowd that had come to the feast heard that Jesus was coming to Jerusalem. So they took branches of palm trees and went out to meet him, crying out, "Hosanna! Blessed is he who comes in the name of the Lord, even the King of Israel!" And Jesus found a young donkey and sat on it, just as it is written, "Fear not, daughter of Zion; behold, your king is coming, sitting on a donkey's colt!" (John 12:12–15 ESV)

13. Do not let your heart be troubled; believe in God, believe also in Me. (John 14:1 NASB)

14. Peace I leave with you; my peace I give to you. Not as the world gives do I give to you. Let not your hearts be troubled, neither let them be afraid. (John 14:27 ESV)

15. When the Helper comes, whom I shall send to you from the Father, the Spirit of truth who proceeds from the Father, He will testify of Me. (John 15:26 NKJV)

16. I have said these things to you, that in me you may have peace. In the world you will have tribulation. But take heart; I have overcome the world. (John 16:33 ESV)

17. Let the peace of God rule in your hearts, to which also you were called in one body; and be thankful. (Colossians 3:15 NKJV)

Chapter 31: How can we share our faith inoffensively?

1. Love is patient and kind. Love is not jealous, it does not brag, and it is not proud. Love is not rude, is not selfish, and does not get upset with others. Love does not count up wrongs that have been done. Love takes no pleasure in evil but rejoices over the truth. Love patiently accepts all things. It always trusts, always hopes, and always endures. (1 Corinthians 13:4–7 NCV)

2. He will be as a sanctuary, but a stone of stumbling and a rock of offense to both the houses of Israel, as a trap and a snare to the inhabitants of Jerusalem. (Isaiah 8:14 NKJV)

3. As it is written, "Behold, I lay in Zion a stone of stumbling and a rock of offense, and he who believes in Him will not be disappointed." (Romans 9:33 NASB)

4. We preach Christ crucified, to the Jews a stumbling block and to the Greeks foolishness. (1 Corinthians 1:23 NKJV)

5. Whatever you do, do it all for the glory of God. Don't give offense to Jews or Gentiles or the church of God. I, too, try to please everyone in everything I do. I don't just do what is best for me; I do what is best for others so that many may be saved. (1 Corinthians 10:31–33 NLT)

6. Even though I am free of the demands and expectations of everyone, I have voluntarily become a servant to any and all in order to reach a wide range of people: religious, nonreligious, meticulous moralists, loose-living immoralists, the defeated, the demoralized—whoever. I didn't take on their way of life. I kept my bearings in Christ—but I entered their world and tried to experience things from their point of view. I've become just about every sort of servant there is in my attempts to lead those I meet into a God-saved life. I did all this because of the Message. I didn't just want to talk about it; I wanted to be *in* on it! (1 Corinthians 9:19–23 MSG)

7. He went to the Jewish meeting place to speak to the Jews and to anyone who worshiped with them. Day after day he also spoke to everyone he met in the market. (Acts 17:17 CEV)

8.   They took him and brought him to the Areopagus, saying, "May we know what this new teaching is which you are proclaiming?" (Acts 17:19 NASB)

9.   As I was going through your city and looking at the things you worship, I found an altar with the words, "To an Unknown God." You worship this God, but you don't really know him. So I want to tell you about him. This God made the world and everything in it. He is Lord of heaven and earth, and he doesn't live in temples built by human hands. (Acts 17:23–24 CEV)

10.   In Him we live and move and have our being, as also some of your own poets have said, "For we are also His offspring." (Acts 17:28 NKJV)

11.   When the people heard about Jesus being raised from the dead, some of them laughed. But others said, "We will hear more about this from you later." So Paul went away from them. But some of the people believed Paul and joined him. Among those who believed was Dionysius, a member of the Areopagus, a woman named Damaris, and some others. (Acts 17:32–34 NCV)

12.   Walk in wisdom toward those who are outside, redeeming the time. Let your speech always be with grace, seasoned with salt, that you may know how you ought to answer each one. (Colossians 4:5–6 NKJV); Always be prepared to give an answer to everyone who asks you to give the reason for the hope that you have. But do this with gentleness and respect. (1 Peter 3:15 NIV)

13.   See the stories of the prostitute in Luke 7:36–50 and of Zacchaeus, a despised tax collector in Luke 19:1–10.

14.   You will know the truth, and the truth will set you free. (John 8:32 CEV)

15.   Live clean, innocent lives as children of God, shining like bright lights in a world full of crooked and perverse people. (Philippians 2:15 NLT); Here's another way to put it: You're here to be light, bringing out the God-colors in the world. God is not a secret to be kept. We're going public with this, as public as a city on a hill. If I make you light-bearers, you don't think I'm going to hide you under a bucket, do you? I'm putting you on a light stand. Now that I've put you there on a hilltop, on a light stand—shine! Keep open house; be generous with your lives. By opening up to others, you'll prompt people to open up with God, this generous Father in heaven. (Matthew 5:14–16 MSG)

Chapter 32: God, how can we know You're listening?

1.   "Can anyone hide from me in a secret place? Am I not everywhere in all the heavens and earth?" says the LORD. (Jeremiah 23:24 NLT)

2.   Blessed are those you choose and bring near to live in your courts! We are filled with the good things of your house, of your holy temple. (Psalm 65:4 NIV)

3.   The LORD is near to the brokenhearted and saves those who are crushed in spirit. (Psalm 34:18 NASB)

4.   The LORD is near to all who call on him, to all who call on him in truth. (Psalm 145:18 NIV).

5.   Psalm 55:17 NLT.

6.   Psalm 34:17 NKJV.

7. This is the confidence which we have before Him, that, if we ask anything according to His will, He hears us. (1 John 5:14 NASB)

8. Pray without ceasing. (1 Thessalonians 5:17 NKJV)

9. When you pray, say: "Father, hallowed be your name, your kingdom come. Give us each day our daily bread. Forgive us our sins, for we also forgive everyone who sins against us. And lead us not into temptation." (Luke 6:2–4 NIV)

10. Jesus wept. So the Jews were saying, "See how He loved him!" But some of them said, "Could not this man, who opened the eyes of the blind man, have kept this man also from dying?" (John 11:35–37 NASB)

11. Jesus said, "Remove the stone." Martha, the sister of the deceased, said to Him, "Lord, by this time there will be a stench, for he has been dead four days." Jesus said to her, "Did I not say to you that if you believe, you will see the glory of God?" (John 11:39–40 NASB)

12. John 11:41–43 NASB.

13. The man who had died came forth, bound hand and foot with wrappings, and his face was wrapped around with a cloth. Jesus said to them, "Unbind him, and let him go." (John 11:44 NASB)

14. The chief priests and the Pharisees convened a council, and were saying, "What are we doing? For this man is performing many signs." (John 11:47 NASB)

15. In the same way, the Spirit helps us in our weakness. We do not know what we ought to pray for, but the Spirit himself intercedes for us with groans that words cannot express. (Romans 8:26 NIV)

16. Who is he that condemns? Christ Jesus, who died—more than that, who was raised to life—is at the right hand of God and is also interceding for us. (Romans 8:34 NIV)

Chapter 33: Do You hear everybody's prayers?

1. "When I called, they did not listen; so when they called, I would not listen," says the LORD Almighty. (Zechariah 7:13 NIV)

2. I scattered them with a whirlwind among all the nations which they had not known. Thus the land became desolate after them, so that no one passed through or returned; for they made the pleasant land desolate. (Zechariah 7:14 NKJV)

3. The eyes of the Lord are on the righteous, and his ears are open to their prayer. But the face of the Lord is against those who do evil. (1 Peter 3:12 ESV)

4. If I had cherished sin in my heart, the Lord would not have listened. (Psalm 66:18 NIV)

5. The LORD is far from the wicked but he hears the prayer of the righteous. (Proverbs 15:29 NIV)

6. Peter opened his mouth and said: "Truly I understand that God shows no partiality, but in every nation anyone who fears him and does what is right is acceptable to him." (Acts 10:34–35 ESV)

7. So it was, when Ahab heard those words, that he tore his clothes and put

sackcloth on his body, and fasted and lay in sackcloth, and went about mourning. (1 Kings 21:27 NKJV)

8.   I, the LORD, search the heart, I test the mind, even to give to each man according to his ways, according to the results of his deeds. (Jeremiah 17:10 NASB)

9.   At Iconium Paul and Barnabas went as usual into the Jewish synagogue. There they spoke so effectively that a great number of Jews and Gentiles believed. (Acts 14:1 NIV)

10.   At Caesarea there was a man named Cornelius, a centurion in what was known as the Italian Regiment. He and all his family were devout and God-fearing; he gave generously to those in need and prayed to God regularly. (Acts 10:1–2 NIV)

11.   While Peter was still thinking about the vision, the Spirit said to him, "Simon, three men are looking for you. So get up and go downstairs. Do not hesitate to go with them, for I have sent them." (Acts 10:19–20 NIV)

12.   Acts 10:31 NIV.

13.   While Peter was still speaking these words, the Holy Spirit came on all who heard the message . . . The gift of the Holy Spirit had been poured out even on the Gentiles. For they heard them speaking in tongues and praising God. Then Peter said, "Can anyone keep these people from being baptized with water? They have received the Holy Spirit just as we have." So he ordered that they be baptized in the name of Jesus Christ. (Acts 10:44–48 NIV)

14.   The apostles and brethren who were in Judea heard that the Gentiles had also received the word of God. And when Peter came up to Jerusalem, those of the circumcision contended with him, saying, "You went in to uncircumcised men and ate with them!" (Acts 11:1–3 NKJV)

15.   When they heard these things they became silent; and they glorified God, saying, "Then God has also granted to the Gentiles repentance to life." (Acts 11:18 NKJV)

Chapter 34: Why aren't some prayers answered?

1.   The LORD's hand is not shortened, that it cannot save; nor His ear heavy, that it cannot hear. But your iniquities have separated you from your God; and your sins have hidden His face from you, so that He will not hear. (Isaiah 59:1–2 NKJV)

2.   If we confess our sins, He is faithful and righteous to forgive us our sins and to cleanse us from all unrighteousness. (1 John 1:9 NASB)

3.   When they cry out, God does not answer because of their pride. But it is wrong to say God doesn't listen, to say the Almighty isn't concerned. (Job 35:12–13 NLT)

4.   He gives us more grace. That is why Scripture says: "God opposes the proud but gives grace to the humble." Submit yourselves, then, to God. Resist the devil, and he will flee from you. Come near to God and he will come near to you.

Wash your hands, you sinners, and purify your hearts, you double-minded. Grieve, mourn and wail. Change your laughter to mourning and your joy to gloom. Humble yourselves before the Lord, and he will lift you up. (James 4:6–10 NIV)

5.   Whoever shuts his ears to the cry of the poor will also cry himself and not be heard. (Proverbs 21:13 NKJV)

6.   Be good husbands to your wives. Honor them, delight in them. As women they lack some of your advantages. But in the new life of God's grace, you're equals. Treat your wives, then, as equals so your prayers don't run aground. (1 Peter 3:7 MSG)

7.   You do not have because you do not ask. (James 4:2 NASB)

8.   This is the confidence we have in approaching God: that if we ask anything according to his will, he hears us. And if we know that he hears us—whatever we ask—we know that we have what we asked of him. (1 John 5:14–15 NIV)

9.   If God is for us, who can be against us? He who did not spare His own Son, but delivered Him up for us all, how shall He not with Him also freely give us all things? (Romans 8:31–32 NKJV)

10.   If any of you lacks wisdom, let him ask God, who gives generously to all without reproach, and it will be given him. But let him ask in faith, with no doubting, for the one who doubts is like a wave of the sea that is driven and tossed by the wind. For that person must not suppose that he will receive anything from the Lord. (James 1:5–7 ESV)

11.   We walk by faith, not by sight. (2 Corinthians 5:7 NASB)

12.   We know that in all things God works for the good of those who love him, who have been called according to his purpose. (Romans 8:28 NIV)

13.   God can do anything, you know—far more than you could ever imagine or guess or request in your wildest dreams! He does it not by pushing us around but by working within us, his Spirit deeply and gently within us. (Ephesians 3:20 MSG)

14.   Even before there is a word on my tongue, behold, O LORD, You know it all. (Psalm 139:4 NASB)

15.   I have loved you with an everlasting love; therefore I have drawn you with lovingkindness. (Jeremiah 31:3 NASB)

16.   The LORD is pleased only with those who worship him and trust his love. (Psalm 147:11 CEV)

17.   The LORD will wait, that He may be gracious to you; and therefore He will be exalted, that He may have mercy on you. For the LORD is a God of justice; blessed are all those who wait for Him. (Isaiah 30:18 NKJV)

18.   Our LORD and our God, you are like the sun and also like a shield. You treat us with kindness and with honor, never denying any good thing to those who live right. (Psalm 84:11 CEV)

19.   Ask, and it will be given to you; seek, and you will find; knock, and it will be opened to you. (Matthew 7:7 NASB)

20.   You can pray for anything, and if you have faith, you will receive it. (Matthew 21:22 NLT)

21. Just then a woman who had suffered for twelve years with constant bleeding came up behind him. She touched the fringe of his robe, for she thought, "If I can just touch his robe, I will be healed." Jesus turned around, and when he saw her he said, "Daughter, be encouraged! Your faith has made you well." And the woman was healed at that moment. (Matthew 9:20–22 NLT)

22. When Jesus had entered Capernaum, a centurion came to Him, pleading with Him, saying, "Lord, my servant is lying at home paralyzed, dreadfully tormented." And Jesus said to him, "I will come and heal him." The centurion answered and said, "Lord, I am not worthy that You should come under my roof. But only speak a word, and my servant will be healed. For I also am a man under authority, having soldiers under me. And I say to this *one*, 'Go,' and he goes; and to another, 'Come,' and he comes; and to my servant, 'Do this,' and he does it.'" When Jesus heard it, He marveled, and said to those who followed, "Assuredly, I say to you, I have not found such great faith, not even in Israel!" . . . Then Jesus said to the centurion, "Go your way; and as you have believed, so let it be done for you." And his servant was healed that same hour. (Matthew 8:5–10, 13 NKJV)

23. When you are praying, first forgive anyone you are holding a grudge against, so that your Father in heaven will forgive your sins, too. (Mark 11:25 NLT)

24. When you pray, don't be like the hypocrites who love to pray publicly on street corners and in the synagogues where everyone can see them. I tell you the truth, that is all the reward they will ever get. (Matthew 6:5 NLT)

25. My Father! If it is possible, let this cup of suffering be taken away from me. Yet I want your will to be done, not mine. (Matthew 26:9 NLT)

Chapter 35: Can prayer really make a difference?

1. Remember the things I have done in the past. For I alone am God! I am God, and there is none like me. Only I can tell you the future before it even happens. Everything I plan will come to pass, for I do whatever I wish. (Isaiah 46:9–10 NLT)

2. Call together everyone from Israel and have them meet me on Mount Carmel. Be sure to bring along the four hundred fifty prophets of Baal and the four hundred prophets of Asherah who eat at Jezebel's table . . . Bring us two bulls. Baal's prophets can take one of them, kill it, and cut it into pieces. Then they can put the meat on the wood without lighting the fire. I will do the same thing with the other bull, and I won't light a fire under it either. (1 Kings 18:19, 23 CEV)

3. They chose their bull, then they got it ready and prayed to Baal all morning, asking him to start the fire. They danced around the altar and shouted, "Answer us, Baal!" But there was no answer . . . The prophets kept shouting louder and louder, and they cut themselves with swords and knives until they were bleeding. This was the way they worshiped, and they kept it up all afternoon. But there was no answer of any kind. (1 Kings 18:26, 28–29 CEV)

4. "Fill four large jars with water and pour it over the meat and the wood."

After they did this, he told them to do it two more times. They did exactly as he said until finally, the water ran down the altar and filled the ditch . . . The LORD immediately sent fire, and it burned up the sacrifice, the wood, and the stones. It scorched the ground everywhere around the altar and dried up every drop of water in the ditch. (1 Kings 18:33–35, 38 CEV)

5.   When the crowd saw what had happened, they all bowed down and shouted, "The LORD is God! The LORD is God!" (1 Kings 18:39 CEV)

6.   A few minutes later, it got very cloudy and windy, and rain started pouring down. So Elijah wrapped his coat around himself, and the LORD gave him strength to run all the way to Jezreel. Ahab followed him. (1 Kings 18:45–46 CEV)

7.   I was caught up to the third heaven fourteen years ago. Whether I was in my body or out of my body, I don't know—only God knows. Yes, only God knows whether I was in my body or outside my body. But I do know that I was caught up to paradise and heard things so astounding that they cannot be expressed in words, things no human is allowed to tell. That experience is worth boasting about, but I'm not going to do it. (2 Corinthians 12:2–5 NLT)

8.   To keep me from becoming proud, I was given a thorn in my flesh, a messenger from Satan to torment me and keep me from becoming proud. (2 Corinthians 12:7 NLT)

9.   Three different times I begged the Lord to take it away. Each time he said, "My grace is all you need. My power works best in weakness." So now I am glad to boast about my weaknesses, so that the power of Christ can work through me. (2 Corinthians 12:8–9 NLT)

10.   If I wanted to boast, I would be no fool in doing so, because I would be telling the truth. But I won't do it, because I don't want anyone to give me credit beyond what they can see in my life or hear in my message. (2 Corinthians 12:6 NLT)

11.   Pray for us that God will give us an opportunity to tell people his message. Pray that we can preach the secret that God has made known about Christ. This is why I am in prison. (Colossians 4:3 NCV)

12.   He did rescue us from mortal danger, and he will rescue us again. We have placed our confidence in him, and he will continue to rescue us. And you are helping us by praying for us. Then many people will give thanks because God has graciously answered so many prayers for our safety. (2 Corinthians 1:10–11 NLT)

13.   With all prayer and petition pray at all times in the Spirit, and with this in view, be on the alert with all perseverance and petition for all the saints, and pray on my behalf, that utterance may be given to me in the opening of my mouth, to make known with boldness the mystery of the gospel, for which I am an ambassador in chains; that in proclaiming it I may speak boldly, as I ought to speak. (Ephesians 6:18–20 NASB)

14.   I know that this will turn out for my deliverance through your prayers and the provision of the Spirit of Jesus Christ, according to my earnest expectation and hope, that I will not be put to shame in anything, but that with all boldness,

Christ will even now, as always, be exalted in my body, whether by life or by death. For to me, to live is Christ and to die is gain. (Philippians 1:19–21 NASB)

15. Lord All-Powerful, see how sad I am. Remember me and don't forget me. If you will give me a son, I will give him back to you all his life, and no one will ever cut his hair with a razor. (1 Samuel 1:9–11 NCV)

16. Go! I wish you well. May the God of Israel give you what you asked of him. (1 Samuel 1:15–17 NCV)

17. "Samuel was born in answer to your prayers. Now you have given him to the LORD. I pray that the LORD will bless you with more children to take his place." After Eli had blessed them, Elkanah and Hannah would return home. The LORD was kind to Hannah, and she had three more sons and two daughters. But Samuel grew up at the LORD's house in Shiloh. (1 Samuel 2:20–21 CEV)

Chapter 36: Is there one right way to pray?

1. There is one Lord, one faith, one baptism, and one God and Father, who is over all and in all and living through all. (Ephesians 4:5–6 NLT)

2. Behold, heaven and the highest heaven cannot contain You. (2 Chronicles 6:18 NASB)

3. Where can I go to get away from your Spirit? Where can I run from you? If I go up to the heavens, you are there. If I lie down in the grave, you are there. If I rise with the sun in the east and settle in the west beyond the sea, even there you would guide me. With your right hand you would hold me. (Psalm 139:7–10 NCV)

4. When you pray, do not keep on babbling like pagans, for they think they will be heard because of their many words. Do not be like them, for your Father knows what you need before you ask him. (Matthew 6:7–8 NIV)

5. In the same way the Spirit also helps our weakness; for we do not know how to pray as we should, but the Spirit Himself intercedes for us with groanings too deep for words. (Romans 8:26 NASB)

6. When Daniel knew that the document had been signed, he went to his house where he had windows in his upper chamber open toward Jerusalem. He got down on his knees three times a day and prayed and gave thanks before his God, as he had done previously. (Daniel 6:10 ESV); Evening and morning and at noon I utter my complaint and moan, and he hears my voice. (Psalm 55:17 ESV)

7. Pray without ceasing. (1 Thessalonians 5:17 ESV)

8. Let us therefore come boldly to the throne of grace, that we may obtain mercy and find grace to help in time of need. (Hebrews 4:16 NKJV)

9. The LORD has heard my supplication; the LORD will receive my prayer. (Psalm 6:9 NKJV)

10. This is the confidence we have in approaching God: that if we ask anything according to his will, he hears us. And if we know that he hears us—whatever we ask—we know that we have what we asked of him. (1 John 5:14–15 NIV)

11. Don't worry about anything, but pray about everything. With thankful hearts offer up your prayers and requests to God. (Philippians 4:6 CEV)

12. Immediately He made His disciples get into the boat and go before Him to the other side, to Bethsaida, while He sent the multitude away. And when He had sent them away, He departed to the mountain to pray. (Mark 6:45–46 NKJV)

13. At that time Jesus went off to a mountain to pray, and he spent the night praying to God. The next morning, Jesus called his followers to him and chose twelve of them, whom he named apostles. (Luke 6:12–13 NCV)

14. When you pray, go away by yourself, shut the door behind you, and pray to your Father in private. Then your Father, who sees everything, will reward you. (Matthew 6:6 NLT)

15. I also tell you this: If two of you agree here on earth concerning anything you ask, my Father in heaven will do it for you. For where two or three gather together as my followers, I am there among them. (Matthew 18:19–20 NLT)

16. Matthew 6:9 NCV.

17. May your kingdom come and what you want be done, here on earth as it is in heaven. (Matthew 6:10 NCV)

18. Give us the food we need for each day. Forgive us for our sins, just as we have forgiven those who sinned against us. And do not cause us to be tempted, but save us from the Evil One. (Matthew 6:11–13 NCV)

19. The kingdom, the power, and the glory are yours forever. Amen. (Matthew 6:13 NCV)

20. Whatever you ask in My name, that will I do, so that the Father may be glorified in the Son. If you ask Me anything in My name, I will do it. (John 14:13–14 NASB)

21. In that day you will not question Me about anything. Truly, truly, I say to you, if you ask the Father for anything in My name, He will give it to you. Until now you have asked for nothing in My name; ask and you will receive, so that your joy may be made full. (John 16:23–24 NASB)

Chapter 38: Should we pray about only major problems?

1. The tongue is a small part of the body, and yet it boasts of great things. See how great a forest is set aflame by such a small fire! (James 3:5 NASB).

2. Water wears away stones. (Job 14:19 NASB)

3. You are children of GOD, your God. (Deuteronomy 14:1 MSG)

4. The Spirit Himself bears witness with our spirit that we are children of God. (Romans 8:16 NKJV)

5. If your children ask for a fish, which of you would give them a snake instead? Or, if your children ask for an egg, would you give them a scorpion? (Luke 11:11–12 NCV)

6. Will you sweep away both the righteous and the wicked? Suppose you find fifty righteous people living there in the city—will you still sweep it away and not spare it for their sakes? Surely you wouldn't do such a thing, destroying the righteous along with the wicked. Why, you would be treating the righteous and the wicked exactly the same! Surely you wouldn't do that! Should not the Judge of all the earth do what is right? (Genesis 18:23 25 NLT)

7. The righteous are bold as a lion. (Proverbs 28:1 NKJV)

8. How can I describe the Kingdom of God? What story should I use to illustrate it? It is like a mustard seed planted in the ground. It is the smallest of all seeds, but it becomes the largest of all garden plants; it grows long branches, and birds can make nests in its shade. (Mark 4:30–32 NLT)

9. To what shall I liken the kingdom of God? It is like leaven, which a woman took and hid in three measures of meal till it was all leavened. (Luke 13:20–21 NKJV)

10. He shall give His angels charge over you, to keep you in all your ways. In their hands they shall bear you up, lest you dash your foot against a stone. You shall tread upon the lion and the cobra, the young lion and the serpent you shall trample underfoot. (Psalm 91:11–13 NKJV)

11. Come to me, all of you who are tired and have heavy loads, and I will give you rest. Accept my teachings and learn from me, because I am gentle and humble in spirit, and you will find rest for your lives. The burden that I ask you to accept is easy; the load I give you to carry is light. (Matthew 11:28–30 NCV)

Chapter 38: Is it okay to pray repetitious prayers?

1. When you pray, do not use vain repetitions as the heathen do. For they think that they will be heard for their many words. (Matthew 6:7 NKJV)

2. Matthew 27:46 NKJV.

3. My God, My God, why have You forsaken Me? Why are You so far from helping Me, and from the words of My groaning? (Psalm 22:1 NKJV)

4. Luke 23:46 NASB.

5. Into Your hand I commit my spirit; You have ransomed me, O LORD, God of truth. (Psalm 31:5 NASB)

6. Acts 4:24–26 NKJV.

7. God, who made heaven and earth, the seas, and all that is in them. (Psalm 146:5–6 NKJV)

8. Why do the nations rage, and the people plot a vain thing? The kings of the earth set themselves, and the rulers take counsel together, against the LORD and His Anointed. (Psalm 2:1–2 NKJV)

9. Psalm 51:1–4 NLT.

10. In a town there was once a judge who didn't fear God or care about people. In that same town there was a widow who kept going to the judge and saying, "Make sure that I get fair treatment in court." For a while the judge refused to do anything. Finally, he said to himself, "Even though I don't fear God or care about people, I will help this widow because she keeps on bothering me. If I don't help her, she will wear me out." (Luke 18:2–5 CEV)

11. Think about what that crooked judge said. Won't God protect his chosen ones who pray to him day and night? Won't he be concerned for them? He will surely hurry and help them. But when the Son of Man comes, will he find on this earth anyone with faith? (Luke 18:6–8 CEV)

12.   Suppose one of you goes to a friend in the middle of the night and says, "Let me borrow three loaves of bread. A friend of mine has dropped in, and I don't have a thing for him to eat." And suppose your friend answers, "Don't bother me! The door is bolted, and my children and I are in bed. I cannot get up to give you something." He may not get up and give you the bread, just because you are his friend. But he will get up and give you as much as you need, simply because you are not ashamed to keep on asking. (Luke 11:5–8 CEV)

13.   Luke 11:9 CEV.

14.   Everyone who asks will receive, everyone who searches will find, and the door will be opened for everyone who knocks. (Luke 11:10 CEV)

Chapter 39: How can we love unlovable people?

1.   If I speak with the tongues of men and of angels, but do not have love, I have become a noisy gong or a clanging cymbal. If I have the gift of prophecy, and know all mysteries and all knowledge; and if I have all faith, so as to remove mountains, but do not have love, I am nothing. And if I give all my possessions to feed the poor, and if I surrender my body to be burned, but do not have love, it profits me nothing. Love is patient, love is kind and is not jealous; love does not brag and is not arrogant, does not act unbecomingly; it does not seek its own, is not provoked, does not take into account a wrong suffered, does not rejoice in unrighteousness, but rejoices with the truth; bears all things, believes all things, hopes all things, endures all things. Love never fails . . . But now faith, hope, love, abide these three; but the greatest of these is love. (1 Corinthians 13:1–8, 13 NASB)

2.   Love one another, just as I have loved you. (John 15:12 NASB)

3.   By this all men will know that you are My disciples, if you have love for one another. (John 13:35 NASB)

4.   Mark 12.29–31 NKJV.

5.   He, wanting to justify himself, said to Jesus, "And who is my neighbor?" (Luke 10:29 NKJV)

6.   This parable is found in Luke 10:30–37.

7.   Luke 10:37 NKJV.

Chapter 40: How can we trust anyone following betrayal?

1.   Cain talked with Abel his brother; and it came to pass, when they were in the field, that Cain rose up against Abel his brother and killed him. (Genesis 4:8 NKJV)

2.   I said, "Oh, that I had the wings of a dove! I would fly away and be at rest—I would flee far away and stay in the desert; I would hurry to my place of shelter, far from the tempest and storm." (Psalm 55:6–8 NIV)

3.   It is not an enemy who reproaches me; then I could bear it. nor is it one who hates me who has exalted himself against me; then I could hide from him

But it was you, a man my equal, my companion and my acquaintance. We took sweet counsel together, and walked to the house of God in the throng. (Psalm 55:12–14 NKJV)

4.   His speech is smooth as butter, yet war is in his heart; his words are more soothing than oil, yet they are drawn swords. (Psalm 55:21 NIV)

5.   I call to God, and the LORD saves me. Evening, morning and noon I cry out in distress, and he hears my voice. He ransoms me unharmed from the battle waged against me, even though many oppose me . . . Cast your cares on the LORD and he will sustain you; he will never let the righteous fall. But you, O God, will bring down the wicked into the pit of corruption; bloodthirsty and deceitful men will not live out half their days. But as for me, I trust in you. (Psalm 55:16–18, 22–23 NIV)

6.   He heals the brokenhearted and bandages their wounds. (Psalm 147:3 NCV)

7.   First forgive anyone you are holding a grudge against. (Mark 11:25 NLT)

8.   God . . . is able, through his mighty power at work within us, to accomplish infinitely more than we might ask or think. (Ephesians 3:20 NLT)

9.   If any of you lacks wisdom, he should ask God, who gives generously to all without finding fault, and it will be given to him. (James 1:5 NIV)

10.   [God] comforts us in all our troubles so that we can comfort others. When others are troubled, we will be able to give them the same comfort God has given us. (2 Corinthians 1:4 NLT)

11.   At that very moment, the party of high priests and religious leaders was meeting in the chambers of the Chief Priest named Caiaphas, conspiring to seize Jesus by stealth and kill him. They agreed that it should not be done during Passover Week. "We don't want a riot on our hands," they said. (Matthew 26:3–5 MSG)

12.   If the bull kills a slave, you must pay the slave owner thirty pieces of silver for the loss of the slave, and the bull must be killed by stoning. (Exodus 21:32 CEV)

13.   Judas, already turned traitor, said, "It isn't me, is it, Rabbi?" Jesus said, "Don't play games with me, Judas." (Matthew 26:25 MSG)

14.   The words were barely out of his mouth when Judas (the one from the Twelve) showed up, and with him a gang from the high priests and religious leaders brandishing swords and clubs. The betrayer had worked out a sign with them: "The one I kiss, that's the one—seize him." He went straight to Jesus, greeted him, "How are you, Rabbi?" and kissed him. Jesus said, "Friend, why this charade?" Then they came on him—grabbed him and roughed him up. (Matthew 26:47–50 MSG)

15.   "You've done it this way to confirm and fulfill the prophetic writings." Then all the disciples cut and ran. (Matthew 26:56 MSG)

16.   Bear with each other, and forgive each other. If someone does wrong to you, forgive that person because the Lord forgave you. (Colossians 3:13 NCV)

17.   In me you may have peace. In this world you will have trouble. But take heart! I have overcome the world. (John 16:33 NIV)

18. Bless those who persecute you; bless and do not curse . . . Live in harmony with one another. (Romans 12:14, 16 NIV)

19. A gentle answer turns away wrath, but a harsh word stirs up anger. (Proverbs 15:1 NASB)

20. Brothers and sisters, do not tell evil lies about each other. (James 4:11 NCV)

21. Do not repay anyone evil for evil . . . If it is possible, as far as it depends on you, live at peace with everyone. Do not take revenge . . . "I will repay," says the Lord. (Romans 12:17–19 NIV)

22. I tell you not to resist an evil person. But whoever slaps you on your right cheek, turn the other to him also. (Matthew 5:39 NKJV)

23. Just as the Father has loved Me, I have also loved you; abide in My love. (John 15:9 NASB)

24. I thank my God always concerning you for the grace of God which was given you in Christ Jesus. (1 Corinthians 1:4 NASB)

Chapter 41: How can You expect us to forgive?

1. When the LORD began speaking through Hosea, the LORD said to him, "Go, and marry an unfaithful woman and have unfaithful children, because the people in this country have been completely unfaithful to the LORD." (Hosea 1:2 NCV)

2. Behold, I will allure her, bring her into the wilderness and speak kindly to her. Then I will give her her vineyards from there, and the valley of Achor as a door of hope. And she will sing there as in the days of her youth, as in the day when she came up from the land of Egypt. (Hosea 2:14–15 NASB)

3. In that day I will also make a covenant for them with the beasts of the field, the birds of the sky and the creeping things of the ground. And I will abolish the bow, the sword and war from the land, and will make them lie down in safety. I will betroth you to Me forever; yes, I will betroth you to Me in righteousness and in justice, in lovingkindness and in compassion, and I will betroth you to Me in faithfulness . . . And I will say to those who were not My people, "You are My people!" And they will say, "You are my God!" (Hosea 2:18–20, 23 NASB)

4. I will love them lavishly. My anger is played out. I will make a fresh start with Israel. (Hosea 14:4–5 MSG)

5. Manasseh led Judah and the citizens of Jerusalem off the beaten path into practices of evil exceeding even the evil of the pagan nations that GOD had earlier destroyed. When GOD spoke to Manasseh and his people about this, they ignored him. (2 Chronicles 33:9–10 MSG)

6. Now that he was in trouble, he went to his knees in prayer asking for help—total repentance before the God of his ancestors. As he prayed, GOD was touched; GOD listened and brought him back to Jerusalem as king. That convinced Manasseh that GOD was in control. (2 Chronicles 33:12–13 MSG)

7. Be even-tempered, content with second place, quick to forgive an offense. Forgive as quickly and completely as the Master forgave you. (Colossians 3:13 MSG)

8.   In prayer there is a connection between what God does and what you do. You can't get forgiveness from God, for instance, without also forgiving others. If you refuse to do your part, you cut yourself off from God's part. (Matthew 6:14–15 MSG)

9.   Freely you have received, freely give. (Matthew 10:8 NKJV)

10.   At that point Peter got up the nerve to ask, "Master, how many times do I forgive a brother or sister who hurts me? Seven?" Jesus replied, "Seven! Hardly. Try seventy times seven." (Matthew 18:21–22 MSG)

11.   The master called his servant in and said, "You evil servant! Because you begged me to forget what you owed, I told you that you did not have to pay anything. You should have showed mercy to that other servant, just as I showed mercy to you." The master was very angry and put the servant in prison to be punished until he could pay everything he owed. (Matthew 18:32–34 NCV)

12.   Whenever you stand praying, forgive, if you have anything against anyone so that your Father who is in heaven will also forgive you your transgressions. But if you do not forgive, neither will your Father who is in heaven forgive your transgressions. (Mark 11:25–26 NASB)

13.   I say to you who are listening, love your enemies. Do good to those who hate you, bless those who curse you, pray for those who are cruel to you . . . But love your enemies, do good to them, and lend to them without hoping to get anything back. Then you will have a great reward, and you will be children of the Most High God, because he is kind even to people who are ungrateful and full of sin. Show mercy, just as your Father shows mercy. (Luke 6:27–28, 35–36 NCV)

14.   Be kind to one another, tender-hearted, forgiving each other, just as God in Christ also has forgiven you. (Ephesians 4:32 NASB)

Chapter 42: How can we have deeper friendships?

1.   My child, listen to your father's teaching and do not forget your mother's advice. Their teaching will be like flowers in your hair or a necklace around your neck. My child, if sinners try to lead you into sin, do not follow them. (Proverbs 1:8–10 NCV)

2.   You will say the wrong thing if you talk too much—so be sensible and watch what you say. (Proverbs 10:19 CEV); The tongue can bring death or life; those who love to talk will reap the consequences. (Proverbs 18:21 NLT)

3.   He who goes about as a talebearer reveals secrets, but he who is trustworthy conceals a matter. (Proverbs 11:13 NASB)

4.   Good people take advice from their friends, but an evil person is easily led to do wrong. (Proverbs 12:26 NCV); Wise friends make you wise, but you hurt yourself by going around with fools. (Proverbs 13:20 CEV)

5.   The start of an argument is like a water leak—so stop it before real trouble breaks out. (Proverbs 17:14 CEV); Pride leads to conflict; those who take advice are wise. (Proverbs 13:10 NLT); People with quick tempers cause trouble, but those who control their tempers stop a quarrel. (Proverbs 15:18 NCV)

6.   An unlucky loser is shunned by all, but everyone loves a winner. (Proverbs

14:20 MSG); Wealthy people are always finding more friends, but the poor lose all theirs . . . Many people want to please a leader, and everyone is friends with those who give gifts. (Proverbs 19:4, 6 NCV)

7.   Friends love through all kinds of weather, and families stick together in all kinds of trouble. (Proverbs 17:17 MSG); There are "friends" who destroy each other, but a real friend sticks closer than a brother. (Proverbs 18:24 NLT); Don't forget your friend or your parent's friend. Don't always go to your family for help when trouble comes. A neighbor close by is better than a family far away. (Proverbs 27:10 NCV)

8.   Follow the example of good people and live an honest life. (Proverbs 2:20 CEV); Faithful are the wounds of a friend, but deceitful are the kisses of an enemy. (Proverbs 27:6 NASB); Just as iron sharpens iron, friends sharpen the minds of each other. (Proverbs 27:17 CEV)

9.   Two people are better off than one, for they can help each other succeed. If one person falls, the other can reach out and help. But someone who falls alone is in real trouble. Likewise, two people lying close together can keep each other warm. But how can one be warm alone? A person standing alone can be attacked and defeated, but two can stand back-to-back and conquer. Three are even better, for a triple-braided cord is not easily broken. (Ecclesiastes 4:9–12 NLT)

10.   I've told you these things for a purpose: that my joy might be your joy, and your joy wholly mature. This is my command: Love one another the way I loved you. This is the very best way to love. Put your life on the line for your friends. You are my friends when you do the things I command you. I'm no longer calling you servants because servants don't understand what their master is thinking and planning. No, I've named you friends because I've let you in on everything I've heard from the Father. (John 15:11–15 MSG)

11.   When others are happy, be happy with them, and when they are sad, be sad. (Romans 12:15 CEV)

12.   You will call in your friends and neighbors and say, "Let's celebrate! I've found my lost sheep." Jesus said, "In the same way there is more happiness in heaven because of one sinner who turns to God than over ninety-nine good people who don't need to." Jesus told the people another story: What will a woman do if she has ten silver coins and loses one of them? Won't she light a lamp, sweep the floor, and look carefully until she finds it? Then she will call in her friends and neighbors and say, "Let's celebrate! I've found the coin I lost." (Luke 15:6–9 CEV)

13.   Your love must be real. Hate what is evil, and hold on to what is good. Love each other like brothers and sisters. Give each other more honor than you want for yourselves. (Romans 12:9–10 NCV); God loves you and has chosen you as his own special people. So be gentle, kind, humble, meek, and patient. Put up with each other, and forgive anyone who does you wrong, just as Christ has forgiven you. Love is more important than anything else. It is what ties everything completely together. (Colossians 3:12–14 CEV)

14.   Do not be shaped by this world; instead be changed within by a new way

of thinking. Then you will be able to decide what God wants for you; you will know what is good and pleasing to him and what is perfect. (Romans 12:2 NCV)

15. Of course, your former friends are surprised when you no longer plunge into the flood of wild and destructive things they do. So they slander you. (1 Peter 4:4 NLT)

16. Remember the root command: Love one another. (John 15:17 MSG); "I will never fail you. I will never abandon you." So we can say with confidence, "The LORD is my helper, so I will have no fear. What can mere people do to me?" (Hebrews 13:5–6 NLT)

17. Naomi's husband, Elimelech, died, and she was left with her two sons. These sons married women from Moab. One was named Orpah, and the other was named Ruth. Naomi and her sons had lived in Moab about ten years when Mahlon and Kilion also died. So Naomi was left alone without her husband or her two sons. (Ruth 1:3–5 NCV)

18. Ruth said, "Don't beg me to leave you or to stop following you. Where you go, I will go. Where you live, I will live. Your people will be my people, and your God will be my God. And where you die, I will die, and there I will be buried. I ask the LORD to punish me terribly if I do not keep this promise: Not even death will separate us." (Ruth 1:16–17 NCV)

19. I am also taking Ruth, the Moabite who was the wife of Mahlon, as my wife. I am doing this so her dead husband's property will stay in his name and his name will not be separated from his family and his hometown. You are witnesses today. (Ruth 4:10 NCV)

20. The neighbors gave the boy his name, saying, "This boy was born for Naomi." They named him Obed. Obed was the father of Jesse, and Jesse was the father of David. (Ruth 4:17 NCV)

21. She loves you more than seven sons of your own would love you. (Ruth 4:15 CEV)

22. When Elizabeth heard Mary's greeting, the baby leaped in her womb, and Elizabeth was filled with the Holy Spirit. In a loud voice she exclaimed: . . . "As soon as the sound of your greeting reached my ears, the baby in my womb leaped for joy." (Luke 1:41, 44 NIV)

Chapter 43: What's so bad about gossip?

1. He who conceals a transgression seeks love, but he who repeats a matter separates intimate friends. (Proverbs 17:9 NASB)

2. An offended friend is harder to win back than a fortified city. Arguments separate friends like a gate locked with bars. (Proverbs 18:19 NLT)

3. Gossips can't keep secrets, so avoid people who talk too much. (Proverbs 20:19 NCV)

4. Since these people refused even to think about God, he let their useless minds rule over them. That's why they do all sorts of indecent things. They are evil, wicked, and greedy, as well as mean in every possible way. They want what

others have, and they murder, argue, cheat, and are hard to get along with. They gossip, say cruel things about others, and hate God. (Romans 1:28–30 CEV)

5. For lack of wood the fire goes out, and where there is no whisperer, contention quiets down. (Proverbs 26:20 NASB)

6. In the heat of an argument, don't betray confidences; word is sure to get around, and no one will trust you . . . A north wind brings stormy weather, and a gossipy tongue stormy looks. (Proverbs 25:9–10, 23 MSG)

7. Watch your tongue and keep your mouth shut, and you will stay out of trouble. (Proverbs 21:23 NLT)

8. They arrived at Geliloth on the Jordan (touching on Canaanite land). There the Reubenites, Gadites, and the half-tribe of Manasseh built an altar on the banks of the Jordan—a huge altar! (Joshua 22:10 MSG)

9. The People of Israel heard of it: "What's this? The Reubenites, Gadites, and the half-tribe of Manasseh have built an altar facing the land of Canaan at Geliloth on the Jordan, across from the People of Israel!" When the People of Israel heard this, the entire congregation mustered at Shiloh to go to war against them. (Joshua 22:11–12 MSG)

10. We built this altar as a witness between us and you and our children coming after us, a witness to the Altar where we worship GOD in his Sacred Dwelling with our Whole-Burnt-Offerings and our sacrifices and our Peace-Offerings. This way, your children won't be able to say to our children in the future, "You have no part in GOD." We said to ourselves, "If anyone speaks disparagingly to us or to our children in the future, we'll say: Look at this model of GOD's Altar which our ancestors made. It's not for Whole-Burnt-Offerings, not for sacrifices. It's a witness connecting us with you." (Joshua 22:27–28 MSG)

11. If you want good fruit, you must make the tree good. If your tree is not good, it will have bad fruit. A tree is known by the kind of fruit it produces . . . Good people have good things in their hearts, and so they say good things. But evil people have evil in their hearts, so they say evil things. And I tell you that on the Judgment Day people will be responsible for every careless thing they have said. (Matthew 12:33, 35–36 NCV)

12. Don't use foul or abusive language. Let everything you say be good and helpful, so that your words will be an encouragement to those who hear them . . . Get rid of all bitterness, rage, anger, harsh words, and slander, as well as all types of evil behavior. (Ephesians 4:29, 31 NLT)

13. If they are on the list, they will learn to be lazy and will spend their time gossiping from house to house, meddling in other people's business and talking about things they shouldn't. (1 Timothy 5:13 NLT)

14. If we could control our tongues, we would be perfect and could also control ourselves in every other way. We can make a large horse go wherever we want by means of a small bit in its mouth. And a small rudder makes a huge ship turn wherever the pilot chooses to go, even though the winds are strong. In the same way, the tongue is a small thing that makes grand speeches. (James 3:2–5 NLT)

15. Can clean water and dirty water both flow from the same spring? (James 3:11 CEV)

16. Kind words are like honey—sweet to the soul and healthy for the body. (Proverbs 16:24 NLT); Timely advice is lovely, like golden apples in a silver basket. (Proverbs 25:11 NLT)

17. The heart of the godly thinks carefully before speaking; the mouth of the wicked overflows with evil words. (Proverbs 15:28 NLT)

18. You will be well rewarded for saying something kind, but all some people think about is how to be cruel and mean. Keep what you know to yourself, and you will be safe; talk too much, and you are done for. (Proverbs 13:2–3 CEV)

19. He who guards his mouth and his tongue, guards his soul from troubles. (Proverbs 21:23 NASB)

Chapter 44: Why are there restrictions on sex?

1. This explains why a man leaves his father and mother and is joined to his wife, and the two are united into one. (Genesis 2:24 NLT)

2. God created man in His own image, in the image of God He created him; male and female He created them. (Genesis 1:27 NASB)

3. God blessed them, and God said to them, "Be fruitful and multiply; fill the earth and subdue it; have dominion over the fish of the sea, over the birds of the air, and over every living thing that moves on the earth." (Genesis 1:28 NKJV)

4. They were both naked, the man and his wife, and were not ashamed. (Genesis 2:25 NKJV)

5. God looked at everything he had made, and it was very good. Evening passed, and morning came. This was the sixth day. (Genesis 1:31 NCV)

6. I am the LORD your God! So don't follow the customs of Egypt where you used to live or those of Canaan where I am bringing you. (Leviticus 18:2–3 CEV)

7. Don't have sex with any of your close relatives, especially your own mother. This would disgrace your father. And don't disgrace him by having sex with any of his other wives. Don't have sex with your sister or stepsister, whether you grew up together or not. Don't disgrace yourself by having sex with your granddaughter or half sister or a sister of your father or mother. Don't disgrace your uncle by having sex with his wife. Don't have sex with your daughter-in-law or sister-in-law. (Leviticus 18:6–16 CEV)

8. Don't have sex with another man's wife—that would make you unclean. (Leviticus 18:20 CEV).

9. You shall not commit adultery. (Exodus 20:14 NKJV)

10. Promise me, O women of Jerusalem, by the gazelles and wild deer, not to awaken love until the time is right. (Song of Songs 2:7 NLT)

11. Let your fountain be blessed, and rejoice in the wife of your youth. As a loving hind and a graceful doe, let her breasts satisfy you at all times; be exhilarated always with her love. (Proverbs 5:18–19 NASB)

12. The husband should fulfill his marital duty to his wife, and likewise the wife to her husband. The wife's body does not belong to her alone but also to her husband. In the same way, the husband's body does not belong to him alone but also to

his wife. Do not deprive each other except by mutual consent and for a time, so that you may devote yourselves to prayer. Then come together again so that Satan will not tempt you because of your lack of self-control. (1 Corinthians 7:3–5 NIV)

13.   To everything there is a season, a time for every purpose under heaven . . . A time to embrace, and a time to refrain from embracing. (Ecclesiastes 3:1, 5 NKJV)

14.   Jesus answered, "Surely you have read in the Scriptures: When God made the world, 'he made them male and female.' And God said, 'So a man will leave his father and mother and be united with his wife, and the two will become one body.' So there are not two, but one. God has joined the two together, so no one should separate them." (Matthew 19:4–6 NCV)

15.   For husbands, this means love your wives, just as Christ loved the church. He gave up his life for her . . . In the same way, husbands ought to love their wives as they love their own bodies. For a man who loves his wife actually shows love for himself. (Ephesians 5:25, 28 NLT)

16.   A man shall leave his father and mother and shall be joined to his wife, and the two shall become one flesh. This mystery is great; but I am speaking with reference to Christ and the church. (Ephesians 5:31–32 NASB)

17.   It is said, "The two will become one flesh." But he who unites himself with the Lord is one with him in spirit. (1 Corinthians 6:16–17 NIV)

18.   Run away from sexual sin! No other sin so clearly affects the body as this one does. For sexual immorality is a sin against your own body. (1 Corinthians 6:18 NLT)

19.   It is actually reported that there is sexual immorality among you, and such sexual immorality as is not even named among the Gentiles—that a man has his father's wife! (1 Corinthians 5:1 NKJV)

20.   The body is not for sexual sin but for the Lord, and the Lord is for the body. (1 Corinthians 6:13 NCV)

21.   Don't you realize that those who do wrong will not inherit the Kingdom of God? Don't fool yourselves. Those who indulge in sexual sin, or who worship idols, or commit adultery, or are male prostitutes, or practice homosexuality, or are thieves, or greedy people, or drunkards, or are abusive, or cheat people— none of these will inherit the Kingdom of God. Some of you were once like that. But you were cleansed; you were made holy; you were made right with God by calling on the name of the Lord Jesus Christ and by the Spirit of our God. (1 Corinthians 6:9–11 NLT)

22.   Because of immoralities, each man is to have his own wife, and each woman is to have her own husband. (1 Corinthians 7:2 NASB)

23.   Marriage is honorable among all, and the bed undefiled; but fornicators and adulterers God will judge. (Hebrews 13:4 NKJV)

24.   He has delivered us from the power of darkness and conveyed *us* into the kingdom of the Son of His love, in whom we have redemption through His blood, the forgiveness of sins. (Colossians 1:13–14 NKJV); Put to death your members which are on the earth: fornication, uncleanness, passion, evil desire, and covetousness, which is idolatry. (Colossians 3:5 NKJV)

25. God's will is for you to be holy, so stay away from all sexual sin. (1 Thessalonians 4:3 NLT)

26. You are God's people, so don't let it be said that any of you are immoral or indecent or greedy. (Ephesians 5:3 CEV)

27. Yes, I am afraid that when I come again, God will humble me in your presence. And I will be grieved because many of you have not given up your old sins. You have not repented of your impurity, sexual immorality, and eagerness for lustful pleasure. (2 Corinthians 12:21 NLT)

28. Peter said to them, "Repent, and let every one of you be baptized in the name of Jesus Christ for the remission of sins; and you shall receive the gift of the Holy Spirit." (Acts 2:38 NKJV)

29. If we confess our sins, He is faithful and just to forgive us our sins and to cleanse us from all unrighteousness. (1 John 1:9 NKJV)

30. How much more shall the blood of Christ, who through the eternal Spirit offered Himself without spot to God, cleanse your conscience from dead works to serve the living God? (Hebrews 9:14 NKJV)

31. No test or temptation that comes your way is beyond the course of what others have had to face. All you need to remember is that God will never let you down; he'll never let you be pushed past your limit; he'll always be there to help you come through it. (1 Corinthians 10:13 MSG)

Chapter 45: What's wrong with relationships with unbelieving men?

1. Abraham said to his servant, the oldest of his household, who had charge of all that he owned, "Please place your hand under my thigh, and I will make you swear by the LORD, the God of heaven and the God of earth, that you shall not take a wife for my son from the daughters of the Canaanites, among whom I live, but you will go to my country and to my relatives, and take a wife for my son Isaac." (Genesis 24:2–4 NASB)

2. When Esau was forty years old, he married Judith daughter of Beeri the Hittite, and also Basemath daughter of Elon the Hittite. They were a source of grief to Isaac and Rebekah. (Genesis 26:34–35 NIV)

3. Rebekah said to Isaac, "I am weary of my life because of the daughters of Heth; if Jacob takes a wife of the daughters of Heth, like these who are the daughters of the land, what good will my life be to me?" Then Isaac called Jacob and blessed him, and charged him, and said to him: "You shall not take a wife from the daughters of Canaan." (Genesis 27:46–28:1 NKJV)

4. They named the place Bokim. There they offered sacrifices to the Lord. Then Joshua sent the people back to their land. (Judges 2:5–6 NCV)

5. The Israelites did what the Lord said was wrong. They forgot about the Lord their God and served the idols of Baal and Asherah. So the Lord was angry with Israel and allowed Cushan-Rishathaim king of Northwest Mesopotamia to rule over the Israelites for eight years. (Judges 3:7–8 NCV)

6. When the people of Israel cried out to the LORD for help, the LORD raised

up a rescuer to save them. His name was Othniel, the son of Caleb's younger brother, Kenaz . . . So there was peace in the land for forty years. Then Othniel son of Kenaz died. (Judges 3:9, 11 NLT)

7.   King Solomon loved many foreign women along with the daughter of Pharaoh: Moabite, Ammonite, Edomite, Sidonian, and Hittite women, from the nations concerning which the LORD had said to the sons of Israel, "You shall not associate with them, nor shall they associate with you, for they will surely turn your heart away after their gods." Solomon held fast to these in love. He had seven hundred wives, princesses, and three hundred concubines, and his wives turned his heart away. (1 Kings 11:1–3 NASB)

8.   I have done according to your words; see, I have given you a wise and understanding heart, so that there has not been anyone like you before you, nor shall any like you arise after you. (1 Kings 3:12 NKJV)

9.   Solomon built a high place for Chemosh the abomination of Moab, on the hill that *is* east of Jerusalem, and for Molech the abomination of the people of Ammon. And he did likewise for all his foreign wives, who burned incense and sacrificed to their gods. (1 Kings 11:7–8 NKJV)

10.   The LORD was very angry with Solomon, for his heart had turned away from the LORD, the God of Israel, who had appeared to him twice. He had warned Solomon specifically about worshiping other gods, but Solomon did not listen to the LORD's command. So now the LORD said to him, "Since you have not kept my covenant and have disobeyed my decrees, I will surely tear the kingdom away from you and give it to one of your servants." (1 Kings 11:9–11 NLT)

11.   He forsook the counsel of the elders which they had given him, and consulted with the young men who grew up with him and served him. (1 Kings 12:8 NASB)

12.   Some people think they are doing right, but in the end it leads to death. (Proverbs 14:12 NCV)

13.   Do not be unequally yoked together with unbelievers. (2 Corinthians 6:14 NKJV)

14.   Anyone who knows the right thing to do, but does not do it, is sinning. (James 4:17 NCV)

Chapter 46: God, why did You create families?

1.   God blessed them and said, "Be fruitful and multiply. Fill the earth and govern it. Reign over the fish in the sea, the birds in the sky, and all the animals that scurry along the ground." (Genesis 1:28 NLT)

2.   This explains why a man leaves his father and mother and is joined to his wife, and the two are united into one. (Genesis 2:24 NLT)

3.   One day Cain suggested to his brother, "Let's go out into the fields." And while they were in the field, Cain attacked his brother, Abel, and killed him. Afterward the LORD asked Cain, "Where is your brother? Where is Abel?" "I don't know," Cain responded. "Am I my brother's guardian?" But the LORD said, "What have you done? Listen! Your brother's blood cries out to me from the ground!" (Genesis 4:8–10 NLT)

4. I will establish My covenant with you; and you shall enter the ark—you and your sons and your wife, and your sons' wives with you. (Genesis 6:18 NASB)

5. The LORD had said to Abram, "Leave your country, your people and your father's household and go to the land I will show you." . . . So Abram left, as the LORD had told him; and Lot went with him. Abram was seventy-five years old when he set out from Haran. (Genesis 12:1, 4 NIV)

6. I will bless those who bless you, and I will curse him who curses you; and in you all the families of the earth shall be blessed. (Genesis 12:3 NKJV)

7. From now on when a baby boy is eight days old, you will circumcise him. This includes any boy born among your people or any who is your slave, who is not one of your descendants. Circumcise every baby boy whether he is born in your family or bought as a slave. Your bodies will be marked to show that you are part of my agreement that lasts forever. (Genesis 17:12–13 NCV)

8. Honor your father and mother. Then you will live a long, full life in the land the LORD your God is giving you. (Exodus 20:12 NLT)

9. You must not commit adultery. (Exodus 20:14 NLT)

10. He was bringing up Hadassah, that is Esther, his uncle's daughter, for she had no father or mother. Now the young lady was beautiful of form and face, and when her father and her mother died, Mordecai took her as his own daughter. (Esther 2:7 NASB)

11. Every day Mordecai paced in front of the court of the women's quarters, to learn of Esther's welfare and what was happening to her. (Esther 2:11 NKJV)

12. He sent back this answer: "Do not think that because you are in the king's house you alone of all the Jews will escape. For if you remain silent at this time, relief and deliverance for the Jews will arise from another place, but you and your father's family will perish. And who knows but that you have come to royal position for such a time as this?" (Esther 4:13–14 NIV)

13. The king's decree gave the Jews in every city authority to unite to defend their lives. They were allowed to kill, slaughter, and annihilate anyone of any nationality or province who might attack them or their children and wives, and to take the property of their enemies. (Esther 8:11 NLT)

14. While He was still speaking to the crowds, behold, His mother and brothers were standing outside, seeking to speak to Him. Someone said to Him, "Behold, Your mother and Your brothers are standing outside seeking to speak to You." (Matthew 12:46–47 NASB)

15. Matthew 12:48 NKJV.

16. Stretching out His hand toward His disciples, He said, "Behold My mother and My brothers! For whoever does the will of My Father who is in heaven, he is My brother and sister and mother." (Matthew 12:49–50 NASB)

17. Jesus saw his mother and the disciple he loved standing near her. He said to his mother, "Woman, here is your son." Then to the disciple, "Here is your mother." From that moment the disciple accepted her as his own mother. (John 19:26–27 MSG)

18. God is Spirit, and those who worship Him must worship in spirit and truth. (John 4:24 NKJV)

19. Peter said to them, "Change your hearts and lives and be baptized, each one of you, in the name of Jesus Christ for the forgiveness of your sins. And you will receive the gift of the Holy Spirit. (Acts 2:38 NCV)

20. His Spirit joins with our spirit to affirm that we are God's children. (Romans 8:16 NLT)

21. One of them was Lydia, who was from the city of Thyatira and sold expensive purple cloth. She was a worshiper of the Lord God, and he made her willing to accept what Paul was saying. Then after she and her family were baptized, she kept on begging us, "If you think I really do have faith in the Lord, come stay in my home." Finally, we accepted her invitation. (Acts 16:14–15 CEV)

22. Suddenly a strong earthquake shook the jail to its foundations. The doors opened, and the chains fell from all the prisoners. When the jailer woke up and saw that the doors were open, he thought that the prisoners had escaped. He pulled out his sword and was about to kill himself. But Paul shouted, "Don't harm yourself! No one has escaped." (Acts 16:26–28 CEV)

23. After he had led them out of the jail, he asked, "What must I do to be saved?" They replied, "Have faith in the Lord Jesus and you will be saved! This is also true for everyone who lives in your home." Then Paul and Silas told him and everyone else in his house about the Lord. While it was still night, the jailer took them to a place where he could wash their cuts and bruises. Then he and everyone in his home were baptized. They were very glad that they had put their faith in God. After this, the jailer took Paul and Silas to his home and gave them something to eat. (Acts 16:30–34 CEV)

Chapter 47: What's up with the teaching on submission?

1. God said, "Let us make human beings in our image, to be like ourselves. They will reign over the fish in the sea, the birds in the sky, the livestock, all the wild animals on the earth, and the small animals that scurry along the ground." So God created human beings in his own image. In the image of God he created them; male and female he created them. (Genesis 1:26–27 NLT)

2. God looked over everything he had made; it was so good, so very good! It was evening, it was morning. (Genesis 1:31 MSG)

3. God blessed them and said, "Be fruitful and multiply. Fill the earth and govern it. Reign over the fish in the sea, the birds in the sky, and all the animals that scurry along the ground." (Genesis 1:28 NLT)

4. The LORD God said, "It isn't good for the man to live alone. I need to make a suitable partner for him" (Genesis 2:18 CEV)

5. I look to the hills! Where will I find help? It will come from the LORD, who created the heavens and the earth. (Psalm 121:1–2 CEV)

6. The man exclaimed, "Here is someone like me! She is part of my body, my own flesh and bones. She came from me, a man. So I will name her Woman!" That's why a man will leave his own father and mother. He marries a woman, and the two of them become like one person. (Genesis 2:23–24 CEV)

7. The woman was convinced. She saw that the tree was beautiful and its fruit looked delicious, and she wanted the wisdom it would give her. So she took some of the fruit and ate it. Then she gave some to her husband, who was with her, and he ate it, too. (Genesis 3:6 NLT)

8. Care for the flock that God has entrusted to you. Watch over it willingly, not grudgingly—not for what you will get out of it, but because you are eager to serve God. Don't lord it over the people assigned to your care, but lead them by your own good example. (1 Peter 5:2–3 NLT)

9. Be filled with the Spirit. (Ephesians 5:18 ESV)

10. I say, walk by the Spirit, and you will not gratify the desires of the flesh. (Galatians 5:16 ESV)

11. If you are led by the Spirit, you are not under the law. (Galatians 5:18 ESV)

12. No one can serve two masters. Either he will hate the one and love the other, or he will be devoted to the one and despise the other. (Matthew 6:24 NIV)

13. Peter and the apostles replied, "We must obey God rather than any human authority." (Acts 5:29 NLT)

14. There is one God and one mediator so that human beings can reach God. That way is through Christ Jesus, who is himself human. (1 Timothy 2:5 NCV)

15. Submit to one another out of reverence for Christ. (Ephesians 5:21 NLT)

16. As the church submits to Christ, so you wives should submit to your husbands in everything. (Ephesians 5:24 NLT)

17. Each individual among you also is to love his own wife even as himself, and the wife must see to it that she respects her husband. (Ephesians 5:33 NASB)

18. All who have been united with Christ in baptism have put on the character of Christ, like putting on new clothes. There is no longer Jew or Gentile, slave or free, male and female. For you are all one in Christ Jesus. (Galatians 3:27–28 NLT)

19. Ephesians 5:23 NCV.

20. The head of every man is Christ, the head of a woman is the man, and the head of Christ is God. (1 Corinthians 11:3 NCV)

21. In the Lord, however, woman is not independent of man, nor is man independent of woman. For as woman came from man, so also man is born of woman. But everything comes from God. (1 Corinthians 11:11–12 NIV)

22. If some husbands do not obey God's teaching, they will be persuaded to believe without anyone's saying a word to them. They will be persuaded by the way their wives live. Your husbands will see the pure lives you live with your respect for God . . . Your beauty should come from within you—the beauty of a gentle and quiet spirit that will never be destroyed and is very precious to God. (1 Peter 3:1–2, 4 NCV)

Chapter 48: How can we respect an ungodly boss?

1. Peter and the apostles replied, "We must obey God rather than any human authority." (Acts 5:29 NLT)

2. Go and make disciples of all the nations, baptizing them in the name of the Father and the Son and the Holy Spirit. Teach these new disciples to obey all the commands I have given you. (Matthew 28:19–20 NLT)

3. Pharaoh, the king of Egypt, gave this order to the Hebrew midwives, Shiphrah and Puah: "When you help the Hebrew women as they give birth, watch as they deliver. If the baby is a boy, kill him; if it is a girl, let her live." But because the midwives feared God, they refused to obey the king's orders. They allowed the boys to live, too . . . So God was good to the midwives, and the Israelites continued to multiply, growing more and more powerful. And because the midwives feared God, he gave them families of their own. (Exodus 1:15–17, 20–21 NLT)

4. The king of Jericho sent word to Rahab, saying, "Bring out the men who have come to you, who have entered your house, for they have come to search out all the land." But the woman had taken the two men and hidden them, and she said, . . . " When it was time to shut the gate at dark, . . . the men went out; I do not know where the men went. Pursue them quickly, for you will overtake them." (Joshua 2:3–5 NASB)

5. [Rahab] said to the men, "I know that the LORD has given you the land, and that the terror of you has fallen on us, and that all the inhabitants of the land have melted away before you. For we have heard how the LORD dried up the water of the Red Sea before you when you came out of Egypt, and what you did to the two kings of the Amorites who were beyond the Jordan, to Sihon and Og, whom you utterly destroyed. When we heard it, our hearts melted and no courage remained in any man any longer because of you; for the LORD your God, He is God in heaven above and on earth beneath." (Joshua 2:9–11 NLT)

6. Slaves, obey your masters here on earth with fear and respect and from a sincere heart, just as you obey Christ. You must do this not only while they are watching you, to please them. With all your heart you must do what God wants as people who are obeying Christ. (Ephesians 6:5–6 NCV)

7. Do your work with enthusiasm. Work as if you were serving the Lord, not as if you were serving only men and women. Remember that the Lord will give a reward to everyone, slave or free, for doing good. (Ephesians 6:7–8 NCV)

8. Masters, in the same way, be good to your slaves. Do not threaten them. Remember that the One who is your Master and their Master is in heaven, and he treats everyone alike. (Ephesians 6:9 NCV)

9. Slaves, yield to the authority of your masters with all respect, not only those who are good and kind, but also those who are dishonest. A person might have to suffer even when it is unfair, but if he thinks of God and can stand the pain, God is pleased . . . This is what you were called to do, because Christ suffered for you and gave you an example to follow. So you should do as he did . . . People insulted Christ, but he did not insult them in return. Christ suffered, but he did not threaten. He let God, the One who judges rightly, take care of him. (1 Peter 2:18–19, 21–23 NCV)

10. Be strong in the Lord and in his great power. Put on the full armor of God so that you can fight against the devil's evil tricks. Our fight is not against people

311

on earth but against the rulers and authorities and the powers of this world's darkness, against the spiritual powers of evil in the heavenly world. (Ephesians 6:10–12 NCV)

11.   Stand strong, with the belt of truth tied around your waist and the protection of right living on your chest. (Ephesians 6:14 NCV)

12.   On your feet wear the Good News of peace to help you stand strong. And also use the shield of faith with which you can stop all the burning arrows of the Evil One. (Ephesians 6:15–16 NCV)

13.   Accept God's salvation as your helmet, and take the sword of the Spirit, which is the word of God. (Ephesians 6:17 NCV)

14.   On the day of evil you will be able to stand strong. And when you have finished the whole fight, you will still be standing. (Ephesians 6:13 NCV)

Chapter 49: How can evil coexist with Your love?

1.   The human heart is the most deceitful of all things, and desperately wicked. Who really knows how bad it is? (Jeremiah 17:9 NLT)

2.   He is the One who makes everything agree with what he decides and wants. (Ephesians 1:11 NCV)

3.   The story of Joseph is found in Genesis 37–50.

4.   As for you, you meant evil against me, but God meant it for good in order to bring about this present result, to preserve many people alive. (Genesis 50:20 NASB)

5.   This is how God showed his love among us: He sent his one and only Son into the world that we might live through him. This is love: not that we loved God, but that he loved us and sent his Son as an atoning sacrifice for our sins. (1 John 4:9–10 NIV)

6.   [Peter and John prayed]: "Indeed Herod and Pontius Pilate met together with the Gentiles and the people of Israel in this city to conspire against your holy servant Jesus, whom you anointed. They did what your power and will had decided beforehand should happen." (Acts 4:27–28 NIV)

Chapter 50: Why do Your followers have to suffer?

1.   Cursed is the ground because of you; through painful toil you will eat of it all the days of your life. (Genesis 3:17 NIV)

2.   The preceding portion of the story is found in Job 1:1–2:8.

3.   His wife said to him, "Are you still holding on to your integrity? Curse God and die!" (Job 2:9 NIV)

4.   I am young in years, and you are old; that is why I was fearful, not daring to tell you what I know . . . I am full of words, and the spirit within me compels me; inside I am like bottled-up wine, like new wineskins ready to burst. (Job 32:6, 18–19 NIV)

5.   Elihu's entire speech is found in Job 32–37.

6. Why do you accuse God of not answering anyone? God does speak—sometimes one way and sometimes another—even though people may not understand it. He speaks in a dream or a vision of the night when people are in a deep sleep, lying on their beds. (Job 33:13–15 NCV)

7. These portions are found in Job 34; 36–37.

8. Where were you when I laid the foundations of the earth? Tell Me, if you have understanding Who determined its measurements? Surely you know! Or who stretched the line upon it? To what were its foundations fastened? Or who laid its cornerstone, when the morning stars sang together, and all the sons of God shouted for joy? Or who shut in the sea with doors, when it burst forth and issued from the womb; When I made the clouds its garment, and thick darkness its swaddling band; when I fixed My limit for it, and set bars and doors; when I said, This far you may come, but no farther, and here your proud waves must stop! (Job 38:4–11 NKJV)

9. Surely I spoke of things I did not understand, things too wonderful for me to know. (Job 42:3 NIV)

10. My ears had heard of you but now my eyes have seen you. Therefore I despise myself and repent in dust and ashes. (Job 42:5–6 NIV)

11. Dear friends, I urge you, as aliens and strangers in the world, to abstain from sinful desires, which war against your soul. (1 Peter 2:11 NIV)

12. Here we do not have an enduring city, but we are looking for the city that is to come. (Hebrews 13:14 NIV)

13. Our light and momentary troubles are achieving for us an eternal glory that far outweighs them all. (2 Corinthians 4:17 NIV)

14. I consider that the sufferings of this present time are not worthy to be compared with the glory that is to be revealed to us. (Romans 8:18 NASB)

15. Beloved, do not be surprised at the fiery ordeal among you, which comes upon you for your testing, as though some strange thing were happening to you; but to the degree that you share the sufferings of Christ, keep on rejoicing, so that also at the revelation of His glory you may rejoice with exultation. (1 Peter 4:12–13 NASB)

16. In this you greatly rejoice, though now for a little while you may have had to suffer grief in all kinds of trials. These have come so that your faith—of greater worth than gold, which perishes even though refined by fire—may be proved genuine and may result in praise, glory and honor when Jesus Christ is revealed. (1 Peter 1:6–7 NIV)

17. The God of all grace, who called you to his eternal glory in Christ, after you have suffered a little while, will himself restore you and make you strong, firm and steadfast. (1 Peter 5:10 NIV)

18. We also rejoice in our sufferings, because we know that suffering produces perseverance; perseverance, character; and character, hope. (Romans 5:3–4 NIV)

19. My brothers and sisters, when you have many kinds of troubles, you should be full of joy, because you know that these troubles test your faith, and

this will give you patience. Let your patience show itself perfectly in what you do. Then you will be perfect and complete and will have everything you need. (James 1:2–4 NCV)

20.   Cast your cares on the LORD and he will sustain you; he will never let the righteous fall. (Psalm 55:22 NIV)

21.   Psalm 46:1–3 NKJV.

22.   Romans 12:15 NKJV.

23.   Do not be anxious about anything, but in everything, by prayer and petition, with thanksgiving, present your requests to God. And the peace of God, which transcends all understanding, will guard your hearts and your minds in Christ Jesus. (Philippians 4:6–7 NIV)

24.   Who will separate us from the love of Christ? Will tribulation, or distress, or persecution, or famine, or nakedness, or peril, or sword? (Romans 8:35 NASB)

25.   Romans 8:38–39 NASB.

Chapter 51: Are all sins the same to You?

1.   The carved images of their gods you shall burn with fire. You shall not covet the silver or the gold that is on them or take it for yourselves, lest you be ensnared by it, for it is an abomination to the LORD your God. (Deuteronomy 7:25 ESV)

2.   You shall not bring the fee of a prostitute or the wages of a dog into the house of the LORD your God in payment for any vow, for both of these are an abomination to the LORD your God. (Deuteronomy 23:18 ESV)

3.   There are six things that the LORD hates, seven that are an abomination to him: haughty eyes, a lying tongue, and hands that shed innocent blood, a heart that devises wicked plans, feet that make haste to run to evil, a false witness who breathes out lies, and one who sows discord among brothers. (Proverbs 6:16–19 ESV)

4.   The person who is joined to the Lord is one spirit with him. Run from sexual sin! No other sin so clearly affects the body as this one does. For sexual immorality is a sin against your own body. Don't you realize that your body is the temple of the Holy Spirit, who lives in you and was given to you by God? You do not belong to yourself, for God bought you with a high price. So you must honor God with your body. (1 Corinthians 6:17–20 NLT)

5.   Talk and act like a person expecting to be judged by the Rule that sets us free. For if you refuse to act kindly, you can hardly expect to be treated kindly. Kind mercy wins over harsh judgment every time. (James 2:12–13 MSG)

6.   I tell you, unless your righteousness exceeds that of the scribes and Pharisees, you will never enter the kingdom of heaven. (Matthew 5:20 ESV)

7.   You have heard that it was said to those of old, "You shall not murder; and whoever murders will be liable to judgment." But I say to you that everyone who is angry with his brother will be liable to judgment; whoever insults his brother will be liable to the council; and whoever says, 'You fool!' will be liable to the hell of fire. (Matthew 5:21–22 ESV)

8.   You have heard that it was said, "You shall not commit adultery." But I say to you that everyone who looks at a woman with lustful intent has already committed adultery with her in his heart. (Matthew 5:27–28 ESV)

9.   You brood of snakes! How could evil men like you speak what is good and right? For whatever is in your heart determines what you say. A good person produces good things from the treasury of a good heart, and an evil person produces evil things from the treasury of an evil heart. (Matthew 12:34–35 NLT)

10.   Beware of the scribes, who like to walk around in long robes, and love respectful greetings in the market places, and chief seats in the synagogues and places of honor at banquets, who devour widows' houses, and for appearance's sake offer long prayers. These will receive greater condemnation. (Luke 20:46–47 NASB)

11.   What sorrow awaits you teachers of religious law and you Pharisees. Hypocrites! For you are careful to tithe even the tiniest income from your herb gardens, but you ignore the more important aspects of the law—justice, mercy, and faith. You should tithe, yes, but do not neglect the more important things. Blind guides! You strain your water so you won't accidentally swallow a gnat, but you swallow a camel! What sorrow awaits you teachers of religious law and you Pharisees. Hypocrites! For you are so careful to clean the outside of the cup and the dish, but inside you are filthy—full of greed and self-indulgence! You blind Pharisee! First wash the inside of the cup and the dish, and then the outside will become clean, too. (Matthew 23:23–26 NLT)

12.   This king did what my heavenly Father will do to you if you do not forgive your brother or sister from your heart. (Matthew 18:35 NCV)

Chapter 52: How can some unbelievers be so good?

1.   God said, "Let us make human beings in our image, to be like ourselves. They will reign over the fish in the sea, the birds in the sky, the livestock, all the wild animals on the earth, and the small animals that scurry along the ground." So God created human beings in his own image. In the image of God he created them; male and female he created them. (Genesis 1:26–27 NLT)

2.   God looked over everything he had made; it was so good, so very good! It was evening, it was morning. (Genesis 1:31 MSG)

3.   Merely listening to the law doesn't make us right with God. It is obeying the law that makes us right in his sight. Even Gentiles, who do not have God's written law, show that they know his law when they instinctively obey it, even without having heard it. They demonstrate that God's law is written in their hearts, for their own conscience and thoughts either accuse them or tell them they are doing right. (Romans 2:13–15 NLT)

4.   Just as he who called you is holy, so be holy in all you do; for it is written: "Be holy, because I am holy." (1 Peter 1:15–16 NIV)

5.   A man came to Jesus and asked, "Teacher, what good thing must I do to have life forever?" Jesus answered, "Why do you ask me about what is good? Only God is good." (Matthew 19:16–17 NCV)

6.   Every good and perfect gift is from above, coming down from the Father of the heavenly lights, who does not change like shifting shadows. (James 1:17 NIV)

7.   By his power we live and move and exist. (Acts 17:28 NCV)

Chapter 53: How can You forgive truly evil criminals?

1.   The LORD doesn't see things the way you see them. People judge by outward appearance, but the LORD looks at the heart. (1 Samuel 16:7 NLT)

2.   He is the atoning sacrifice for our sins, and not only for ours but also for the sins of the whole world. (1 John 2:2 NIV)

3.   We have redemption through His blood, the forgiveness of sins. (Colossians 1:14 NKJV)

4.   When they had come to the place called Calvary, there they crucified Him, and the criminals, one on the right hand and the other on the left. Then Jesus said, "Father, forgive them, for they do not know what they do." And they divided His garments and cast lots. (Luke 23:33–34 NKJV)

5.   Jesus went to the Mount of Olives. Now early in the morning He came again into the temple, and all the people came to Him; and He sat down and taught them. Then the scribes and Pharisees brought to Him a woman caught in adultery. And when they had set her in the midst, they said to Him, "Teacher, this woman was caught in adultery, in the very act. Now Moses, in the law, commanded us that such should be stoned. But what do You say?" This they said, testing Him, that they might have *something* of which to accuse Him. But Jesus stooped down and wrote on the ground with *His* finger, as though He did not hear. So when they continued asking Him, He raised Himself up and said to them, "He who is without sin among you, let him throw a stone at her first." And again He stooped down and wrote on the ground. Then those who heard *it*, being convicted by *their* conscience, went out one by one, beginning with the oldest *even* to the last. And Jesus was left alone, and the woman standing in the midst. When Jesus had raised Himself up and saw no one but the woman, He said to her, "Woman, where are those accusers of yours? Has no one condemned you?" She said, "No one, Lord." And Jesus said to her, "Neither do I condemn you; go and sin no more." (John 8:1–11 NKJV)

Chapter 54: What about people who continue to sin?

1.   My people are destroyed for lack of knowledge. (Hosea 4:6 ESV)

2.   All Scripture is inspired by God and is useful to teach us what is true and to make us realize what is wrong in our lives. It corrects us when we are wrong and teaches us to do what is right. God uses it to prepare and equip his people to do every good work. (2 Timothy 3:16–17 NLT)

3.   The Law has shown me that something in me keeps me from doing what I know is right. With my whole heart I agree with the Law of God. But in every part of me I discover something fighting against my mind, and it makes me a prisoner of sin that controls everything I do. What a miserable person I am. Who

will rescue me from this body that is doomed to die? Thank God! Jesus Christ will rescue me. (Romans 7:21–25 CEV)

4.　If people's thinking is controlled by the sinful self, there is death. But if their thinking is controlled by the Spirit, there is life and peace . . . But you are not ruled by your sinful selves. You are ruled by the Spirit, if that Spirit of God really lives in you. But the person who does not have the Spirit of Christ does not belong to Christ. Your body will always be dead because of sin. But if Christ is in you, then the Spirit gives you life, because Christ made you right with God . . . The true children of God are those who let God's Spirit lead them. (Romans 8:6, 9–10, 14 NCV)

5.　Those who are God's children do not continue sinning, because the new life from God remains in them. They are not able to go on sinning, because they have become children of God. So we can see who God's children are and who the devil's children are: Those who do not do what is right are not God's children, and those who do not love their brothers and sisters are not God's children. (1 John 3:9–10 NCV)

6.　Your word is a lamp to my feet and a light to my path. (Psalm 119:105 NKJV)

7.　Your word I have hidden in my heart, that I might not sin against You. (Psalm 119:11 NKJV)

8.　Those who enter into Christ's being-here-for-us no longer have to live under a continuous, low-lying black cloud. A new power is in operation. The Spirit of life in Christ, like a strong wind, has magnificently cleared the air, freeing you from a fated lifetime of brutal tyranny at the hands of sin and death. (Romans 8:1–2 MSG)

9.　Whoever causes one of these little ones who believe in Me to stumble, it would be better for him to have a heavy millstone hung around his neck, and to be drowned in the depth of the sea. (Matthew 18:6 NASB)

10.　Woe to the world because of the things that cause people to sin! Such things must come, but woe to the man through whom they come! If your hand or your foot causes you to sin, cut it off and throw it away. It is better for you to enter life maimed or crippled than to have two hands or two feet and be thrown into eternal fire. And if your eye causes you to sin, gouge it out and throw it away. It is better for you to enter life with one eye than to have two eyes and be thrown into the fire of hell. (Matthew 18:7–9 NIV)

11.　Proverbs 6:27–28 MSG.

12.　If we confess our sins, He is faithful and righteous to forgive us our sins and to cleanse us from all unrighteousness. (1 John 1:9 NASB)

13.　My little children, I am writing these things to you so that you may not sin. And if anyone sins, we have an Advocate with the Father, Jesus Christ the righteous. (1 John 2:1 NASB)

14.　Do you think we should continue sinning so that God will give us even more grace? No! We died to our old sinful lives, so how can we continue living with sin? (Romans 6:1–2 NCV)

Chapter 55: How can anybody find good in tragedy?

1. Habakkuk 3:18–19 NASB.
2. Blessed be the God and Father of our Lord Jesus Christ, the Father of mercies and God of all comfort. (2 Corinthians 1:3 NASB)
3. Five times I received from the Jews the forty lashes minus one. Three times I was beaten with rods, once I was stoned, three times I was shipwrecked, I spent a night and a day in the open sea, I have been constantly on the move. I have been in danger from rivers, in danger from bandits, in danger from my own countrymen, in danger from Gentiles; in danger in the city, in danger in the country, in danger at sea; and in danger from false brothers. I have labored and toiled and have often gone without sleep; I have known hunger and thirst and have often gone without food; I have been cold and naked. (2 Corinthians 11:24–27 NIV)
4. [God] comforts us in all our affliction so that we will be able to comfort those who are in any affliction with the comfort with which we ourselves are comforted by God. For just as the sufferings of Christ are ours in abundance, so also our comfort is abundant through Christ. (2 Corinthians 1:4–5 NASB)
5. Every good and perfect gift is from above, coming down from the Father of the heavenly lights, who does not change like shifting shadows. (James 1:17 NIV)
6. God has said, "Never will I leave you; never will I forsake you." (Hebrews 13:5 NIV)